OFF THE BEATEN PATH® PENNSYLVANIA →

Help Us Keep This Guide Up to Date

We would love to hear from you concerning your experiences with this guide and how you feel it could be improved and kept up to date. Please send your comments and suggestions to:

editorial@GlobePequot.com

Thanks for your input, and happy travels!

OFF THE BEATEN PATH® SERIES

ELEVENTH EDITION

OFF THE BEATEN PATH®
PENNSYLVANIA ➡

A GUIDE TO UNIQUE PLACES

CHRISTINE H. O'TOOLE

gpp®

travel

Guilford, Connecticut

All the information in this guidebook is subject to change. We recommend that you call ahead to obtain current information before traveling.

To buy books in quantity for corporate use or incentives, call **(800) 962-0973** or e-mail **premiums@GlobePequot.com**.

Editor: Kevin Sirois
Project Editor: Lynn Zelem
Layout: Joanna Beyer
Text design by Linda R. Loiewski
Maps: Equator Graphics © Morris Book Publishing, LLC

ISSN 1536-6197
ISBN 978-0-7627-7953-6

Printed in the United States of America
10 9 8 7 6 5 4

To Jim, James, and Bill: great Pennsylvanians.

Contents

About the Author

Christine O'Toole writes for *National Geographic Traveler*, the *New York Times, International Herald-Tribune, Hemispheres, Washington Post, USA Today, Pittsburgh Magazine, Pittsburgh Post-Gazette*, and other publications. A native of Newtown Square, Delaware County, she has lived and worked in Philadelphia, Harrisburg, Washington, D.C., and Pittsburgh. She contributed to *Travelers Tales: Prague and the Czech Republic* (Travelers Tales, 2006) and is a co-author of Pennsylvania's *Forbes Trail: Gateways and Getaways Along the Legendary Route from Philadelphia to Pittsburgh* (Taylor Trade Press, 2008).

Acknowledgments

This book has helped me relive some favorite moments in Pennsylvania history—my own.

As a native who started east, moved west, and eventually became a travel writer, my personal and professional footprints run all through the state. For their help in mapping every opportunity along the way, I thank fellow writers like my twin, Carol Denny, and Jim O'Toole of the *Pittsburgh Post-Gazette,* my husband, intrepid companion, and best editor. Dave Floyd provided valuable fact checking.

To my father, Ned Hoffner, who bundled up seven kids and took them skiing in the Poconos, camping at French Creek, skating on frozen Delaware County ponds, and leaf-hiking at Ridley Creek, I owe a debt of gratitude for his boundless energy, example, and encouragement. He started me on this path.

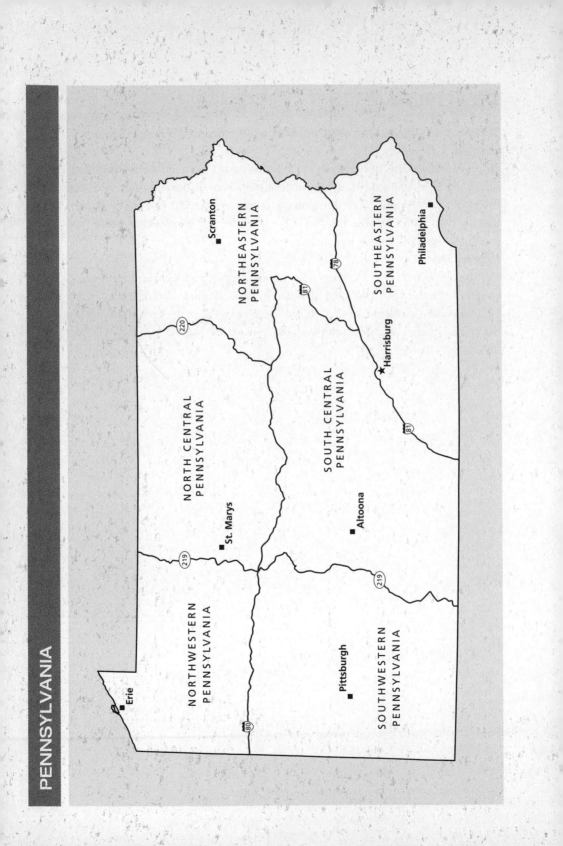

Introduction

When I think of Pennsylvania, I think green.

Driving home to Philadelphia after a weekend at the beach, I used to roll down the window as I crossed the Delaware River and sniff the humid fragrance of an August night, so different from south Jersey's parched sand. On a spring drive down Route 6, I'll see a golden mountainside and know it's a week away from leafing out (unless it snows, of course—a distinct possibility in the Pennsylvania mountains). Whether observed from a bike seat in York County or a trail along the Chestnut Ridge, this state has simply terrific photosynthesis.

The natural end of all that transpiration is, of course, fall, and it's fabulous here. In October you bask in what I think is its most memorable weather: warm days, deep blue skies, and a palette of colors that Crayola (a Pennsylvania company) would kill for. Throw a few elk, bear, bikers, or golfers into that picture, and you've got the state at its finest.

Pennsylvania is an old state. Its central ridges and valleys are mind-bendingly ancient—about 250 million years old, geologically speaking. Evidence of human life in rock shelters in Washington County goes back at least 16,000 years. Ten thousand years ago Indians hunted mammoths and mastodons. Europeans first settled here in 1643. All those layers of history mean that however you slice it, there's always something new to enjoy and digest.

Spend lots of time in Philadelphia—it's as youthful as it is historic and has a collection of fabulous museums that would take weeks to visit. Walk around Old City, an authentic 18th-century neighborhood where young locals push strollers and bikes. In-line skate down Kelly Drive (but remove the skates when you get to the *Rocky* steps at the Museum of Art). Boo the sports teams—it's a tradition here—and ride the Market Street El, the Broad Street subway, or the trains to Suburban Station, because the Schuylkill Expressway can be a nightmare.

But Pennsylvania is a broad state. So, in planning your jaunt here, be broad-minded.

If you think state capitols are a snore, you'll be pleasantly surprised by Pennsylvania's neoclassical masterpiece on the banks of the Susquehanna. If you've ever seen the Grand Canyon, you owe it to yourself to compare it to Pennsylvania's version, a gorgeous gorge in Tioga County. And if you think Pennsylvania military history is all Gettysburg and Valley Forge, find out why the French and Indians battled for this land before the nation even existed—and why the British hacked their way through hundreds of miles of deep, mountainous forest (more greenery) to claim their fort at Pittsburgh.

Pennsylvania is green because it's well watered. Between the peaceful upper Delaware and Lake Erie, ribbons of white water and terrific trout streams cut through the woods. In the valleys of Susquehanna and Lancaster Counties, lush farms snuggle against every rolling hillside, enjoying magnificent thunderstorms. And streamside county seats like Franklin abide like Brigadoon, charmingly unchanged.

Although Pennsylvania's tourist attractions often focus on industry, agriculture is still its biggest business. So, since you're being broad-minded, try a U-pick orchard or produce from a roadside stand. Visit the annual Farm Show in Harrisburg, which celebrates everything that grows in the state, from apples to zucchini. (Sweet-faced kids leading sweet-faced cows, butter sculptures, and rodeos, too—all for free every January.) Give Pennsylvania—specifically, recent governors Ridge and Rendell—credit for the steady improvements in the state's 116 parks. Over the past few decades, the Department of Conservation of Natural Resources (DCNR) has worked to groom them and to create interpretive signs and exhibits. Nice job, DCNR (and thank you, commonwealth taxpayers).

Old industries have new purposes here. Many abandoned short lines built to haul coal are now being converted to trails. A bonus: Most of them run alongside streams. Hundreds of peaceful miles that used to be rusting steel are now long, restful water-level pathways. (The state's prettiest country roads have also been linked in biking networks.) And in Elk County former strip mines have been converted to verdant meadows, creating a resurgence of elk. The herd is now one of the largest in the eastern United States—a rustbelt story with a wild ending.

Quick: What's the state's website address? If you're tailing a car with a Pennsylvania license plate, the answer's right in front of you: www.state.pa.us. Use that ubiquitous URL to find all things Pennsylvanian. Select the tourism page, "Visit PA" (www.visitpa.com), and type a keyword—say, apple—and you'll find museums devoted to apples, farm markets galore, even restaurants with apple desserts to die for. It really works.

Twenty years ago the state had a slogan that promised "You've Got a Friend in Pennsylvania." (Today you'll see front license plates in the same blue-and-gold style that say "You've Got a Friend in Jesus," a play on that old catchphrase. When you see one now, you'll catch the reference. That's true native lore.) The old ad campaign caught on because it's common sense and the real thing. With 12 million residents, you really are bound to know someone here. And I can vouch for the part about friends, most recently while writing this book.

In Donegal a fellow in a pickup truck tugged my car out of a snowdrift and simply drove off with a friendly wave. Dennis Tice of the Bedford Visitors

Brief History of Early Pennsylvania

King Charles II of England gave William Penn, a Quaker, a large tract of land in the New World as repayment of a debt the king owed to William's father. The tract of land that became known as Pennsylvania, or "Penn's Woods," was settled in 1643. William Penn encouraged the Quakers and other persecuted groups to settle in Pennsylvania, saying, "No person shall be molested or prejudiced for his or her conscientious persuasion or practice." In Pennsylvania, he promised, they could practice their religious beliefs in a democratic way. Over time, Pennsylvania's freedom appealed not only to Quakers but also to Amish, Moravians, Slovaks, Poles, Jews, Catholics, Hungarians, Italians, Irish, Greeks, and many other religious and ethnic groups.

Penn established a legislature, making his mark as one of America's great visionaries. "He was the greatest law-giver the world has produced," said Thomas Jefferson. Penn originally intended the capital of Pennsylvania to be located in Upland, now known as Chester. In 1682 the capital moved upriver to Philadelphia. But as settlers in Pennsylvania began pushing westward, legislators decided that the capital should be in a more central location, so they moved it to Lancaster in 1799 and finally to Harrisburg in 1810.

Bureau insisted that my family drive to Gravity Hill, the most memorable of all my off-the-beaten-path destinations. Two shy Smethport teenagers, the only employees, kept me, the only dinner guest, company at the Courtyard Restaurant while I ate. And Ken Fosco made the early US Navy come alive for me on the Flagship *Niagara* while he guided me around. Ken's an enthusiast who'll never set sail (he gets seasick).

More help came from other authors. *Diners of Pennsylvania,* by Brian Butko and Kevin Patrick, is a great side dish for *Off the Beaten Path*. So is *Weird Pennsylvania,* Matt Lake's compendium of ghost stories, local legends, and other oddities from across the commonwealth.

You might say that hospitality is a cornerstone of the state, but in Pennsylvania we prefer that you say "keystone."

During colonial times Pennsylvania was the middle colony of the original 13 colonies. It held the colonies together as the keystone supports the arch above a window or door, so it's the Keystone State and has been at least since 1800. Actually, technically, it's not a state at all. Officially Pennsylvania is a commonwealth, as are only three other states—Kentucky, Massachusetts, and Virginia. The word comes from Old English and means the "common weal," or well-being of the public. In Pennsylvania all legal processes are carried out in the name of the commonwealth, although the word does not appear on the state seal.

Navigating the State

Pennsylvania's hills come in three flavors. From west to east, the state's topography slides from the Allegheny Plateau (an Ice Age leftover) through the central Ridge and Valley region, and southeast through the Piedmont, until it flattens at the coastal plain along the Delaware River.

From above, the Ridge and Valley region looks like folds in a blanket. The long, wooded ridges run southwest to northeast, with beautiful farm valleys in between. Roads generally run along those ridgetops or through the valleys. That's why the six slices of the state—three northern segments and three southern—don't follow a grid. In most cases they are bounded by the major roads (more about them later), which, in turn, find a way around the state's rivers and valleys that can seem a bit slanted. If you want straight lines, go west; if you want surprises, stick around.

YOU TAKE THE HIGH ROAD, AND I'LL TAKE ROUTE 30

Pennsylvania has the nation's fourth-largest highway system—more than 44,000 miles of highways under state control. And the Keystone State has the eighth highest count of highway miles—nearly 119,000 miles. Bottom line: It's real easy to get around. From four-lane highways with limited access to country roads that pass more cows than people, Pennsylvania has its share of concrete, macadam, and tarmac.

Most of Pennsylvania's busiest highways started out as Indian paths, as Indians had a genius for picking the most direct and level paths everywhere they went. The paths they created were no more than a foot or two wide, but they were later followed by European foot soldiers, then settlers with wagons, then modern road builders. Next stop: the interstates. When you drive any of the roads described below, you'll notice they often follow a ridgeline, a stream, a valley, or a mountain pass. You'll now know why.

Among all these roadways, five highways deserve special attention:

- **The National Road (Route 40)** was the first federally funded highway (1818 to 1835). It connected Washington, D.C., with points west, traversing Maryland, cutting across the southwest corner of Pennsylvania, running through Ohio and Indiana, and ending in Illinois. The National Road opened up land west of the Alleghenies and allowed a budding nation to expand westward. In the state's southwestern corner, Indians had long used what is now Route 40 before the European settlers paved it. In those early days the route was called Nemacolin's Path for the chief who controlled these parts. (He was, in turn, controlled by the mighty Iroquois nation to the north.) You can see tollhouses in Petersburg and Searights and nearly

50 more structures that served as taverns and inns during the road's early years. The Stone House in Farmington and the Century Inn in Scenery Hill still welcome travelers after 200 years.

- **The Lincoln Highway (Route 30)** was the first coast-to-coast highway. When it was established in 1913, it was merely a line on a map, stretching from New York City to San Francisco by connecting existing roads. In 1925 the government began numbering highways. In 1928 the Lincoln Highway Association fabricated and installed (with the help of Boy Scouts) more than 3,000 concrete markers—one at almost every mile—across the entire country. Bands of red, white, and blue (with a big L) were painted on telephone poles to designate the highway. Alas, road widenings, snow plows, and natural disasters have destroyed all but about 20 markers. The Lincoln Highway Heritage Corridor LHHC (www.lhhc.org), a nonprofit organization, aims to encourage you to follow this ribbon of highway, where you'll discover nifty attractions that your grandparents might have seen. Within Pennsylvania, Route 30 covers 320 miles and 13 counties. At its westernmost Pennsylvania point, it's 4 miles west of Hookstown; it runs east through the state and crosses the Benjamin Franklin Bridge, connecting Philadelphia to Camden, New Jersey. Reach LHHC at Box 582, Ligonier 15658. You can also call (724) 238-9030, fax (724) 238-9310, or visit www.lhhc.org.

- **Route 6** starts out mountainous in the east, then flattens out to a 2-lane highway that strings together all the county seats of what's called the "northern tier." This is one of those in-between Indian paths: big mountains flank your car as you drive through the Brokenstraw Valley, near the Allegheny National Forest. It may be a national road, but the speed limit is still a leisurely 50 miles per hour most of the way.

- **Route 1** is a mostly stop-and-don't-go path through dreary suburban strip malls around Philadelphia—but be patient. Follow it south into Chester County and you'll find the heart of the Brandywine Valley—home to Wyeths, mushrooms, universities (Cheney and Lincoln), and farmland.

- **The Pennsylvania Turnpike.** Talk about the beaten path—this one's been beaten just about to death. Those who drive it may frequently admire the feats of engineering that took it through four mountains (and over a few more), two rivers, and the state's major cities. But they can't bring themselves to admire its congestion, seemingly constant summer construction, and frequently foggy conditions. (I won't even mention the tolls.) The Pennsylvania Turnpike developed the Sonic Nap Alert Pattern

(SNAP), which is the placement of rumble strips along the edge of the right lane to alert drivers who are falling asleep. A better way to stay awake: Grab a map and plot a route that takes you off the turnpike as much as possible.

DELIGHTFUL DRIVING TOURS

If you shun turnpikes, the state has some suggestions specifically for you in its "PA Roadtrips" page on the state website. Among the ideas to whet your appetite are visits to artisanal cheesemakers in the Cumberland Valley or the best pizza joints in Old Forge. For classic country roads, consider the routes dubbed "Scenic Byways." My favorite, among a baker's dozen of quiet 2-lane excursions, is the 60-mile meander through the Laurel Highlands, home to Fallingwater and handsome mountaintop vistas. See the suggestions at www.visitpa.com.

funfoodfact

Chocolate factories in Pennsylvania include Blommer, in East Greenville; Godiva, in Reading; Goldenberg, in Philadelphia; Hershey, in Hershey; Mars, in Elizabethtown; R. M. Palmer, in West Reading; and Wilbur, in Lititz. How sweet it is.

THE MASON-DIXON LINE

The English astronomers Charles Mason and Jeremiah Dixon surveyed parts of the colonies in the 1760s and drew a straight line—the stripe that became the Mason-Dixon line. Pennsylvania touches the north side of the line; Delaware, Maryland, and West Virginia touch the south. During the Civil War the North,

When Autumn Leaves Start to Fall

In autumn 127 varieties of trees change from summer green into 127 spectacularly brilliant fall colors. Choose this time to hike or bike Pennsylvania's trails. If you know where to look, Pennsylvania offers hundreds of miles of scenic biking paths. Kudos to former Governor Tom Ridge, an avid cyclist, for asking engineers to link the commonwealth's most level country roads. The result is a network of 6 less-traveled routes that take you near major cities but keep you far from clogged highways. You share the road, but safely. Routes A, E, G, L, S, Y, and Z are well marked. Check out the map at www.bikepa.com/routes. For off-road riding, get some trail tips at www.explorepatrails.com. And check the regional chapters of this book for local ideas.

the Union, comprised the "free states," and the South, the Confederacy, comprised the "slave states."

WELCOME CENTERS

The Pennsylvania Department of Transportation (PennDOT) and the Pennsylvania Turnpike Commission operate welcome centers at highway entrances to the Keystone State. Knowledgeable and friendly hosts at the centers can offer directional assistance; provide detailed information about Pennsylvania's culture, history, scenic attractions, and activities; give you the weather forecast; report on road conditions; and arrange overnight accommodations. The centers have vending machines, picnic tables, restrooms, and pet areas. The welcome centers operate from 7 a.m. to 7 p.m., 7 days a week, including most holidays. Following is a list of welcome center locations.

- **Allegheny Mountains:** Warfordsburg, I-70 westbound, 0.5 mile north of Maryland border

- **Brandywine Valley:** Linwood, I-95 northbound, 0.5 mile north of Delaware border

- **Delaware Water Gap:** I-80 westbound, 0.5 mile west of New Jersey border

- **Dutch Country:** State Line, I-81 northbound, 1.5 miles north of Maryland border

- **Endless Mountains:** Great Bend, I-81 southbound, 0.5 mile south of New York border

- **Gateway to Route 6:** Matamoras, I-84 at exit 53, 0.5 mile south of New York border

- **I-83 North:** Shrewsbury, I-83 northbound, 2.5 miles north of Maryland border

- **Laurel Highlands:** Mount Morris, I-79 northbound, 5 miles north of West Virginia border

- **Lehigh Valley:** Easton, I-78 westbound, 0.5 mile west of New Jersey border

- **Pennsylvania Great Lakes:** North East, I-90, 0.5 mile west of New York border

- **Shenango Valley:** West Middlesex, I-80 eastbound, 0.5 mile east of Ohio border

- **Tioga:** Route 15 southbound, 7 miles south of New York border

- **Washington:** Claysville, I-70 eastbound, 5 miles east of West Virginia border

Kids Welcome

Children and inner children will find plenty of play time in Pennsylvania. Zoos abound (Philadelphia's is the oldest in the country, with 1,600 creatures; others in Pittsburgh, Hershey, and Erie are large and thriving). Philadelphia's Please Touch Museum is world-class; Pittsburgh's Children's Museum includes a salute to a local hero, TV's Mister Rogers. Sesame Place, in Bucks County, has been voted one of *Parents* magazine's top picks for its rides and Muppets. The Crayola Factory in Easton is a rainbow of markers, stickers, glitter, and color. And amusement parks? Pennsylvania boasts some that are twirled and true: Kennywood and Idlewild in the west, Hersheypark and Dorney Park in the east. Daredevils love Camp Woodward's skateboarding ramps and classes for extreme sports near State College, while toddlers prefer to feed the

Eleven Keystone Food Firsts

- 1861: Julius Sturgis Pretzel Company, Lititz, becomes America's first commercial baker.

- 1894: Cracker Jacks are first manufactured in Philadelphia.

- 1900: Frank Fleer coats chewing gum in sugar. *Voilà:* Chiclets.

- 1902: Fast food is born at the Horn & Hardart Automat, 818 Chestnut St., Philadelphia.

- 1904: The banana split makes its first appearance in Latrobe.

- 1918: Frank Fleer does it again: Dubble Bubble.

- 1920: Emil's, 1800 S. Broad St., Philadelphia, makes sandwiches for Hog Island workers and calls them hoagies.

- 1929: Sam Isaly of Pittsburgh creates the Klondike, the first ice-cream bar, selling it for a nickel.

- 1936: Frank Ludens of Reading concocts the Fifth Avenue candy bar.

- 1937: Good 'n' Plenty candy is manufactured in Philadelphia.

- 1968: Jim Delligatti, a McDonald's franchise owner, invents the Big Mac in Uniontown.

ducks at Dutch Wonderland in Lancaster County. And while you're driving the kids from one to the other, tune in to "Kid's Corner," a Sunday-through-Thursday radio show. More than 40,000 kids call in each month, making the Philadelphia-based show the most popular National Public Radio program for under-tens. Find it on WXPN-FM, 88.5, Philadelphia, 88.7, Lancaster, and 104.9, Allentown; WXPH-FM, 88.1, Harrisburg; and WKHS-FM, 90.5, Worton, Maryland. Or listen online at http://kidscorner.org.

Pennsylvania Fast Facts

PENNSYLVANIA'S OFFICIAL DESIGNATIONS

- **Animal:** White-tailed deer
- **Arboretum:** Morris Arboretum, Philadelphia
- **Beverage:** Milk
- **Bird:** Ruffed grouse
- **Dog:** Great Dane
- **Fish:** Brook trout
- **Flower:** Mountain laurel
- **Fossil:** *Phacops rana,* a small water animal
- **Insect:** Firefly
- **Motto:** Virtue, Liberty, and Independence
- **Ship:** Flagship *Niagara*
- **Tree:** Hemlock

GEOGRAPHY

- **Area:** 45,888 square miles
- **Campsites:** 7,000
- **Capital:** Harrisburg, in Dauphin County
- **Counties:** 67
- **Counties with no traffic lights:** Forest and Perry
- **Geographic center:** Centre County, 2.5 miles southwest of Bellefonte

- **Highest point:** Mt. Davis, 3,213 feet

- **Lakes:** 1 Great Lake (Lake Erie), 50 natural lakes (over 20 acres wide), and 2,500 artificial lakes

- **Largest county:** Lycoming, which is larger than Rhode Island

- **Lowest point:** Delaware River

- **Miles of Appalachian Trail:** 230 (The midpoint of the 2,144-mile Appalachian Trail, where it's traditional for hikers to eat a half-gallon of ice cream, is in Pine Grove Furnace State Park, Cumberland County.)

- **Rivers and streams:** 54,000 miles, more flowing water than any other continental state

- **Rivers with the hardest-to-pronounce names:** Schuylkill (say SCHOOL-kill) and Youghiogheny (rhymes with sock-a-SAY-knee) Rivers

- **Size:** 44,820 square miles of land, plus 735 square miles of Lake Erie

- **Species of fish:** 159

- **Species of trees:** 127

- **State forest districts:** 20; 2,200,000 acres

- **State game lands:** 294; 1,379,002 acres

- **State parks:** 116; 282,500 acres; 5,000 miles of trails

GOVERNMENT

- **US representatives:** 18

- **State representatives:** 203

- **State senators:** 50

- **Municipalities:** 2,566 (more than any other state)

- **Sales tax on clothing and shoes:** Zero

PENNSYLVANIA FIRSTS

- **First hospital**—Pennsylvania Hospital, Philadelphia, 1751

- **First newspaper**—*Pennsylvania Packet,* Philadelphia, 1784

- **First national capital**—Philadelphia, 1790

- **First American theater**—Walnut Street Theater, Philadelphia, 1809

- **First brewery**—Yuengling Brewery, Pottsville, 1829

- **First zoo**—Zoological Society of Philadelphia, 1874

- **First all motion-picture theater**—Nickelodeon, Pittsburgh, 1905

- **First Jeep**—Bantam Car Company, Butler, 1940

- **First computer**—University of Pennsylvania, Philadelphia, 1946

- **First educational public television station**—WQED, Pittsburgh, 1954

AGRICULTURE (THE STATE'S LARGEST INDUSTRY)

- **Farmland:** 7.7 million acres

- **Farms:** 59,000

- **Leading farm products:** dairy products, mushrooms, apples, tobacco, grapes, peaches, cut flowers, Christmas trees, and eggs

- **Rural population:** 3,560,000

MASCOTS OF MAJOR SPORTS TEAMS

- **Philadelphia Eagles**—Eagle

- **Philadelphia Phantoms**—Phantom

- **Philadelphia Phillies**—Phanatic

- **Philadelphia 76ers**—Hot Shot

- **Pittsburgh Pirates**—Parrot

- **Pittsburgh Penguins**—Iceberg

- **Pittsburgh Steelers**—Steely McBeam

FAMOUS NATIVES & RESIDENTS

- Christina Aguilera, *recording artist*

- Louisa May Alcott, *novelist*

- Marian Anderson, *contralto*

- Kevin Bacon, *actor*

- Samuel Barber, *composer*

- John Barrymore, *actor*

- Donald Barthelme, *author*

- Stephen Vincent Benét, *poet and story writer*

- Daniel Boone, *frontiersman*

- Ed Bradley, *TV anchorman*

- James Buchanan, *US president*

- Alexander Calder, *sculptor*

- Rachel Carson, *biologist and author*

- Mary Cassatt, *painter*

- Henry Steele Commager, *historian*

- Bill Cosby, *actor*

- Jimmy and Tommy Dorsey, *bandleaders*

- W. C. Fields, *comedian*

ANNUAL TEMPERATURE AVERAGES (FAHRENHEIT): MAXIMUM/MINIMUM

	Allentown	Erie	Harrisburg	Philadelphia
January	35/20	33/20	37/23	39/24
April	61/39	54/37	62/42	63/43
July	85/64	79/62	86/66	87/68
October	64/43	61/44	65/45	67/47
	Pittsburgh	Scranton	Wayne County*	Williamsport
January	35/20	33/19	34/19	29/15
April	61/40	58/38	61/39	54/35
July	83/62	82/62	84/62	79/60
October	63/43	62/42	63/41	58/40

*Closest city: Binghamton, New York

Are You Feeling Lucky?

Pennsylvania now allows table gaming and slot machines at select locations around the state. Five of the casinos are located at race courses: Parx Casino in Bensalem; Presque Isle Downs & Casino in Erie; Hollywood Casino at Penn National in Grantville, near Harrisburg; the Meadows in Washington; and Mohegan Sun at Pocono Downs. The Poconos resort area also boasts the Mount Airy Casino (www.mountairy casino.com). Rivers Casino commands a waterfront location in Pittsburgh as the name suggests, and Bethlehem's Sands Casino occupies the site of a former steel mill. In the Philadelphia area, there's Sugarhouse Casino and Harrah's Chester, with Valley Forge Convention Center set to begin gaming in 2012. Nemacolin Resort in Fayette County is also set to open a casino in 2012.

- Stephen Foster, *composer*

- Robert Fulton, *inventor*

- Martha Graham, *choreographer*

- Alexander Haig, *former US secretary of state*

- Marilyn Horne, *mezzo-soprano*

- Lee Iacocca, *auto executive*

- Reggie Jackson, *baseball player*

- Wiz Khalifa, *rapper*

- Gene Kelly, *dancer and actor*

- Grace Kelly, *Princess of Monaco*

- S. S. Kresge, *merchant*

- Mario Lanza, *actor and singer*

- Man Ray, *painter*

- Margaret Mead, *anthropologist*

- Andrew Mellon, *financier*

- Tom Mix, *actor*

- Arnold Palmer, *golfer*

- Robert E. Peary, *explorer*

- Betsy Ross, *flag maker*

- B. F. Skinner, *psychologist*

- John Sloan, *painter*

- Will Smith, *actor*

- Gertrude Stein, *author*

- James Stewart, *actor*

- John Updike, *novelist*

- Wallis Warfield, *Duchess of Windsor*

- Andy Warhol, *artist*

- Fred Waring, *bandleader*

- Ethel Waters, *singer and actress*

- Anthony Wayne, *military officer*

- August Wilson, *poet, writer, and playwright*

- Andrew Wyeth, *painter*

Philadelphia

As a native of the Philadelphia region, I love coming back to visit this historic city. To me, it's not only a place with lots of Revolutionary history—it's a hip, youthful city with wonderful art and architecture. Did I mention the fabulous food scene?

Philadelphia has the fifth-largest metropolitan area in the country. The region comprises 5 counties in Pennsylvania (Bucks, Chester, Delaware, Montgomery, and Philadelphia) plus 2 in New Jersey (Camden and Gloucester). In the 1960s Walter Annenberg, who then owned the *Philadelphia Inquirer* and *Daily News,* coined the phrase "Delaware Valley," essentially for marketing purposes. The term stuck for decades but has recently fallen out of favor. Now it's safe, once again, to refer to the Philadelphia region or to the Philadelphia metropolitan area.

Philadelphia was not always a bustling urban center of 5 million people. When William Penn received a gift of a lot of forestland in the New World—hence, Penn's Woods, or Pennsylvania—he became a 17th-century urban planner. The

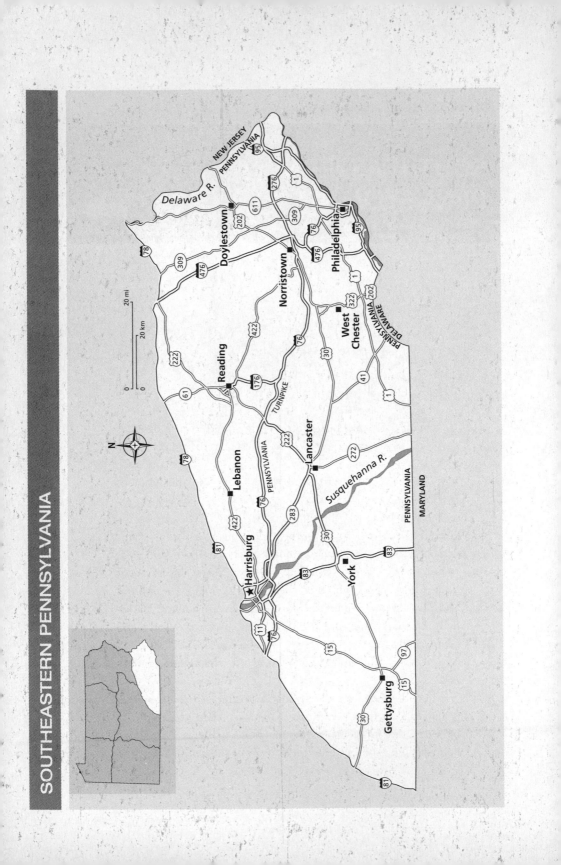

SOUTHEASTERN PENNSYLVANIA

orderly street plan he created for Philadelphia is replicated in several other Pennsylvania towns, notably Lancaster and Carlisle.

Penn envisioned Philadelphia as a modern "greene countrie towne." Within his 2-mile-wide-by-1-mile-north/south street grid, he designated 5 squares to remain forever verdant. In the central square, cleverly called Center Square, the city built its *City Hall* in 1871. The surrounding 4 squares—Logan to the northwest, Rittenhouse to the southwest, Washington to the southeast, and Franklin to the northeast—remain delightful spots to stroll, meet a friend, or picnic.

trivia

What better postmark than the signature of the nation's first postmaster? Get Benjamin Franklin's John Hancock on letters mailed from the US Post Office at 316 Market St., next to his home.

Atop City Hall, crowning a 548-foot tower, William Penn surveys his city. He faces northeast, toward the spot where he made a legendary treaty with the *Lenni-Lenape Indians* in 1682. For the next four generations, the Penn Family and the Quakers dominated the city. You can find out more at the *Arch Street Friends Meeting House* (320 Arch St.; 215-627-2667; www.archstreetfriends .org). Still in regular use, the meeting house profiles Pennsylvania's amazing founder in "Penn the Peacemaker," a small permanent exhibit. A few blocks south, at Second and Walnut Streets, a small plaza called Welcome Park offers a small-scale version of Penn's city plan and a timeline of his tumultuous life. He died in England in 1718.

Liberty Bell? Check. Independence Hall? Ditto. Most of Philadelphia's most popular attractions lie within Independence National Historical Park. Start your visit there with a stop at the *Independence Visitor Center,* a perfect

AUTHOR'S TOP 10 FAVORITES IN SOUTHEASTERN PENNSYLVANIA

American Philosophical Society	Franklin Square
Brandywine River Museum	Mt. Gretna
Chanticleer	Rosenbach Museum
distelfinks	Wright's Ferry Mansion
Fairmount Waterworks Interpretive Center	USA Weightlifting Hall of Fame

orientation to the neighborhood. Check out the free movies, plot your itinerary on a giant map, get your timed admission tickets to free attractions, and quiz the helpful staff for suggestions. It's open daily at 1 N. Independence Mall West.

For more information phone (800) 537-7676 or (215) 925-7676, or visit www.independencevisitorcenter.com. Hours are 8:30 a.m. to 7 p.m. from Memorial Day through Labor Day; 8:30 a.m. to 6 p.m. during the months of Apr, May, and Sept; and for the rest of the year, 8:30 a.m. to 5 p.m.

Just north of the Visitor Center, stop by the *National Constitution Center* (525 Arch St., Independence Mall). The building by I. M. Pei, opened for the document's 220th birthday in 2003, includes a hectic first floor with high-tech, interactive displays that interpret all 8 articles and 27 amendments. Civic-minded kids can take the presidential oath in front of the capitol on live TV or don Supreme Court judicial robes. In Signers' Hall, mingle with clustered,

How to Order a Cheesesteak

Ordering a cheesesteak—that overstuffed hot sandwich of paper-thin sliced beef on a long, freshly baked Italian roll—can be intimidating, and not just because the counter man usually looks greasy and vaguely unhappy. This toothsome favorite, known elsewhere as a Philly steak, will hit your stomach like a hunk o' hunk o' burnin' love.

Most Philadelphians pledge allegiance to a preferred vendor—just ask the nearest local for the best shop within walking distance.

Cheesesteaks are messy. They're usually wrapped in paper for takeout (you should also grab lots of napkins and remove your tie). They are best eaten when you are absolutely famished, and washed down with a birch beer—a favorite local soda that tastes a bit like a Dr. Pepper.

Here's what you want to decide before that scary cook barks questions at you:

Half or whole? A half sandwich is a 6-inch slab; a whole is the equivalent of roughly 2 full meals.

Cheese? Complicated. First decide if you want the cheese; if not, order a steak. If you want the classic provolone topping, order cheese. If you like soft processed cheese from an aerosol can, order with Whiz.

Green stuff? A cheesesteak hoagie means topped with chopped lettuce and tomato. Specify your onions cooked or raw. Peppers can be either sweet or hot; mushrooms, always cooked.

Sauce? In Philly parlance, sauce means spicy tomato sauce (feel free to specify lots or a little). You could ask for ketchup instead. Go for the burn.

After all that, don't be surprised if your order turns out wrong. Somehow, it's all good.

lifelike statues of the document's 43 signatories—authentic to their well-polished brass fingertips. Because it's often quite crowded, with many school groups on weekdays, book your timed admission tickets ahead, either here or at the Visitor Center. Open daily. Admission is $12 for adults and $11 for seniors (extra for other special exhibits); student tickets range from $8 to $11, while children under 4 get in free. For more information call (215) 923-0004, or visit www.constitutioncenter.org.

A new open-air attraction on the Mall is ***The President's House: Freedom and Slavery in the Making of a New Nation.*** The site, with archeological artifacts, commemorates life at the nation's first executive mansion, where George Washington—with nine slaves—and John Adams lived. Admission is free.

Franklin Square, the most recently restored of Penn's original city parks, is an instant kids' antidote to Too Much History. Located a block north of the Constitution Center at Sixth and Race Street, it offers a cool fountain, an antique carousel, a playground, and a minigolf course (look for the pint-sized replicas of Philly landmarks that mark some of the 18 holes).

Franklin Square is also one of the best places in town to hear a good story—the true stories of the struggle for independence. Costumed re-enactors invite passersby to join them on free storytelling benches around Old City, or join them for ticketed themed walking tours through ***Once Upon a Nation.*** My personal favorite: the Tipplers' Tour, an evening stroll through the 18th-century pubs near the waterfront. Activities are seasonal; get details and buy tickets at Historic Philadelphia, which also sells tickets to Lights of Liberty and the ***Betsy Ross House.*** Find them at 600 Chestnut St., (215) 629-4026. Hours vary, but the center is open daily and also sells tickets online at www.historicphiladelphia.org.

phlashforward

Park your car and ride the *Phlash,* a small van that makes 18 touristic stops in Center City. It operates every fifteen minutes from 10 a.m. to 6 p.m. spring through fall, and costs $2 per trip or $10 for an all-day family pass. Call (215) 440-5500 or visit www.gophila.com/phlash for more details.

Most Old City tourists grab their souvenirs and meals along Market Street. Since 1745, locals have done their shopping a few blocks south, at ***Head House Square.*** Originally dubbed "The Shambles," meaning a butcher's lane, the brick arcade at Second and Pine Street still hosts Sunday farmers' markets in warm weather. A block away, South Street offers one of the city's funkiest shopping and dining scenes, with everything from antiques to tattoo parlors. My favorite Christmas ornament—a papier-mâché Mexican wrestler—came from ***Eyes Gallery*** (402 South St.,

215-925-0193; www.eyesgallery.com). There are dozens of other one-of-a-kind boutiques; get the details at www.southstreet.com.

"Music is the most magical form of communication among people," said Wolfgang Sawallisch, former music director of the *Philadelphia Orchestra.* For more than 100 years the orchestra has been creating musical magic in Philadelphia and beyond. With Leopold Stokowski, Eugene Ormandy, and Riccardo Muti among its noted conductors, the orchestra has commissioned dozens of works of art, recorded scores of others, and entertained audiences from Ottawa to Osaka. By 1988 it was calculated that the orchestra had traveled enough to circle the Earth a hundred times. Its current home, the Kimmel Center for the Performing Arts, opened in 2001 at Broad and Spruce Streets. It's a block away from the century-old Academy of Music, called the "Grand Old Lady of Broad Street." For more information and detailed schedules, visit the Fabulous Philadelphians at www.philorch.org.

The *Philadelphia Museum of Art* is a must-see. For an off-the-beaten-time opportunity try Friday evenings, when, in addition to seeing the artwork, you can order a cocktail, catch a live performance, and mingle with other aficionados—all for the normal museum entrance fee of $16 per adult (students over 12 pay $12). The museum includes the Perelman Building, across the street from the 200-gallery main building. On the first Sunday of each month, admission fees are pay-what-you-wish (but blockbuster exhibits require a separate ticket). Call (215) 763-8100 or visit www.philamuseum.org to find out what's on tap.

trivia

The majestic plateau now topped by the Philadelphia Museum of Art was formerly a giant reservoir. Powered by the river, pumps raised water into reservoirs high atop the hill, which gave its name to the city park: Faire Mount.

In addition to the grand Swann Memorial Foundation, below the museum on the Benjamin Franklin Parkway, Philadelphia has plenty of impressive public art. Claes Oldenburg is represented by four fanciful works. The newest is his **Paint Torch** on Lenfest Plaza at the Pennsylvania Academy of Fine Art (118 N. Broad St.; follow the signs to North Broad and Cherry Streets). His **Clothespin** stands at the corner of Fifteenth and Market Streets. **Split Button** lies on the campus of the University of Pennsylvania, nearest the intersection of Thirty-fourth and Walnut Streets. **Giant Three-Way Plug, Scale A, 3/3,** perches next to the Museum of Art itself.

A few blocks west, at the pedestrian-only intersection of Locust Walk and Thirty-seventh Street, take a seat on the bronze bench next to the bronze statue of Benjamin Franklin, founder of the university. Ben's reading his *Pennsylvania*

Gazette, leaning on his cane, and waiting for you to sit down and relax. He knows he's a photo op extraordinaire.

For lunch you can't beat the **Reading Terminal Market.** Founded in 1892 at the terminus of the Reading Railroad, this is a traditional stall market with 85 merchants selling usual and unique kinds of fish, meat, produce, pastries, flowers, and more. That's far fewer than the 800 stalls that lined the place on opening day, but it's big enough to find precisely the spice or the sourdough roll you want. The market is particularly known for its Pennsylvania Dutch vendors, who bring fresh-this-morning produce and treats from the surrounding countryside each day. It's open daily from 8 a.m. to 6 p.m. and on Sun from 9 a.m. to 5 p.m. Restaurant and individual merchant hours may vary (see www .readingterminalmarket.org). Many stands sell delicious lunches at reasonable prices. Get your Philadelphia soft pretzel here.

Another in-your-face Philadelphia shopping tradition is the loud, messy, and lively **Italian Market.** It sprawls on both sides of South Ninth Street between Fitzwater and Wharton Streets, with 4 cheese stores, 4 fish stores, 7 butcher shops, 40 different international food vendors, and a larger-than-life mural of beloved former mayor Frank Rizzo, here called the Big Bambino. For more than 100 years, this district has been the city's favorite place to rub elbows and pinch tomatoes. Open every day but Sun. Get the details at www .phillyitalianmarket.com.

Don't overlook the excitement of other ethnic neighborhoods. The city's Jews, Asians, Latinos, and African Americans welcome you, too.

The **National Museum of American Jewish History** is the only museum in the nation dedicated exclusively to exploring and interpreting the American Jewish experience. The NMAJH was originally founded by the members of historic Congregation Mikveh Israel, established in 1740. Its new home at 101 S. Independence Mall East opened in 2010. Visit anytime except Mon and Jewish holidays, but note that tickets ($12) cannot be purchased within the museum on Sat. Book online at www.nmajh.org instead.

Enter Chinatown at **Friendship Gate,** at Tenth and Arch Streets, and grab a meal and your bearings at **Joseph Poon Chef Kitchen** at 1010 Cherry St. Poon, a larger-than-life celebrity chef, leads 3-hour "Wok 'n' Walk" tours of his neighborhood by appointment. They include a 4-course lunch and local color: everything from a Tai Chi demonstration to a vegetable-carving lesson. Lunch and the tour cost $60 per adult. For more details call (215) 928-9333 or visit www.josephpoon.com.

Nearby at 700 Arch St., explore the African-American community's heritage at the **African-American Museum in Philadelphia,** with 4 galleries. Open Tues through Sat, 10 a.m. to 5 p.m., Sun noon to 5 p.m. Admission is $10 for

The Philadelphia Negro

In 1899 W. E. B. DuBois published *The Philadelphia Negro,* a meticulously researched, groundbreaking study of African-American life. The book, now a recognized classic in its field, was ignored by the people who sponsored it. The 27-year-old, spats-wearing, cane-carrying, Victorian-looking gentleman researched the 40,000 African Americans who lived amid more than a million whites in Philadelphia, then the second-largest city in the nation.

adults, $8 for seniors and children. Call (215) 574-0380, or visit www.aamp museum.org. The Philadelphia Dance Company, known locally as Philadanco, is one of the country's foremost African-American performing groups; it's headquartered at 9 N. Preston St. in West Philadelphia.

The Philadelphia Latino community calls the Fifth Street and Lehigh Avenue corridor "El Centro de Oro," or its heart of gold. Here you'll find Taller Puertorriqueño, a Puerto Rican cultural education organization; Asociación de Musicos Latinos Americanos (AMLA), a center for Latin music; and great bodegas and cafes.

One of Philly's toughest neighborhoods is lightening up. *Fishtown,* a two-fisted stretch of abandoned factories and warehouses just northeast of center city, is adding new restaurants and art galleries. One sweet spot for the tattooed and trendy is *Johnny Brenda's* (1201 Frankford Ave.; 215-739-9684; www.johnnybrendas.com). It's a gastropub named after a famous local boxer, and indie rock bands play upstairs. Locals pick up produce at Greensgrow, an urban farm stand on Cumberland Street. New shops dot nearby blocks on Frankford Avenue. But the sentimental favorite among local eateries is still *Johnny's Hots* (1234 N. Delaware Ave.; 215-423-2280), with award-winning cheesesteaks and a local sandwich specialty: hot sausage with a fishcake smashed on top. Don't ask.

The Benjamin Franklin Parkway holds some of the jewels of Philadelphia—the majestic Museum of Art, the Franklin Institute, the Rodin Museum, the Museum of Natural Sciences, and the Free Library (founded by Ben himself).

In May 2012, the *Barnes Foundation,* a private collection formerly housed in suburban Merion, moves next door to the Rodin. Now this spectacular collection of Impressionist and early modernist masterworks can be seen by a wider public at 2025 Benjamin Franklin Pkwy. Call (215) 640-0171 or visit www.barnesfoundation.org.

While in the city, don't overlook some smaller gems with world-class special collections.

One of the city's oddest museums is preserved, quite literally, off North Broad Street, 3 blocks from the Temple University campus. The *Wagner Free Institute of Science* (1700 W. Montgomery Ave.) is an institution housing the private collections of the altruistic William Wagner. Since its founding in 1855, it has offered free public education courses. Fossils, taxidermy mounts, skeletons, insects, minerals, geodes, and shells—Wagner meticulously amassed a collection now displayed in a grand 3-story Victorian library. It even claims the first American saber-toothed tiger. It's both spooky and spectacular, a perfect setting for a horror movie. Admission is still free, though the institute suggests a donation. Hours are Tues through Fri 9 a.m. to 4 p.m. Visit www.wagner freeinstitute.org.

Just a few blocks from the Wagner, visit the only museum in the country dedicated to the collection and preservation of black dolls: the *Philadelphia Doll Museum,* which highlights the story of how African-American people have been perceived throughout world history by exploring the subtle cultural messages conveyed by its 300 handmade and manufactured dolls from Africa, Europe, and America. It's open Thurs through Sat from 10 a.m. to 4 p.m. and Sun from noon to 4 p.m. at 2253 N. Broad St., (215) 787-0220, philadollmuseum .com. Admission is $4 for adults, $3 for all others.

In the Rittenhouse Square area, a beautiful spot for strolling and shopping, stop by the *Rosenbach Museum* at 2008–10 Delancey Place. It's the palatial town home formerly owned by two brothers: Philip Rosenbach, who collected rare furnishings, and A. S. W. Rosenbach, who collected rare books and manuscripts. Today you can gape at rarities on display from the museum's vast holdings: the original manuscript of James Joyce's *Ulysses,* Shakespeare folios, rare Americana, and works by

roamifyou wantto

Roll along the Benjamin Franklin Parkway aboard an invention he'd adore: a Segway scooter. Tour the museum district and the Kelly Drive waterfront on these self-balancing scooters. Reservations only. For more information call (877) 454-3381 or glide to www .iglidetours.com.

children's author/illustrator Maurice Sendak (for whom the museum's new addition was named). The museum opens at noon Tues through Sun; closed Mon and national holidays. Admission is $10, $8 for seniors, and $5 for students, and free for children under 5. Guided tours are required for most galleries. Call (215) 732-1600, or visit www.rosenbach.org.

Like the Rosenbach, the *Pennsylvania College of Physicians Mutter Museum* is housed in a Rittenhouse Square town house and has its own

A Case of Nerves

The anatomical model outside the bookstore at Drexel University College of Medicine's East Falls campus looks eerily true to form, with good reason: It's the remains of a real human body. What appears to be string art is actually the nervous system of a college cleaning woman who willed her body to science in 1888. The school's foremost anatomy professor at the time spent five months manually picking out every piece of bone and flesh from the cadaver before wrapping each strand of the nervous system in wet gauze and preserving it with paint and shellac. See it at 2900 Queen Ln., (215) 991-8100, drexelmed.edu.

unique niche, but there all similarities end. In fact, "endings" might be a good theme for this bizarre collection of skulls, lesions, a giant distended colon, the secretly removed tumor of Grover Cleveland, and much more. Both medical and morbid, for certain members of certain families (parents of teenage boys, are you listening?) it would be engrossing, as well as gross. The museum at 19 S. Twenty-second St. is open daily from 10 a.m. to 5 p.m. and till 9 p.m. Fri. Adult admission is $14. Call (215) 563-3737, or visit www.collegeofphysicians.org.

The *Philadelphia Art Alliance,* located on ultra-fashionable Rittenhouse Square, displays innovative visual art. Built as a private home in 1906, the building was given to the Art Alliance in 1925. People initially joined the organization so they could imbibe alcohol on Sundays—the building was a speakeasy during Prohibition. The facility at 251 S. Eighteenth St. is open Tues through Sun from 11 a.m. to 5 p.m. Admission is $5 for adults and $3 for seniors and students. Fri is pay as you wish. The Gardenia Restaurant on the premises serves lunch from 11:30 a.m. to 2:30 p.m. For more information call the alliance at (215) 545-4302, or visit www.philartalliance.org.

For those intrigued by Lewis and Clark, a visit to Independence National Park is definitely in order—not to gawk at the Declaration, but to view artifacts of the famous 1803–04 expedition at the *American Philosophical Society* next door at 105 S. Fifth St. Among the society's founders were Benjamin Franklin and Thomas Jefferson. The society, which directed scientific preparations for the Corps of Discovery, owns Lewis's original journals and exhibits them each summer. Rembrandt Peale's famous portraits of the explorers are displayed with those of other early American heroes a block away. (Pick up a nifty walking guide detailing other neighborhood sites connected to the historic journey at the park's visitor center.) The society presents displays in the library lobby and the next-door Philosophical Hall. The library's displays are open Mon through Fri from 9 a.m. to 4:45 p.m. Philosophical Hall's museum opens at 10 a.m. either Thurs through Sun (Mar 25 to Labor Day) or Fri through Sun (Labor Day to Dec 31). Admission is supposedly free, but a $1 donation is requested. For more information call (215) 440-3400, or visit www.amphilsoc.org.

Go to jail. Go directly to jail. Do not pass Go, and do not miss a tour of the **Eastern State Penitentiary** at Twenty-second Street and Fairmount Avenue. You can stay for a short time, unlike Willie Sutton (who robbed banks because, he said, that's where the money was) and Al Capone. This was the world's first *penitentiary,* a place where criminals could be *penitent.* Constructed in the 1820s to rehabilitate criminals through solitary confinement, the castlelike penitentiary that was once the most expensive building and most famous prison in the world is now a crumbling, empty block of sky-lit cells and guard towers. The Halloween events—well, they're a scream. Eastern State Penitentiary is open daily 10 a.m. to 5 p.m. and stays open until 8 p.m. on Fri in June, July, and Aug. Groups of 20 or more can book ahead. Call (215) 236-3300, or visit www.easternstate.org.

At Forty-third Street and Baltimore Avenue, in the pocket-sized Clark Park, is a **statue of Charles Dickens,** the only known sculpture in the world of the English author of classics such as *David Copperfield* and *Great Expectations.*

For over a hundred years, men (and, of late, women and children) have strutted along Philadelphia's Broad Street on the first day of the year, commemorating winter with costumes, comedy, and uncommon music. It's the internationally recognized **Mummers Parade.** The annual parade is an hours-long extravaganza of otherwise-normal people dressed in glitter, feathers, and organza. They march, dance, strut, and vie for prizes (and bragging rights). Thousands of enthusiastic revelers line city sidewalks at dawn each Jan 1 as the clubs, or "brigades," of Mummers dance to the music of banjos. Think of it as Carnival, with overdressed middle-aged men instead of underdressed hotties. Visit www.mummers.com or the **Mummers Museum,** 1100 S. Second St. The phone number is (215) 336-3050.

Philadelphia boasts **Fairmount Park,** the biggest planned urban park system in the world, with more than 8,700 acres of parkland, including natural and historical features, cultural attractions, recreation areas, and waterways.

The park comes within a 5-minute walk from downtown along Kelly Drive. Renamed for a famous Philadelphia rower (and brother of Princess Grace of Monaco), the road closes to traffic on Sunday so bikers, runners, and bladers can enjoy the riverfront scene from its east bank. Alongside are crew teams practicing for the city's many regattas; they finish their races close to **Boathouse Row,** the oft-photographed stretch of Victorian riverfront buildings. Bathed in floodlights at night, they're best seen either from West River Drive

The Mural Tour

Early in 1999 Philadelphia surpassed Los Angeles as having the most urban murals of any city in the country. On exhibit 24 hours a day, with no admission fee and no waiting lines, 2,300 murals tell the story of the city's vitality, history, and dreams. The brainchild of Jane Golden, the **Mural Arts Program** (215-685-0750; www.muralarts.org) has created 1,900 of those murals, inspiring hundreds of disadvantaged youths to work with professional artists. To everyone's pleasure, as the murals go up, graffiti decreases. Here, with permission from the Mural Arts Program, is a self-guided tour of 11 popular murals. By car this tour takes about an hour. Or take the tour by trolley from Apr to Oct. Tickets are $25 for adults, $23 for seniors, and $15 for children 3 through 10.

Start at the Tourist Center at Sixteenth Street and J. F. Kennedy Boulevard.

Go west on Kennedy Boulevard toward Twentieth Street, moving into the left lane as you drive.

Turn left on Twentieth Street.

In 1 block turn right on Market Street.

Continue 0.9 mile, across the Schuylkill River. Turn right on Thirty-third Street.

In 0.4 mile turn right on Hamilton Street.

In 2 blocks turn left on Thirty-first Street.

In 1 block turn left at Spring Garden Street.

Look for **Tuscan Landscape** on your left.

Get in left lane and turn left at light on Thirty-second Street (sign may be missing).

In 4 blocks turn right at Powelton Avenue.

In 0.7 mile, look across Fortieth Street for **Boy with Raised Arm.**

Continue west on Powelton Avenue to third light, where it intersects with Market Street and Forty-fourth Street. Look across the intersection for **A Celebration of Community.**

Turn left onto Market Street. Go 1.7 miles, crossing the Schuylkill River, and turn right on Twenty-third Street.

In 0.6 mile cross South Street. Continue south, as Twenty-third Street bears right and becomes Grays Ferry Avenue.

Go 0.7 mile and turn left on Twenty-ninth Street.

Go to second stop sign (Wharton Street) and look across intersection for **Peace Wall.**

Continue on Twenty-ninth Street to second stop sign; turn left on Dickinson Street. Go 1.3 miles and turn left on Broad Street (which would be Fourteenth Street).

At first light (Reed Street), look across intersection to see **Mario Lanza.**

Continue on Broad Street about 0.8 mile; turn right on South Street.

At Sixth Street turn right and face **Brazilian Rainforest.**

Continue on Sixth Street and turn right on Christian Street.

Cross Seventh Street and look right for **Moonlit Landscape.**

Continue on Christian Street and turn right on Ninth Street.

Go 6 blocks and turn right on Pine Street.

Turn left on Seventh Street, and stay on it for 1.9 miles. You will run into Washington Square. Follow Seventh Street clockwise around the square, staying in the right lane.

At Race Street, bear left around Franklin Square. Stay on Seventh, in the middle lane. Go straight, driving under the multilane I-476 overpass.

At Brown Street, look across intersection on left to see **Immigration and the Dignity of Labor.**

Continue north on Seventh. Turn left at Poplar Street.

Turn left on Eighth Street.

In 2 blocks turn right on Fairmount Avenue.

Turn left on Twelfth Street.

In 2 blocks turn right on Mt. Vernon Street.

In 1 block turn sharp left on Ridge Avenue.

In 1 block at Green Street, look left to see **Dr. J.**

Turn left on Green Street.

Turn left on Eleventh Street.

In 1 block turn left on Mt. Vernon Street.

When Mt. Vernon ends at Broad Street, turn left.

Go 3 blocks to intersection of Spring Garden Street. Look across intersection on left for **Common Threads.**

Continue on Broad Street for 8 blocks to intersection with Vine Street. Look across intersection for **A Tribute to the Family.**

When Broad Street ends at City Hall, turn right onto J. F. Kennedy Boulevard. Go straight, crossing Fifteenth Street, to return to Tourist Center on your right.

The mural project also creates 3-dimensional art. See artist Bob Phillips's **Metamorphosis,** a series of forged steel butterflies, chrysalis lamps, ornamental railings, and mosaics on the bridge that crosses the CSX tracks between Thirty-first Street and Fairmount Park.

(where you can't stop your car to enjoy them) or from the promenade outside the Fairmount Waterworks.

The *Fairmount Waterworks Interpretive Center,* located in the largest cream-colored building in the group below the Museum of Art, is a great free introduction to what was once a worldwide wonder. In 1821 the city created an ingenious system that used water power to pump water. Waterwheels, installed in the dam below the Engine House, used 30 gallons of water to lift 1 gallon out of the river. The dam was the largest in the world and created a lake in the Schuylkill that was 6 miles long—which is why it's been a favorite rowing venue ever since.

The center does a lighthearted job of showing kids how water is treated and transported (even the restrooms are educational, with displays on "The Journey of Your Flush"). Don't miss the wonderful short film that explains how the city turned the waterworks into a profit-making venture that beautified the entire riverbank, with parks, fountains, and promenades. The center is at 640 Waterworks Dr. and is open Tues through Sat from 10 a.m. to 5 p.m., Sun from 1 to 5 p.m. (except for city holidays). Call (215) 685-0723 or visit www .fairmountwaterworks.org. The Waterworks Restaurant (www.thewaterworks restaurant.com) alongside offers 5-star dining and views.

On the western side of the Schuylkill, one of Fairmont Park's grandest structures has become its newest museum for kids. In 2008, the *Please Touch Museum* moved to Memorial Hall, built for the 1876 Centennial Exposition, filling the vast, 38,000-square-foot space with exciting exhibits for the under-7 crowd. It's a spectacular transformation. There's a carousel and family-friendly cafe on site. Open daily except Thanksgiving and Christmas; admission is $15, no matter what your age (4231 Ave. of the Republic, 215-581-3181; www.please touchmuseum.org).

> ## trivia
>
> Near Wissahickon Creek in northwest Fairmount Park you'll see Hermit Street, Hermit Lane, and Hermit Terrace. The streets commemorate a brotherhood of 17th-century German mystics led by Johannes Kelpius, who lived in a cave nearby.

The perfect trip to Philadelphia includes a visit to *Valley Green*—if you can find it. A 5-mile-long, dirt-and-gravel path called *Forbidden Drive* passes through Valley Green. It's so called because it forbids automobiles, admitting only walkers, runners, horses, bikers, and bladers. Take Germantown Avenue northwest to #7900, turn left on Springfield Avenue, and follow signs (and the topography downhill) to the valley. Or take Henry Avenue northwest to #7900, then turn right on Wise's Mill Road, following signs to the valley. If you're on foot, access Forbidden Drive anywhere and stop for coffee or crepes at the **Valley Green Inn.** Call (215) 247-1730, or visit www.valleygreeninn.com for reservations.

Northwest of downtown, the neighborhood of **Germantown** was a bustling village well before 1776. Today, it's a community that has fallen on hard times, but several house museums commemorate its past. **Stenton** is the well-preserved Georgian home of James Logan, secretary to William Penn. Logan was a powerful figure and a mentor to Benjamin Franklin, who borrowed his books (the collection was the foundation for Philadelphia's Free Library). Nearby **Wyck,** a Quaker home from 1690, maintains a 175-year-old rose garden. The Battle of Germantown was conducted on the grounds of **Cliveden,** now a National Trust property. Visiting hours for all three are seasonal and limited. For the how-to's, visit www.freedomsbackyard.com.

Follow Germantown Avenue farther north and you'll climb to **Chestnut Hill,** a well-heeled historic district. Cobblestoned, tree-lined Germantown Avenue is loaded with blocks of pleasant shops and cafes; nearby lie the leafy campuses of Germantown Academy and Chestnut Hill College. To browse the many cafes in the neighborhood, visit www.philadelphiarestaurants.com.

Chestnut Hill is also the home of the **Morris Arboretum** of the University of Pennsylvania, a romantic 92-acre garden that emphasizes sculpture, trees, and research. Kids love its Out on a Limb, a treetop canopy walk that includes a suspension bridge and play areas. It's a quarter mile off Germantown Avenue at 100 E. Northwestern Ave. You can enjoy lunch alfresco, or at least under a tent, during warm weather at the cafe next to the Widener Visitor Center. The arboretum opens daily at 10 a.m. Admission is $16 for adults, $14 for seniors, $7 for students; kids under 3 are admitted free. Tip: Get a discount by biking or hiking there. Call (215) 247-5777, or visit www.upenn.edu/arboretum.

In nearby **Elkins Park** (take Route 611 north from the city) is Frank Lloyd Wright's **Beth Sholom Congregation.** Dedicated in 1959, months after Wright's death, the building is a hexagonal pyramid of glass. The design is based, in part, on ideas put forth by the synagogue's distinguished and

Creepy Crawlies

Talk about thousand-leggers: the country's largest bug museum is the **Insectarium,** where swarms of live and mounted insects crawl through the imagination of children and adults. See (and sometimes touch) newly discovered and extinct species, bug out while watching insect movies, and creep through a man-made spiderweb. The museum is at 8046 Frankford Ave., (215) 335-9500, myinsectarium.com.

forward-looking first rabbi, Mortimer Cohen. The building was intended to be self-contained and to stand apart from its suburban surroundings. It succeeds. Wright designed the fittings, too: the lighting, the seating, and the placement of the religious symbols. When the Museum of the Diaspora in Tel Aviv created a permanent exhibit of synagogues to represent 18 centuries of Judaism, it chose Beth Sholom for the 20th century. Tours of the sanctuary, at Old York and Fox-croft Roads, are given Sun, Wed, and Thurs. To visit, check www.bethsholom preservation.org or call (215) 659-3009. To attend religious services, call (215) 887-1342, extension 227.

Nyuk nyuk nyuk! From the sublime to the ridiculous: A few minutes north of Elkins Park lies a monument to the holy trinity of witless comedy. The **Stoogeum** immortalizes the head-knocking, eye-poking genius of the Three Stooges, Larry, Moe and Curly, with exhibits, film clips, and memorabilia tucked into a space in a suburban strip mall off Bethlehem Pike in Gwynedd Valley. Can you tour it? Soitenly. The building is open once a month, so visit www.stoogeum.com to find out exactly which day to visit. For additional information, you can contact curator Gary Lassen at (267) 468-0810, but he far prefers e-mails sent to garystooge@aol.com.

Got a few hours' layover between planes? Go fishing. It's actually possible, from Philadelphia International Airport, to hop in a cab and be transported across the highway into a national wildlife refuge. This one, the **John Heinz National Wildlife Refuge at Tinicum,** was created to save the largest remaining freshwater tidal marsh in the country. As planes soar overhead, 300 species of birds fly below. The interpretive center at 8601 Lindbergh Blvd. is open daily. Additional information can be found at http://heinz.fws.gov.

Another patch of green—one of the city's most venerable—lies a few miles down Lindbergh Boulevard. From its surroundings—the Philadelphia Gas Works and other flat and charmless industrial sites—you'd never guess

ON THE BEATEN PATH ATTRACTIONS WORTH VISITING

Academy of Music, Philadelphia

Independence Hall, Philadelphia

Liberty Bell, Philadelphia

National Constitution Center, Philadelphia

Pennsylvania Academy of Fine Arts, Philadelphia

Philadelphia Zoo

Barnes Foundation, Philadelphia

that the site is a landmark in the history of botany. **Bartram's Garden,** the 18th-century home of the naturalist Bartram family, is an idyllic Schuylkill River plantation that preserves native wildflowers, trees, and wetlands.

Father and son John and William Bartram are credited with sharing the plants of the New World with European scientists; John was named King George III's royal botanist in 1765. Both he and his son identified new species on field trips up and down the East Coast, cultivated more than 200 of them, and saved at least one from extinction: the *Franklinia,* a tree named for their good friend and frequent visitor Benjamin Franklin. (Thomas Jefferson and George Washington stopped by, too). Today visitors can stroll the plantation and river trail, admiring the skyscrapers of downtown Philadelphia from a peaceful meadow. A map brochure identifies the locations of famous specimens, such as the country's oldest living ginkgo tree (circa 1785).

Boat trips along the Schuylkill are available on weekends in warm-weather months. Those tours are run by the Schuylkill River Development Corporation. Check the schedule at their website, schuylkillbanks.org, or call them at (215) 222-6030.

Bartram's Garden is open daily, except for city holidays, and admission to the grounds is free. Garden shop hours are 10 a.m. to 2 p.m. Mon through Thurs and 10 a.m. to 4 p.m. Fri through Sun. Guided garden and house tours leave the Garden Shop Fri through Sun at 10:30 a.m., noon, 1:30 p.m. and 3 p.m. (2 garden tours, 2 house tours). The tours cost $10 for adults, $8 for seniors and students; children 12 and under are free. The garden is located at Fifty-fourth Street and Lindbergh Boulevard but is hard to find; call first for directions at (215) 729-5281, or visit www.bartramsgarden.org.

Philadelphia gave birth to the nation's first horticultural society in 1827 and its first flower show in 1829. At the first show, 25 members of the Pennsylvania Horticultural Society showed off their magnolia bushes, peonies from China, an India rubber tree, the coffee tree of Arabia, and sugarcane from the West Indies. Today the **Philadelphia Flower Show** is an international success: 10 acres of soil, picket fences, orchids, and more—spectacular, enviable gardens created by nurseries and florists enlivening the Pennsylvania Convention Center. Crowds of more than 300,000 people cross-pollinate at the early-March flower show, the world's biggest to be held indoors. For more information call (215) 988-8800, or visit www.theflowershow.com.

Inner Suburbs

Harriton House was the northernmost tobacco plantation operated on the slave economy. It's at 500 Harriton Rd., Bryn Mawr. It's open by appointment from 9 a.m. to 5 p.m. Tues through Sat, so call ahead (610) 525-0201, or visit www.harritonhouse.org.

Right in the middle of the beaten path is *Valley Forge National Historical Park,* where George Washington and his 11,000 soldiers slept fitfully during the winter of 1777–78. If you are a history buff, an enthusiastic kid studying the Revolution, or just a healthy visitor out for a country walk—if you are, in fact, anything but a British loyalist—you'll enjoy the natural and historical beauty of the park. The visitor center offers an excellent short free film introduction and other services, and bike rentals are available in good weather. The park grounds are open daily year-round from dawn till dusk. The visitor center and Washington's Headquarters are open 9 a.m. to 5 p.m. daily except Thanksgiving, Christmas, and New Year's Day. Valley Forge National Historical Park, 1400 N. Outer Line Dr., King of Prussia, (610) 783-1077.

Not far away is the *Mill Grove Audubon Wildlife Sanctuary,* on a bluff overlooking Perkiomen Creek. The museum features an array of wildlife art by *John James Audubon,* in a rural setting with 3 miles of trails. The first American home of Audubon, the museum charges $4 for adult admission, $3 for seniors, and $2 for children. It's open Tues through Sat 10 a.m. to 4 p.m. and Sun 1 to 4 p.m. The grounds are open daily except Mon, from dawn to dusk. Find it at the intersection of Audubon and Pawlings Roads, Audubon. Call (610) 666-5593 for details about naturalist programs, some of which are perfect for children.

Consider, too, a visit to the *Wharton Esherick Museum.* This Philadelphia-born artist spent much of his life in this curious, rustic 5-story structure, creating designs mostly in wood. Like Barcelona's famed Antonio Gaudí, Esherick eschewed straight lines and right angles. The 2-story spiral staircase, carved from a single piece of wood, defies description but begs to be touched, as do many of the displayed pieces the artist designed for the 1940 World's Fair in New York. The hour-long guided tour is not recommended for young children. Tours of this National Historic Landmark for Architecture are available Mar through Dec, 10 a.m. to 5 p.m. Sat, and 1 to 5 p.m. on Sun; groups of 5 or more may tour weekdays from 10 a.m. to 5 p.m. Adult entry is $12 and includes a 1-hour guided tour. The studio is on the Horseshoe Trail near Country Club Road. Check www.whartonesherickmuseum.org or call (610) 644-5822 for reservations and driving directions.

While nearby Longwood Gardens gets the tour buses and big crowds, *Chanticleer,* in Wayne, attracts the folks who garden for fun. Its British designer, Chris Woods, spent 20 years transforming an estate on the city's posh Main Line into a contemporary garden that arouses the senses.

Open to the public since 1993, Chanticleer's 2 manor houses are surrounded with bold shapes, modern contrasts, and a lighthearted approach. The result looks like a hip children's picture book. No placards with Latin plant names here—just oceans of color and shapes, punctuated by witty garden sculpture. Stroll an easy mile-long path, linking 8 separate plantings, that winds down a gentle green slope. Beds close to the circa 1913 house (the former home of the Rosengarten family) are pleasingly structured. Those at a distance, like the Woods and the Water Garden, flourish seemingly undisturbed,

A Day on the Main Line

Built to shuttle the wealthy in and out of Philadelphia in style, the *Main Line* train became synonymous with old money and grand estates. The stops along the way—like Haverford, Bryn Mawr, Rosemont, and Villanova—also correspond to gracious college campuses and chic shopping and are well worth a drive west along Route 30, known here as Lancaster Avenue. One savvy local, Libby O'Toole, shared some of her favorite spots.

Start in Bryn Mawr, where the area's most beloved toy store fronts the street at number 839½. *Pun's Toys* has gotten "best of" honors from local magazines and lots of lucky kids. Skip the cartoon action figures—Pun's has marvelous tin soldiers from centuries of wars, velvety plush creatures, juggling equipment, puzzles, puppets, and more. It opens at 9:30 a.m. Mon through Sat. Visit www.punstoys.com or call (610) 525-9789.

For hand-painted Italian ceramics, try *Via Bellissima,* at 853 W. Lancaster Ave.; it's open Mon through Sat 10 a.m. to 5:30 p.m.; call (610) 581-7414 or visit http://viabellissima.com. One block down the street, grown-up girls love *Skirt,* a tiny boutique crammed with everything from this year's most sophisticated prom dresses to designer flip-flops. It's open Mon through Fri, 10:30 a.m. to 6 p.m., and 10:30 a.m. to 6 p.m. on Sat; call (610) 520-0222, or browse www.shop-skirt.com.

Continue past the gray Gothic Villanova University campus to Wayne. The corner of Conestoga Road and Lancaster is home to *The Flag Lady* (398 W. Lancaster Ave.; (610) 964-6280; www.flagladygifts.com), with Vera Bradley specialties, seasonal decorations, and holiday accessories that Main Line matrons love. The matron's teenage kids prefer *South Moon Under,* with men's and women's clothing and hip dorm-wares like picture frames and candles. Open daily at 205 W. Lancaster Ave.; (610) 964-9064; www.southmoonunder.com.

Stash the shopping bags and relax at *Georges'.* This bistro by Georges Perrier, founder of Philly's 4-star Le Bec-Fin, has a bar with a roaring fire and a casual dining room (503 W. Lancaster Ave.; (610) 964-2588; www.georgesonthemainline.com). Or relax with tea on the Victorian veranda at the *Wayne Hotel.* This restored century-old landmark is a charmer, with 4 floors of elegant guest rooms and a main floor restaurant, *Taquet* (139 E. Lancaster Ave.; 610-687-5000; www.waynehotel.com).

with swaths of single colors, like red clover or blue camas, punctuating the lawns.

Chris Woods's whimsical sensibility takes a theatrical turn in the Ruin Garden, 3 open-air garden rooms that were built on the foundation of a prior residence on the property. A large fountain, inspired by ancient sarcophagi, dominates the Great Hall, mirroring the surrounding trees in its dark waters; huge sculpted stone books spill over the floor of a library; and in the Pool Room, marble faces gaze tranquilly from the watery depths of another fountain.

Chanticleer is located at 786 Church Rd., Wayne; call (610) 687-4163, or visit www.chanticleergarden.org. It's open Apr through Oct, Wed through Sun, 10 a.m. to 5 p.m. (until 8 p.m. Fri, May through Labor Day). Admission is $10 for adults, free for those 12 and under. Docents lead 90-minute group tours twice daily Wed through Fri, but you'll enjoy a solitary stroll just as much.

Art aficionados adore the **Brandywine River Museum** (Route 1, just south of Route 100, Chadds Ford), one of the largest and most comprehensive collections of paintings by three generations of Wyeths (N. C., Andrew, and Jamie) and Howard Pyle. The exhibition, in a 19th-century gristmill overlooking the stream, changes often, so you might see your favorites (like *Jamie's Pig*) next to works you've never seen. It's open every day except Christmas, 9:30 a.m. to 4:30 p.m., and admission is $10 for adults. Call (610) 388-2700, or visit www.brandywinemuseum.org.

At **Longwood Gardens** (Route 1, PO Box 501, Kennett Square 19348), the extravagant, elegant, exquisite horticultural displays are open every day of the year, from 9 a.m. to 5 p.m. Jan to Mar, and staying open until 6 p.m. Apr through Oct, with extended hours in summer and at Christmas. The conservatory opens at 9 a.m. Exotic flowers thrive in hothouses, and illuminated fountains highlight summer concerts. Longwood is a carnival of 20 indoor gardens, 400 performing-arts events each year, a gift shop, and a restaurant. Daily programs and classes ratchet up your green-thumb quotient. Admission is $18 for adults, $15 for seniors, and $8 for children ages 5 to 18. Call (610) 388-1000 or go to www.longwoodgardens.org for details.

Follow Route 1 south until you get to **Lincoln University,** just northeast of Oxford. Lincoln, founded in 1854, is the nation's oldest historically black college. Originally named Ashmun Institute, it was renamed in 1866 to honor President Abraham Lincoln.

In addition to being the cradle of liberty, Philadelphia is also the birthplace of the helicopter industry. That's why you'll find the **American Helicopter Museum,** a sure-fire kids' favorite, 20 minutes from Route 1 in West Chester. You'll learn about the history of the chopper and see vintage machines and the only V-22 Osprey on public display in the United States; some days, you can even hop into a helicopter for a quick flight. Family rides are offered the third Saturday of the month for $40 per person. *Philadelphia Magazine* voted the museum its "best scientific outing for kids" a few years back, for the number of things that they can get into—wind tunnels, instrument cockpits, and hands-on exhibits. The museum is off Route 202 at 1220 American Blvd., adjacent to the Brandywine Airport. It's open Wed through Sat 10 a.m. to 5 p.m., and Sun from noon to 5 p.m., and Mon and Tues by appointment only. Admission is $10 for adults; $8 for seniors, students, and children; and free for little fliers under 2. Call (610) 436-9600, or fly to www.helicoptermuseum.org.

Armchair shoppers love **QVC,** the cable television network that hawks everything from zirconium to cookware. When they leave home, they flock to its West Chester studios for a glimpse into its inner workings. Daily guided walking tours take them to an observation deck overlooking the broadcast area. The station is at 1200 Wilson Dr., near the Helicopter Museum. Tours run 7 days a week at 10:30 a.m., noon, 1 p.m., 2:30 p.m. and 4 p.m.; tickets are $7.50 for adults and $5 for children ages 6 to 12. Call now, as they say: (800) 600-9900, www.qvctours.com. Bring identification.

West Chester's downtown, planned as a neat 18th-century grid by the Penn family, is worth a stroll, with eateries, galleries, and the campus of West Chester University.

If you'd rather bike, walk, or skate than drive, try the **Schuylkill River Trail** to get from here to there. It extends 26 miles from Center City Philadelphia along the Schuylkill River to Phoenixville. (When completed, the trail will be 130 miles long.) If you live in the area, consider walking the trail in spurts till you cover it all.

Nothing could be farther off the beaten path than the **Museum of Mourning Art** at Arlington Cemetery in Drexel Hill (2900 State Rd.). Would you believe emblems of the skull and skeletons, hearses, and mourning jewelry can be found in a museum? Open weekdays from 8 a.m. to 4:30 p.m. Call (610) 259-5800 or check http://arlingtoncemetery.us.

On the northern edge of the metropolis, Doylestown, the Bucks County seat, offers a concrete-and-tile monument to one man's life. It's **Fonthill,** the home of Henry Mercer. Mercer (1856–1930) was a polymath of astounding energy. After training as an attorney and following a career as a globe-trotting archaeologist, he turned artist, designing and producing thousands of tiles at the height of the American Arts and Crafts movement. (The floor of the state capitol is inlaid with some of the results.) Mercer crammed the walls and ceilings of his castlelike abode with his own work and added extensive displays of pottery, lighting, and furniture. One writer called the result "Colonial Williamsburg on amphetamines." It's less crazy when you learn that Mercer always intended his home to be a museum. The next-door Moravian Pottery and Tileworks and the **Mercer Museum** a few blocks away comprise the town's "Mercer Mile."

Both Fonthill and the Mercer Museum are open daily (the museum is open Tues evenings, too) but are closed on certain holidays. Call Fonthill at (215) 348-9461 and the Mercer Museum at (215) 345-0210, or visit www.mercer museum.org. Admission is $12 for Fonthill and $10 for the museum.

Upscale flea market may be a contradiction in terms, but it aptly describes nearby **Rice's Market** (6326 Greenhill Rd., New Hope; 215-297-5993; www .ricesmarket.com). There's been a weekly market on this 30-acre site since 1860; now there are two, on Tues and Sat. It's a Bucks County tradition, located midway between Doylestown and the Delaware River, with vendors hawking everything from antiques to zucchini. Get there early.

As you travel west, drop south to Chester County and **Historic Yellow Springs** (1685 Art School Rd., Yellow Springs). This village "has a connection with every era of American life," says staffer Pat McGlone. During the Revolutionary War, Washington's troops traveled here from Valley Forge for the medicinal waters. During the Civil War, Union troops recuperated at its hospital. Sixty years later, lured by the bucolic surroundings, the Pennsylvania Academy of Fine Arts established its landscape school here. In 1958 Steve McQueen spent his honeymoon at the springs while filming *The Blob* locally. Nowadays the beautifully restored Inn at Yellow Springs serves exquisite French dinners, and the remaining buildings host art programs. For directions and details call (610) 827-7414, or visit www.yellowsprings.org.

Pennsylvania Dutch Country

About 300 years ago, groups of religious refugees from the Rhine region of Germany migrated to southeastern Pennsylvania. These settlers, mostly peasant farmers, came to take advantage of the religious freedom offered by William Penn. They included Amish and Mennonites—people of "plain" dress—and Lutherans and other Reformed groups of more worldly attire, sometimes called "fancy." Over time these people became known as "Pennsylvania Dutch," with the *Dutch* really a misinterpretation of the original *Deutsch*.

Wilkum to Lebanon and Lancaster Counties and the scenic Pennsylvania Dutch Country, where life moves at a slower pace and centers around time-honored traditions and values. Here you find beautiful scenery punctuated with one-room schoolhouses and wooden covered bridges, modern farm machinery pulled by mules, homemade clothing and quilts hanging to dry. You hear the clip-clop of horses' hooves on quiet country roads. The plain folks are less materialistic and less hurried than their urban counterparts, yet the highways through **Lancaster County** have grown touristy, as various people attempt to capitalize on the otherworldliness of these self-effacing settlers. Virtually any T-shirt shop, quilt boutique, or restaurant in the area can hand you a brochure with a self-guided driving tour. For a glimpse of a real Pennsylvania Dutch family, enjoy the movie *Witness* and leave these people alone.

Begin exploring off Route 72 in Lebanon County. It's the less-traveled part of the region, with equal numbers of "English" and Amish residents. While Lancaster County, to the south, hawks its "real Pennsylvania Dutch" attractions with ferocity, Lebanon County treats its Amish neighbors with deference and respect. Farms seated on the richest soil in the country sport immaculate barns and flourishing gardens. Stern Biblical quotes flank mailboxes. In the quiet, a syncopated trot heralds horse-drawn buggies before they come into view.

> ## trivia
>
> **Baldwin's Book Barn** in West Chester is just that: an 1822 barn crammed with 300,000 titles, both new and antique. Call it the anti-Amazon. Open daily; call (610) 696-0816, or visit www .bookbarn.com.

The region's German dissenter roots still flourish. In Schaefferstown, bright signs adorned with distelfinks, the folk-art icons of the region, adorn adjacent museums. The modest **Gemberling-Rex House and Brendle Museum** display 250 years of village history. They're not open often, so plan ahead (717-949-2244; www.hsimuseum.org). A historic tavern operates nearby: the Franklin House (Route 419 on the town square in Schaefferstown; 717-949-2122). It offers German platters and sandwiches for weekend lunches and serves dinner daily except Mon; call for hours.

Three miles west of Reading, there's a place to test an old adage: Give a man a fish, and you feed him for today; teach a man to fish, and you feed him for a lifetime. **Limestone Springs Preserve** (930 Tulpehocken Rd., Richland; 717-866-2461; www.limestonespringspreserve.com) offers recreational trout fishing Apr through Oct. For $1 admission and $4 for each pound you catch, you get your chance to introduce the kids to fun that isn't generated on a video screen.

Pennsylvania has more than 100 private fishing lakes; for a full list, visit www.fish.state.pa.us/lakesreg.htm.

Head north toward Cornwall, a village with charm, history, and a pretty nice bike trail. You may have noticed how many eastern Pennsylvania towns end in "Forge" or "Furnace." There's plenty of iron ore below this land, mined since the 18th century. The **Cornwall Iron Furnace** is the only surviving furnace of its kind in the Western Hemisphere and was put to work during the American Revolution. Now a well-done state museum, it offers thoughtful displays about the region's development. The surrounding homes—grand for the owners, modest for the ironworkers—still stand. The redbrick museum is at Rexmont and Boyd Streets (717-272-9711; www.cornwallironfurnace.org). It is open Thurs through Sat from 9 a.m. to 5 p.m. and Sun from noon until 5 p.m., with the last tour beginning at 4 p.m. each day. Admission is $6 for adults, $5.50 for seniors, and $4 for youths.

Moving all that iron eventually required a short-line railroad that's now gone rails-to-trail. The Lebanon Valley Trail is now about 14.5 miles long between the Lancaster county line to Lebanon. Check progress at www.lvrail trail.com. The 1830-era Cornwall Inn (717-306-6178 or 866-605-6563; www .cornwallinnpa.com), a bed-and-breakfast at the Cornwall trailhead, was once the Cornwall mining company store. It has rooms and family-friendly suites from $139.

In the 1890s the Pennsylvania Chautauqua Society, attracted by the region's natural beauty, founded **Mt. Gretna.** The landscape is still just as inviting—gently wooded mountains, a stream, and a lake. Throughout the summer, the Chautauqua's genteel educational and cultural tradition lives on with music, theater, and arts events, and the Arts and Crafts–style cottages are treasured family heirlooms (a few can be rented, too). Follow Route 72 west from Cornwall to discover its charms.

The most well-known local attraction is the professional summer stock theater at the Gretna Theatre, where plays have been performed since 1927. Within strolling distance, on paths covered with pine needles, are the Greek Revivalist Hall of Philosophy (for lectures and chamber music), a gift boutique, and the Jigger Shop, an old-fashioned soda fountain that feels like the soul of the village. Among the highlights here are old-fashioned birch beer from a keg; fountain drinks you thought you'd forgotten, like lime rickeys; and chrome-bound counter stools that twirl until you're dizzy. The waiters and waitresses sport their colleges on their name tags (tip generously). Enjoy your lunch on the spacious deck.

Mt. Gretna's lake across the road is another throwback—a sand-bottomed freshwater lake with a beach, broad lawns, picnic pavilions, and a stationary diving platform with swing ropes in the middle.

They say you can't revisit the past. Mt. Gretna proves them wrong. Get all the details at www.mtgretna.com.

Heading south, you'll see another monument to religious expression at **Ephrata Cloister.** At the zenith of this community in the 1740s and 1750s, about 300 German members worked and worshiped here. Today the National Historic Landmark is open for tours at 632 W. Main St. in Ephrata.

The charismatic founder of this community, Conrad Beisel, settled along the Cocalico Creek in 1732. He was followed by two groups of followers: celibate men and women, who lived in dormitories, and married couples with families. All expected that the Second Coming was imminent. The monastic Anabaptist community invented its own a cappella music, created Germanic calligraphy known as Frakturschriften, and operated a printing press. By 1813 its celibate members had died; children raised in the community were less enthusiastic about the celibate tradition, and the community dwindled. Its buildings remain. Visit Mon through Sat from 9 a.m. to 5 p.m. and on Sun from noon to 5 p.m. Ephrata Cloister is often closed Mon and Tues in the off-season, as well as on winter holidays. Admission is $9 for adults, $8 for senior citizens, and $6 for youths 3 to 11. For more information call (717) 733-6600, or visit www.ephratacloister.org.

At the **Landis Valley Museum** north of Lancaster, you can see 18 historic buildings filled with artisans demonstrating the crafts, tools, and tales of German immigrants. Its shop stocks an interesting array of heirloom seeds for home gardeners. It's open Mon through Sat 9 a.m. to 5 p.m. and Sun noon to 5 p.m.; closed major holidays. Adult admission is $12. From downtown Lancaster, take Route 272 north to 2451 Kissel Hill Rd. For more details call (717) 569-0401, or visit www.landisvalleymuseum.org.

Landis Valley bills itself as a living history museum, usually a good indication that kids will find it a trifle dull. Little ones will prefer the next-door **Hands-On House,** a farm-themed attraction with an outdoor playground. It's at 721 Landis Valley Rd. Admission is $8.50 and it's open late on Fri. Call (717) 569-5437 or visit www.handsonhouse.org.

The city of **Lancaster** served as the capital of the United States for almost an entire day: September 27, 1777. At the time, British invaders were threatening the capital in Philadelphia. The Continental Congress and the Executive Council of Pennsylvania fled to Lancaster, where they held one session of congress. Believing that the British were in hot pursuit, congress kept moving across the Susquehanna River to York.

The historic heart of town, founded in the 1740s, is handsomely preserved and worth exploring. On Tues, Thurs,

trivia

Where did Pennsylvania's only US president live? Perennial bachelor James Buchanan owned Wheatland, a stately Lancaster home now open to visitors.

and Sat, Lancaster's Central Market sells the best baked goods, flowers, and farm produce around—as it has since 1730, making it America's oldest continuously operated farmers' market. The huge redbrick arcade at 23 N. Market St.

Mind the Gap

As a shortcut between Lancaster and the Delaware River, detour from Route 30. Try Route 41, which drops south from Route 30 through beautiful farmlands. Start at the tiny village of *Gap* (home of the Gap Diner), and continue past West Grove and over the state line to the Delaware Memorial Bridge. As highways go, it's a byway—restful and scenic.

opens at 6 a.m.; call (717) 291-4723. Steps away is the **Lancaster Quilt and Textile Museum,** which gives the most famous local craft its due. It's open seasonally, so call (717) 299-6440 before you go to 37 N. Market St. (www.quilt andtextilemuseum.com). Yes, of course there's a museum store.

A National Historic Monument, the **Fulton Opera House** in Lancaster was built in 1852. A gem of Victorian architecture, the theater's lush interior includes a sweeping staircase and crystal chandelier. Sarah Bernhardt, Al Jolson, W. C. Fields, Mark Twain, and others performed here. Read more history or order tickets at www.fultontheatre.org. For more downtown cultural events, including a "first Friday" evening each month, visit www.lancaster arts.org.

In western and southern Lancaster County, the hills are more pronounced and the views more dramatic. Along the Susquehanna River you'll find many scenic overlooks that offer breathtaking views of the river far below.

Lancaster County features one of the largest concentrations of antiques in the country. In **Adamstown,** the "Sunday Antiques Capital of the United States," more than 7,000 antiques dealers gather to display and sell their merchandise. Every Sunday from 7:30 a.m. to 4 p.m., Adamstown (www.antiques capital.com) becomes the essential antiquers' paradise. Dozens of shops line Route 272, with **Renninger's** (www.renningers.com) one of the best known and best loved. If you crave memories from any bygone era—even the 1990s— here's where to find what you're looking for. Take the Pennsylvania Turnpike to exit 286, then go north on Route 272.

Since 1875 **Groff's Meats** has been selling wholesale and retail meat in Elizabethtown. The fourth generation of Groffs—two brothers and two sisters— now run the business. Groff relatives and employees buy and slaughter cattle and pigs, then lovingly and painstakingly convert them into hams, bacon, sweet bologna, and, in the fall, mincemeat: a super-secret family recipe of beef and suet, local apples, raisins, sherry, rum concentrate, and spices. No minces are killed to make this concoction. Groff's Meats makes 5.5 tons—*tons*—of mincemeat a week during mincemeat season, which coincides roughly with autumn leaves. (If storage space fills up, they might skip a week.) Visit Groff's Meats at 33 N. Market St., Elizabethtown, or place a 2-pound or 35-pound order by calling (717) 367-1246.

You want corn chips? You want onion rings? **Herr Foods** is the third largest snack-food company in the country, employing 1,000 people and distributing its munchies in 10 northeastern states. The factory tour includes a 25-minute video (great for kids). Then you walk through windowed corridors, watching people and machines washing, peeling, slicing, cooking, and seasoning the food—then bagging, boxing, and preparing it for shipment. Reach onto the conveyor belt and pick up a free handful of fresh, warm chips. Yum. Herr's is at the intersection of Herr Drive and Route 272 in Nottingham, just south of Lancaster. The visitor center is open weekdays year-round except for major holidays, 8 a.m. to 5 p.m. Mon through Fri. The free hour-long tour runs on the hour from 9 a.m. to 11 a.m. and again from 1 to 3 p.m. Mon through Thurs, and 9 a.m. to 11 a.m. Fri. Call ahead to (800) 637-6225, or visit www .herrs.com for reservations.

Visit the demonstration garden and see the agricultural experiments taking place at the **Rodale Institute.** Rodale, which publishes *Prevention* and other magazines, welcomes visitors. Take a self-guided tour Tues through Sat 10 a.m. to 4 p.m. (Tues and Fri until 7 p.m.), or take a leisurely stroll through the gardens on your own anytime, 24/7. Call (610) 683-1400, or visit www.rodale institute.org.

People in the East know **Reading** for its outlets, its Pennsylvania Dutch heritage, and its antiques marts. But few people recognize that in some ways, Reading is the East—the East as in Orient, China, and pagodas. At the top of **Mt. Penn,** the 7-story **Pagoda** dominates the town's skyline. In the early 1900s William Abbott Witman bought this land to quarry its stone. But the quarrying operation defaced the mountain, which he hid by building, of all things, a pagoda, hoping it would become a luxury hotel. When Witman's license to serve alcohol was denied, the building fell into the hands of a bank. In 1910 an investor bought the full catastrophe, then sold it to the City of Reading for a dollar. You can visit, free, daily from 11 a.m. to 5 p.m. A gift shop is open Fri, Sat, and Sun on the first level. To get there, start in Reading and drive uphill. For precise driving directions call (610) 375-6399 during operating hours or check www.pagodaskyline.org.

Daniel Boone, the legendary pioneer, was born and raised in **Birdsboro.** You can visit his family's homestead and learn about 18th-century rural Pennsylvania. From Reading, take Route 422 east to 400 Daniel Boone Rd., Birdsboro. From mid-June to mid-Aug, the modest exhibit on his life is open in the visitor center Tues through Sat, 10 a.m. to 4 p.m. and Sun noon to 4 p.m.

Saving Grace

Lancaster County boasts that it has the most productive nonirrigated farmland in the United States. There are more than 4,500 farms here, mostly small and family owned. The pace of urban sprawl severely threatened these farms during the 1980s and 1990s—the *Philadelphia Inquirer* estimated the rate of loss at an acre an hour.

To the rescue came the Lancaster Farmland Trust. The trust helps farm owners obtain conservation easements to preserve their lands for agricultural use forever. And it's stemming the tide of development: since 1994 there have been two county acres saved for every one lost to development. To date, over 18,000 acres of the county's farmland has been preserved, the most successful of all such efforts nationwide.

(reduced hours in the off-season). You may visit part of the grounds for free (on my last visit, there was a Mini Cooper rally in the parking lot) or pay $6 for a guided interior tour. Call (610) 582-4900 or visit www.danielboonehomestead .org for more details.

A cozy and well-done little museum in Womelsdorf pays tribute to a very early American, Conrad Weiser. His amazing gifts as a linguist put him at the center of Pennsylvania history from 1730 to 1758. Fluent in a half-dozen Indian languages, English, and his native German, he negotiated with the Iroquois, served a magistrate and militia leader, and fathered 10 children. Somehow, he also found time to join the Ephrata Cloister for two years. The ***Conrad Weiser Homestead*** is open seasonally at 2588 Weiser Ln.; call (610) 589-2934 or visit www.conradweiserhomestead.org.

I think of "bluestocking" as a term of respect. That's why Susannah Wright, "the bluestocking of the Susquehanna," is one of my heroines. Her riverside home in Columbia, a classic Quaker structure that she built in 1738, has been restored with an outstanding collection of period arts and antiques, and is well worth a visit spring to fall. The home is known as ***Wright's Ferry Mansion.*** Wright never married, but operated a ferry business with her brother (his home on the opposite bank is now called Wrightsville), composed poetry, recorded the language of the local Shawnee people, and established a thriving silk production business by raising her own silkworms. Call (717) 684-4325 for seasonal hours. Down the street is the ***National Watch and Clock Museum,*** a deft and thoughtful look at how humans tell time. Look for the clock tower at 514 Poplar St. Hours vary; admission is $8 for individuals, $20 for the whole family. Call (717) 684-8261 or visit www .nawcc.org.

Capital District

My husband used to joke that my intellect was like the Susquehanna River: broad but shallow. It's a good description, both of my brain and of the river at **Harrisburg.** Here little forested islands dot the stream, and the only boats that can maneuver are of the pontoon variety. But Harrisburg's small downtown makes good use of its waterfront, and its state capitol complex, lavishly restored and expanded over the past few decades, is no snore—it's a stunner.

In 1906 President Theodore Roosevelt dedicated the gleaming granite capitol, declaring it "the handsomest building I ever saw." Lots of folks would argue that it outshines even the US Capitol, which stylistically shares its distinctive flights of steps and domed rotunda.

Free tours start at the foot of the grand staircase, copied from St. Peter's Basilica in Rome and the Paris Opera House. Look up—272 feet—to admire the grand dome. Look down, too: Interspersed with the terra-cotta floor tiles throughout the building are 377 mosaics by Henry Mercer's Moravian Tileworks. These mosaics depict a visual timeline of Pennsylvania, from its native animals, like the elk and robin, to the factory and automobile.

Images of women abound in the capitol, which adopts different styles for its major chambers. In the state senate chamber, you'll find the mural "Unity" by muralist Violet Oakley in which goddesses holding up light fixtures preside in pre-Raphaelite style. In the Italianate house chamber, women representing "The Hours" are featured in the dome painting by Edwin Austin Abbey, and still others are found glowing with light in the stained-glass windows designed by Philadelphian William Brantley Van Ingen.

The capitol's newer east wing houses offices, a skylit cafeteria, and the welcome center's lighthearted interactive introduction to state government (the state dog is the Great Dane because William Penn owned one). Don't miss the wonderful Rube Goldberg contraption called "Making a Bill."

Guided tours are offered every half hour Mon through Fri 8:30 a.m. to 4 p.m. Weekends and most holidays (except major ones), tours are offered at 9 a.m., 11 a.m., 10 p.m., and 3 p.m. Call the tour guide office (800-868-7672), or visit www.legis.state.pacapitol.us.

At the **State Museum of Pennsylvania** (300 North St.) older family members take the capitol tour, while toddlers may enjoy the museum's Curiosity Connection, a cute hands-on space on the ground floor. Closed Mon and Tues; $5 admission for adults, $4 for all others over age 1. Get the details at (717) 787-4980 or www.statemuseumpa.org.

Security precautions prevent visitors from parking in the garage under the capitol, and on-street parking is fiendishly difficult. Leave your car instead on **City Island,** a short walk across the Walnut Street pedestrian bridge from downtown. City Island is the site of Riverside Stadium, the summer home of the Harrisburg Senators, an Eastern League AA pro team (check the schedule at www.senatorsbaseball.com). But it's got plenty of other fun. The *Pride of the Susquehanna* paddleboat departs for river tours from its marina (call 717-234-6500). A miniature steam train, minigolf, food stands, athletic fields, and paved paths are open most of the year. If you're feeling unathletic, just take a horse-drawn carriage ride from the Harrisburg Carriage Company (717-234-1686).

Farther from downtown, Harrisburg's attractions dwindle, but firebugs may enjoy the **Pennsylvania National Fire Museum** in an old Victorian firehouse at 1820 N. Fourth St. ($6 adult admission; 717-232-8915; www.pnfm.org). Continuing the pyrotechnical theme is **The Firehouse,** a bar and restaurant 2 blocks from the capitol at 606 N. Second St. (717-234-6064; www.thefirehouserestaurant.com). The red hydrant behind the bar holds beer taps. Nearby is the capital's answer to Philadelphia's Reading Terminal: the 1860s-era **Broad Street Market** (717-236-7923), with farm-fresh

winetrail

The Susquehanna Valley is wine country, and the new *Mason-Dixon Wine Trail* lets you meander through 14 vineyards. Find maps, seasonal events, and discounts for B&Bs and hotels at www.masondixonwinetrail.com.

food, candies, preserves, and snacks. Open Wed through Sat. Eat here or carry a take-out picnic to the river along Front Street.

Four miles north of the city you'll find the gardens and greens of **Felicita,** an upscale resort with the usual dining and golf amenities. What sets this 650-acre property apart are the spectacular gardens created over 30 years by owners Richard and Alice Angino. Twenty-one gardens, with themes ranging from Alpine to Islamic to Japanese to Monet water lily, culminate in the grand Italianate, a spectacular setting best viewed from the 4-level terrace. The gardens are private property, but if you visit in warm weather, they're generally open for $10 tours on Wed and Sat morning at 10:30 a.m. For garden tours or resort reservations, call (888) 321-3713. Visit www.felicitaresort.com for more information.

While Gettysburg gets the most Civil War tourists, Civil War skirmishes reached right into **Camp Hill,** now part of the Harrisburg suburbs. Harrisburg's bid to lure some of those history buffs is the **National Civil War Museum,** which portrays personal experiences on both sides of the conflict. About 850 artifacts and lots of multimedia illuminate the lives of common soldiers, men and women on the home front, and African Americans in the conflict. It's open Mon through Sat from 10 a.m. to 5 p.m. (until 8 p.m. Wed) and noon to 5 p.m. Sun. The hilltop location, somewhat isolated from town, is One Lincoln Circle at Reservoir Park. Admission is $10 for adults, $9 for seniors, and $8 for students. Call (717) 260-1861, or visit www.nationalcivilwarmuseum.org.

The two giant cooling towers by the airport south of Harrisburg are the site of the country's worst-yet nuclear disaster, at **Three Mile Island.** The affected reactor was shut down immediately after its partial meltdown in March 1979; low levels of radiation were released. Take a photo (from a distance), and continue into Middletown. At **Alfred's Victorian,** the restaurant specialty is the Flaming Victorian Salad, which bears absolutely no relation to other kinds of leaking fuel. The address is 38 N. Union St. For more information call (717) 944-5373, or visit www.alfredsvictorian.com.

A short drive down I-83 from Harrisburg brings you to **York,** a biggish town (or a smallish city) whose history is everywhere. York, briefly the US capital in the 18th century, is now a genteel county seat just north of the Maryland state line. The Articles of Confederation were signed here in 1777. But the northern edge of town gets lots of traffic these days, and not simply because of nearby strip malls. Here stand the muscle-flexing power of two macho monuments: the **Harley-Davidson Vehicle Operations and Tour Center** and the USA Weightlifting Hall of Fame at the York Barbell Company.

The visitor center at Harley-Davidson (1425 Eden Rd.) celebrates the lure of the open road—and the choppers that frequently cost more than 4-wheeled cars. The well-designed exhibits and the factory tour are free. More than 60,000 visitors come by each year—double the number of those touring the town's colonial district. The factory tours are relatively quiet (you'll hear your guide through earphones) and are offered to guests over age 12 from 9 a.m. to 2 p.m. Mon through Fri. A play space at the center entertains younger kids. The gift shop—offering everything from leather jackets and caps to Harley-Davidson Yahtzee games—is open 1 hour earlier and 2 hours later. Call (877) 883-1450, or roar over to www.harleydavidson.com.

Up the road, look for the larger-than-life weightlifter jerking his barbells high over I-83, 5 minutes from the Harley factory. A latter-day Atlas, he lunges forward, twirling continuously above the York Barbell Company. The **USA Weightlifting Hall of Fame** next door chronicles competitive strength from ancient Greece, through its late-19th-century heyday when celebrity strongmen toured the world, to the present.

Really strong guys, at least in cartoons, favor leopard-skin leotards and handlebar mustaches. That's all due to Eugen Sandow and Louis Cyr, the trendsetters whose stunts awed Victorian fairgoers. The exhibit traces them and their descendants to the well-oiled era of Schwarzenegger and Steenrod (as in Vicki, a contemporary Hall of Famer). Most of the memorabilia in the

Hall of Fame was acquired by York Barbell's founder, Bob Hoffman, who advocated weight training, health foods, and isometrics. Practicing what he preached, he lived to the age of 87. Free admission Mon through Sat from 10 a.m. to 5 p.m. at 3300 Board Rd., exit 24 off I-83; (800-358-9675; www.york barbell.com).

York County bills itself as "The Factory Tour Capital of the World." "Conveyor belts are great!" says its guidebook. You'll find Pfalzgraff, the pottery maker; Hope Acres Farm, where robots milk the cows; Snyders, the pretzel people; and more. A good place to sort out all the man-made possibilities is right at the Harley-Davidson Tour Center, where the county maintains an information office (888-858-9675 or visit www.yorkpa.org). One-stop shopping.

Among the kitschy delights of the Lincoln Highway is the *Shoe House,* just off Route 30 at 197 Shoe House Rd. in Hellam, Adams County. It was built in 1948 by Mahlon Haines, who made shoes, then boots, then a house for honeymooners shaped like a shoe. A really big shoe: 48 feet long and 25 feet high. You can tour the shoe June through Oct (or other months by appointment) for $4.50; call (717) 840-8339 or check www.shoehouse.us for hours and directions.

Hersheypark, the famous amusement park, may be too crowded for you, but consider *Chocolate World* at the entrance to Hersheypark in Hershey. A sweet 9-minute ride takes you through a simulated chocolate factory. It's interesting for adults and a treat for kids. Hours vary by season and week; closed Christmas. During some festivals, the hours may be extended. Call (717) 534-4903 or (800) 437-7439, or visit www.hersheypark.com. You can't beat the price (it's free), and you get free candy treats at the end.

The Moorish architecture of *Hotel Hershey* is worth a peek into the lobby, even if you can't afford its 4-star prices. And the fabulous rose garden outside the hotel blooms freely (and is free for public viewing) well into November. For 23 more acres of floral displays, visit *Hershey Gardens* next door (170 Hotel Rd.; 717-534-3492; www.hersheygardens.org).

On Pennsylvania Dutch country barns and signs, you'll see lots of ornamental geometric suns, hearts, stars, and birds (here called distelfinks) These are hex signs, and their happy iconography bespeaks Old World traditions. Sun wheels connote warmth and fertility; tulips stand for faith; blue means protection; and red, emotions. Find an extensive collection at *Will-Char, the Hex Place* (3056 Rte. 30, East Paradise; 717-687-8329; www.hexsigns.com). The brilliant folk-art icons are also interpreted in quilts, and the *Old Country Store* (Route 340, Old Philadelphia Pike, Intercourse) has been called one of the nation's top-10 shops for this time-honored craft.

Battlefield Territory

Don't miss **Gettysburg.** Union and Confederate soldiers fought the bloodiest battle of the Civil War here in 1863. The area is organized for tourism, with the absorbing history communicated in virtually every medium.

War, they say, is hell. That's never more true than on a summer weekend at Gettysburg. The crowds are daunting. If at all possible, plan on a weekday visit, preferably in the off-season.

The Museum and Visitor Center should always be your first stop: It orients you to the war, the battle, and the battlefield. You can stop in for just a snack, restrooms, and free maps, but it's worth paying the $10.50 admission for a fine 20-minute film, a museum with 1,600 artifacts, and—the piece de resistance— the miraculous **Cyclorama.** The latter is the world's largest painting, created in 1884 by Paul Philippoteaux. The 377-foot picture in the round depicts Pickett's Charge in images so realistic the first visitors wept. You can purchase tickets online in advance at www.gettysburgfoundation.org, or upon arrival at the center at 1195 Baltimore Pike. It's open except for Thanksgiving, Christmas, and New Year's days, with extended summer hours.

Make the most of your visit to this well-preserved battlefield with the help of a licensed tour guide—each one must pass a detailed oral exam. Gettysburg offers bus and car tours where experts will accompany lay visitors on 2-hour trips. Car tours start at $55 for up to 6 people; bus tours, which depart from the visitor center, are $28 for adults, $17 for those aged 6 to 12.

Also at Gettysburg the **Eisenhower National Historic Site** commemo-rates Dwight D. Eisenhower's military and presidential years. The only way to get there is on a tour that departs from the visitor center. Your site visit includes the Eisenhowers' 230-acre farm and farmhouse, the only home the First Couple ever owned. The tour costs $7.50 per adult, $5 for youths.

Gettysburg also offers bicycle, horseback, and Segway tours of the battle-field—an ideal way to cover ground and to bypass crowds on the battlefield roads—with guides who know their stuff.

Horseback tours are offered not by the National Park Service but by two local firms: the **National Riding Stable** at Artillery Ridge Camping Resort, 610 Taneytown Rd. (1.5 miles from the visitor center), (717) 334-1288; and **Hickory Hollow Farm,** 219 Crooked Creek Rd., (717) 334-0349. Advance reservations are a must. **Segs in the City** offers 2-hour battlefield safaris on Segway trans-porters, spring through fall, at $70 per person; visit www.segsinthecity.net or call (800) SEGS-393.

Gettysbike offers morning, evening, and sunset tours that beat the heat. They'll rent you bikes, but you can also pedal your own. Call (717) 752-7752,

JANUARY

Mummers Parade

Philadelphia
(215) 599-0776
www.visitphilly.com
Wake up early on New Year's Day and catch the Mummers Parade, the all-Philadelphia strut of 30,000 costumed "Mummers."

Pennsylvania Farm Show

Harrisburg Farm Show Complex
(717) 787-5373
www.farmshow.state.pa.us
The Pennsylvania Farm Show has it all. For 10 days each January, the events at the Harrisburg Farm Show Complex attract human and animal competitors from all over the commonwealth. More than 350,000 people attend the show each year, making this century-old slice of Americana the largest indoor agricultural event in the United States. And it's free.

MARCH

Philadelphia International Flower Show

Pennsylvania Convention Center
(215) 988-8899
www.theflowershow.com
Spring means flowers, but nowhere more so than at the Philadelphia International Flower Show—the largest and most prestigious flower show in the world, with 10 acres of lush gardens and lavish floral settings. There's an admission fee, paid even by the show's judges.

APRIL

Penn Relays

University of Pennsylvania
(215) 898-6145
www.thepennrelays.com

The venerable Penn Relays are held at the University of Pennsylvania the last weekend of April. This track event attracts the country's fastest runners, from high schoolers to Olympic wannabes to the over-80 Masters. Reserved seating is available for Saturday events, which attract crowds of more than 40,000.

MAY

Kensington Kinetic Sculpture Derby

Philadelphia
(215) 427-0350
kinetickensington.org
Alien spaceships mounted on welded bikes, giant pink poodles hurtling through the air, and Mummers riding hand-cranked pirate ships are among the sights of the Kensington Kinetic Sculpture Derby, a Philadelphia neighborhood competition that challenges crack physicists to invent the most outrageous and artistic yet functional human-powered vehicles they can dream up.

Devon Horse Show and Country Fair

Devon Fairgrounds
(610) 964-0550
www.thedevonhorseshow.org
The Devon Horse Show and Country Fair, the nation's largest outdoor horse show, creates traffic jams up and down Route 30 for a week at the end of May.

JULY

Blobfest

Phoenixville
(610) 917-1228
www.thecolonialtheater.com
Do you pride yourself on a truly blood-curdling scream? Test it against others at Phoenixville's Blobfest. The contest is only one of the bizarre features of the

town's celebration of the cheesy horror classic *The Blob*, filmed here in 1958. Held the second weekend of July. Don't forget your own handmade tinfoil hat to ward off evil alien space rays.

AUGUST

Philadelphia Live Arts Festival and Philly Fringe

Philadelphia
(215) 413-9006
www.livearts-fringe.org
Thousands of artists converge on Philly each August for the wild and wacky art party known as Philadelphia Live Arts Festival and Philly Fringe. For 2 weeks, dancers, actors, playwrights, musicians, visual artists, video-makers, and puppeteers roam the city's streets and fill its performance halls. At night, festival-goers head to the Festival Bar for dancing, drink specials, and visual media installations. Location of the bar is to be determined.

Renaissance Faire

Mount Hope Estate and Winery
Route 72, Cornwall
www.parenaissancefaire.com
Her Majesty is at the Renaissance Faire, held weekends from late Aug through mid-Oct. Watch blacksmiths, taste "roasted turkey legges," and let loose your inner groundling. Held at Mount Hope Estate and Winery, Route 72, 0.5 mile south of Pennsylvania Turnpike exit 266 (old exit 20) (Box 685, Cornwall 17016).

SEPTEMBER

World War II Days

The Eisenhower National Historic Site
Gettysburg
(717) 338-9114
www.nps.gov/eise

Gettysburg hosts all kinds of soldiers' reunions. The Eisenhower National Historic Site, home of the Allied commander, observes World War II Days the third weekend of September, with reenactors, demonstrations, tanks, and talks.

OCTOBER

Dracula Festival

Rosenbach Museum & Library
(215) 732-1600
rosenbach.org
Twilight fan alert: A month-long Dracula Festival brings fans of the vampire novel into the light for theatrical readings, cupcake-decorating workshops, and photo booths equipped with costumes at the Rosenbach Museum & Library, which holds Bram Stoker's original *Dracula* outlines and research notes.

DECEMBER

Reenactment of Washington's Crossing

1112 River Rd., Washington Crossing
(215) 493-4076
www.ushistory.org/washingtoncrossing
George Washington crossed the Delaware River on December 25, 1776, to launch his attack on the British in Trenton. The Reenactment of Washington's Crossing launches each Christmas Day from Washington Crossing Historic Park in Bucks County, 35 miles north of Philadelphia. The visitor center displays artifacts and provides details.

stop in at 1995 Baltimore St., or check www.gettysbike.com. Closed Sun and winter months.

In the little town of Gettysburg, stop by the restored old train station on Carlisle Street or the nearby **Wills House,** where Lincoln worked on his famous address. The home of David Wills, a prominent citizen of the town, become ground zero in Gettysburg's recovery effort, with Wills himself fulfilling the roles of the CDC, the Red Cross, and FEMA combined. Exhibits there focus on the aftermath of the battle. Visit the museum at 8 Lincoln Sq.; http:// davidwillshouse.org; (717) 334-2499. Open 7 days a week May through Aug; closed on Tues in the off-season and Tues and Wed in Mar. Admission: $6.50 for adults.

There are plenty of tacky attractions in Gettysburg. Catch a movie at Gateway Gettysburg, a theater off Route 15 near the National Military Park at 20 Presidential Circle. Tickets are $8.50 for adults, $7.50 for students and seniors. Call (717) 334-5575.

The **Hall of Presidents** (717-334-5717) features wax reproductions of 36 presidents who relate American history in their own words. For a complete listing of tourist territories, dining, camping, and lodging, stop by the **Gettysburg Convention and Visitors Bureau** at 35 Carlisle St.; call (717) 334-6274; or visit www.gettysburgcvb.org.

Gettysburg nightlife offers few options except ghost tours. Many of the 51,000 battlefield casualties were carried to homes and buildings in town, and legends of ghostly apparitions have persisted for decades. One place to get into the spirit, so to speak, is **Farnsworth House** (401 Baltimore St.). In addition to selling Civil War memorabilia and books, the house also hosts candlelight evening ghost walks through town and presents the Civil War Mourning Theater, with dramatic and sometimes ghoulish monologues. A dinner theater on the premises offers period music. For details visit www.farnsworthhouseinn .com, or call (717) 334-8838.

Drive to 900 High St., Hanover, and take a deep breath. Fresh air? No. Fresh Utz (the name rhymes with *huts*) potato chips. Here is the factory of **Utz Quality Foods,** and you're welcome to take a free self-guided tour Mon through Thurs 8 a.m. to 4 p.m. Call (717) 637-6644 or (800) 367-7629 for details.

As you head west on Route 30 from Gettysburg, you have an opportunity to see the largest herd of elephants in the country. The rolling farms hereabouts are nothing like the savanna, but you can find a plethora of pachyderms at **Mister Ed's Elephant Museum** in Orrtanna. Owner Ed Gotwalt curates a collection of 6,000 specimens, all his: political, plush, Hindu, and other specimens. Tusks and ivory carvings, too. Most of the items fall into the deliciously kitschy category. So do the old-fashioned penny candies and roasted peanuts on sale in the gift store. Open Sun through Thurs 9 a.m. to 5 p.m., plus Fri and Sat 9 a.m. to 6 p.m., the shop—er, museum—is at 6019 Chambersburg Rd. Call (717) 352-3792, or visit www.mistereds-elephantmuseum.com.

Hickory Bridge Farm B&B in Orrtanna offers 9 rooms, including cottages, all with private baths. Two rooms have private whirlpools, too. Guest rooms are furnished with Pennsylvania Dutch antiques, and the cottages have wood-burning stoves. It's a genuine farmstead that boasts a red barn-turned-restaurant, a country museum with old farm equipment, a spring-fed swimming pond, and a trout stream surrounded by 50 acres of farmland. In the restaurant you're offered amazing quantities of Pennsylvania Dutch cooking in a designer country setting, Fri and Sat night and Sun noon to 3 p.m. Call (717) 642-5261, or visit www.hickorybridgefarm.com for more information.

Places to Stay in Southeastern Pennsylvania

CHESTER HEIGHTS (CHADDS FORD)

Hamanassett Bed & Breakfast
PO Box 366
Chester Heights 19017
(610) 459-3000
www.hamanassett.com
A Federalist-style mansion surrounded by Brandywine hunt country.

LANCASTER

Lancaster Arts Hotel
300 Harrisburg Ave.
(717) 299-3000
www.lancasterartshotel
.com
Chic boutique hotel and restaurant in a historic

tobacco warehouse near Franklin and Marshall College.

GETTYSBURG

Brafferton Inn
44 York St.
(717) 337-3423
www.brafferton.com
This brick-front inn in the historic district dates from 1786.

KEMPTON

Hawk Mountain Bed & Breakfast
221 Stony Run Valley Rd.
(610) 756-4224
www.hawkmountainbb
.com
A contemporary inn with swimming pool and mountain views.

LAMPETER

Australian Walkabout Inn Bed & Breakfast
837 Village Rd.
(717) 464-0707
www.walkaboutinn.com
Ask for a pastry called an Australian tea-ring and if you're brave a dollop of Vegemite on your toast.

PHILADELPHIA

Thomas Bond House
129 S. Second St.
(800) 845-BOND
www.thomasbondhouse
bandb.com
In Independence National Historic Park the home of a Revolutionary-era physician is now a restored bed-and-breakfast with views of the Delaware River.

Places to Eat in Southeastern Pennsylvania

CORNWALL

The Blue Bird Inn
2387 Cornwall Rd.
(717) 273-3000
www.bluebirdinn.com
Casual pub grub. Late-night entertainment on the tiki-torch deck attracts a young crowd on Fri and Sat nights.

DENVER

Park Place Diner
(formerly Zinn's)
Route 272 (just north of exit 286 on the Pennsylvania Turnpike)
(717) 336-2210
Pennsylvania Dutch comfort food in Amish country.

DOYLESTOWN

Paganini Trattoria
81 W. State St.
(215) 348-5922
www.paganiniristorante.com
Homemade pasta and more (plus a casual cafe across the street).

HARRISBURG

Bricco
31 S. Third St.
(717) 724-0222
Elegant Italian trattoria serving lunch and dinner near the capitol.

LEBANON

Trattoria Fratelli
502 E. Lehman St.
(717) 273-1443
www.tratfrat.com
Voted best in central Pennsylvania for a decade. Upscale innovative Italian cuisine served Tues through Sat. Try grilled chicken and polenta or crabmeat specials.

PHILADELPHIA

City Tavern
138 S. Second St.
(215) 413-1443
www.citytavern.com
Located in Independence National Park, this public house was the unofficial meeting spot for the First Continental Congress. Popular with tourists but has authentic decor and menu with venison, cider, and ales.

Dante & Luigi's
Tenth and Catherine Streets
South Philadelphia
(215) 922-9501
The oldest Italian restaurant in America.

DiNardo's
312 Race St.
(215) 925-5115
Best known for hard-shell crabs.

Pat's King of Steaks
1237 E. Passyunk Ave.
(215) 468-1547
www.patskingofsteaks.com
Cheesesteaks and hoagies.

Villa di Roma
936 S. Ninth St.
(215) 592-1295
Italian food in a tacky, brightly lit setting.

White Dog Cafe
3420 Sansom St.
(215) 386-9224
www.whitedog.com
A hip eatery and bar on the University of Pennsylvania campus.

READING

Judy's on Cherry
332 Cherry St.
(610) 374-8511
www.judysoncherry.com
New American–style cuisine and brewpub downtown. Open Tues through Sat.

Red Plate Diner
440 E. Penn Ave.
Wernersville
(610) 678-7721
www.redplatediner.com
Comfortable, friendly all-American eatery.

WEST CHESTER

Dilworthtown Inn
1390 Old Wilmington Pike
(610) 399-1390
www.dilworthtown.com
An inn since 1780 with more than 900 wines on offer. Dinner only.

Jimmy John's
1507 Wilmington-West Chester Pike (Route 202)
(610) 459-3083
A Brandywine hot dog institution. Drop a quarter in the slot to operate the massive model train display.

SOUTH CENTRAL PENNSYLVANIA →

As you head west into south central Pennsylvania, you'll see higher highs and lower lows. The mountains loom higher, the valleys get broader, and the attractions can throw you an unexpected curve. One of the biggest of the latter is the railroad wonder, ***Horseshoe Curve.*** As the early railroads expanded westward, the Pennsylvania Railroad ran into a major snag at Altoona: mountains. The grade in the Alleghenies was far too steep for a run straight up or down. To circumvent the situation and to connect two sides of Kittanning Point, engineers designed a huge, curving track, which opened to train traffic in 1854. Men used picks, shovels, and horses to carve the curve, which is still considered an engineering marvel. The length of the curve is 2,375 feet; the grade is 1.8 percent; the degree of curvature is 9 degrees, 25 minutes; and the central angle is 220 degrees.

When you come to this spot (using the Seventeenth Street exit off I-99/Route 220) where trains make a U-turn, ride the funicular or walk the 194 steps to the top; a sturdy fence protects your body from the trains but leaves your eyes and ears free to enjoy. To imagine what it's like, think of a football stadium 50 times larger than reality. You are sitting at one end

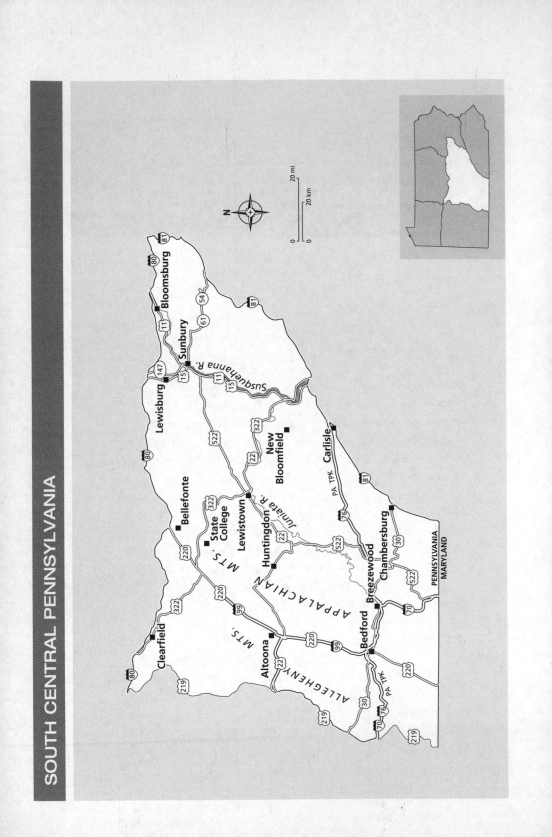

SOUTH CENTRAL PENNSYLVANIA

near the goalpost, two rows down from the top tier. At the topmost level of the stadium, a train approaches from the far end. It chugs on by, wrapping around the curve—and around you—as the engineer waves and toots his whistle. The long train continues on the other side of the stadium so that at one point, an endless iron snake surrounds you. Eventually it disappears around another curve, but you can still hear it, and everyone near you is still smiling. If the weather's nice, you can have a picnic while waiting for a few more of the 60 passenger and freight trains that traverse the curve daily. The curve is open daily in Apr from 11 a.m. to 4 p.m. From May to Oct, it is open 10 a.m. to 6 p.m. Mon through Sat and 11 a.m. to 6 p.m. on Sun. Prior to Thanksgiving, the curve is open weekends only in Nov from 11 a.m. to 4 p.m. From Dec through the end of Mar, the curve is closed. An annual grounds pass to the curve costs $6, but for $10 ($8 for seniors, $7 for children under 12), you can buy a combination pass that also covers the round-trip ride on the curve's funicular railway and a ticket to the *Altoona Railroaders Memorial Museum.* This all-in-one admission can be purchased either at the curve or at the museum, 1300 Ninth Ave. To get to the museum from I-99, take the Seventeenth Street exit, then turn right on Ninth Avenue. It's open daily May through Oct, Mon through Sat 10 a.m. to 5 p.m., and Sun from 11 a.m. to 5 p.m. The museum is also open weekends from the beginning of Nov until mid-Dec. Open only weekends in Nov and Dec; closed Jan 1 through Mar 31. For information on either site, call (814) 946-0834 or visit www.railroadcity.com.

It costs only $2.50 to ride *Leap the Dips,* the historic wooden side-friction roller coaster in Altoona's *Lakemont Park.* The amusement reopened in 1999 after 14 years in mothballs; the Leap the Dips Foundation spent a million bucks restoring the original cars and replacing the superstructure. To get to the park

AUTHOR'S TOP 10 FAVORITES IN SOUTH CENTRAL PENNSYLVANIA

Carlisle

Chambersburg Heritage Center

Coffee Pot

Gravity Hill

Horseshoe Curve

Nature Inn at Bald Eagle State Park

Millersburg Ferry

National Museum of the American Coverlet

Pike to Bike Trail

Road Kill Cafe

from I-80, take Route 220 south; after Route 220 becomes I-99, exit at Frank-stown Road. Call (814) 949-7275 or (800) 434-8006; or visit www.lakemont parkfun.com.

Alongside the park is the new home of the **Altoona Curve,** an AA East-ern League baseball team that also throws fastballs and sliders. This is *Bull Durham*–type baseball, laid-back and family-friendly. The State College Spikes of the New York–Penn League also play here. Check the schedule at (877) 99-CURVE or www.altoonacurve.com.

You'll find another historic landmark at 3205 Sixth Ave. **Reighard's** claims to be America's oldest gasoline station, offering full service to motorists since 1909.

Just 12 miles west of Altoona off Route 22, visit the **Allegheny Portage Railroad,** now a National Historic Site. At this location in 1834, canal boats were loaded onto railcars, reducing the trip between Philadelphia and Pitts-burgh from three weeks by wagon to four days by railroad and canal. At the visitor center you can take a brief history lesson. You can also walk forested trails along the railroad's route or, if you're so inclined, watch a costumed stonecutting demonstration. It's open from 9 a.m. to 5 p.m., closed major holi-days. You'll get a weeklong pass for $4. For more information write Allegheny Portage Railroad, 110 Federal Park Rd., Gallitzin 16641; call (814) 886-6150; or visit www.nps.gov/alpo.

By now, you've got the idea: Railroad buffs love this area. Their hotel of choice is **The Station Inn** in Cresson. It's a little shaky. That's why they like it. The inn's front porch is the perch where enthusiasts can watch 70 trains rumble past each day on the Norfolk Southern line. The trains are just 150 feet from the door of the hotel, built in 1866. Its 7 modest rooms are named for old railroads; the porch is where buffs trade anecdotes and lore. Contact the inn, located at 827 Front St., at (814) 866-4757, or visit www.stationinnpa.com.

caboose with a view

The New Portage, Allegheny, and Gallitzin railroad tunnels were so strategically important that they were guarded during World War II. The bright-red caboose at tiny **Gallitzin Tunnels Park** tells their story. Call (814) 886-8871 to visit.

If you head north on Route 220, then north on Route 360 and west on Route 322, you come to **Clearfield,** which originated as the Indian town of Chinklacamoose. A portion of the Old Town Historic District is listed on the National Register of Historic Places. Several stately Victorian homes offer an interesting self-guided walking tour extending 4 blocks along Front Street.

West of Altoona, along Route 22, visit the **Mt. Assisi Monastery** and the *Holy House of Father Gallitzin* in Loretto. Father Gallitzin was a Russian prince who gave up his title and inheritance; he became the first priest to receive all the orders in the United States, and he served the community of Loretto. Catholics on a pilgrimage find it refreshing to stop there as well as at the Carmelite Monastery and St. Michael's Church. For more information and to schedule a visit to the sunken gardens—open year-round, dawn to dusk—call (814) 693-2800, or write the Mt. Assisi Visitor Center, PO Box 188, Loretto 15940. The monastery is on the campus of St. Francis University. While visiting, stop by its Southern Alleghenies Museum, one of four locations of this regional institution. The permanent collection of American art here includes works by Pennsylvanians Mary Cassatt, Thomas Sully, and John Kane.

Heading northeast from Altoona, you discover the town of *State College,* home of *Pennsylvania State University* (not to be confused with the University of Pennsylvania, which is in Philadelphia). It's a member of the Big Ten football conference, so sports—playing, watching, and wearing blue-and-white outfits—is an important undergraduate major. Penn State was founded in 1855 as the Farmers' High School. It has grown. Beaver Stadium, the fourth-largest stadium in the country, is often packed beyond its 93,967-seat capacity.

Fourteen miles south of the main campus lies the university's *Shaver's Creek Environmental Center* (3400 Discovery Rd., Petersburg). Located off Route 26 in the Stone Valley Recreation Area, it offers lots of painless education programs for kids and adults. The facility has a cool Raptor Center, where birds of prey like owls, hawks, and eagles can be studied up close and personal; a bat colony where more than 1,200 brown bats roost nightly; herb and flower gardens; and picnic areas. One popular annual event is the Maple Harvest Festival the last weekend in March. For more information on that, go to www .shaverscreek.org, or call (814) 863-2000.

Route 522 near Raystown Lake, a huge man-made reservoir, runs along the ridgetop alongside one of Pennsylvania's prettiest streams: the Juniata River. The small village of *Huntingdon* is worth a detour onto Route 26. See a monument to the town's past and glimpse its future in the students at Juniata College.

The Oneida Indians, who once lived in this region, had a custom of erecting a huge monolithic stone—think *2001: A Space Odyssey*—outside their villages. These "standing stones" bore tribal symbols and history. When the first white settlers arrived in Huntingdon County in 1754, they reported a 14-foot standing stone near the Oneida village. Neighboring Tuscarora Indians somehow stole the stone. War erupted. Though the Oneida regained their stone, they moved west as settlers moved in, and the stone vanished. To commemorate Native American history, Huntingdon created a replica of the standing stone in the historic town center. It's still there, surrounded by well-kept century-old homes and the college. A peaceful cemetery crowns the hillside, its grave markers overlooking the town: a different kind of standing stone.

Valleys of the Susquehanna

Due north of State College, although there are no direct roads, is **Bellefonte,** meaning "beautiful fountain." It's best known for its **Big Spring,** which gushes 11.5 million gallons of water each day. Find the spring in Talleyrand Park, named for the French diplomat who supposedly named the town during a US visit.

This diminutive town bred seven governors of Pennsylvania, according to a marker in front of its Palladian courthouse. The Victorian downtown still has lively little shops and restaurants. The friendly folks at the visitor center— located at 320 W. High St. in the 19th-century rail station by the park—will provide a map for a self-guided walking tour. Any evening except Sunday, finish your tour with dinner at the **Gamble Mill,** a microbrewery and fine restaurant located in old town gristmill. It's a real find (814-355-7764, www .gamblemill.com).

Just 12 miles from Bellefonte on Route 150 is Pennsylvania's first "green" resort, the **Nature Inn at Bald Eagle State Park.** Perched on 5,900 acres of forest, the cozy inn is emphatically not a resort. It has just 16 rooms, not hundreds; it offers a patio with a fire pit and gas grills instead of a gourmet dining room. But it has a great lakefront location and LEED Gold certification—that means it's the latest and greatest in energy efficiency. Park rangers offer interpretive hikes for guests, each room offers binoculars for bird-watching, and there's a fun playroom for younger kids. It's a secluded getaway for sure, but since it's only 25 miles from State College, it's also a smart choice for lodging during Penn State football weekends, when Happy Valley can overflow. Get the details on the inn, located at 201 Warbler Way, Howard, at (814) 625-2879 or www.natureinnat baldeagle.com.

trivia

The Statue of Liberty also lifts her lamp over the Susquehanna River near Dauphin Narrows. As you drive along Route 322, you'll see her 25-foot white replica on an abandoned pier in the middle of the river.

Boalsburg is home to the **Pennsylvania Military Museum,** honoring the women and men of Pennsylvania who served their country in war. From Benjamin Franklin's first military unit—the Associators—through the conflict in Vietnam, this museum tells the tale of these patriots. The museum is open Wed through Sat 10 a.m. to

4 p.m., and Sun from noon to 4 p.m. Admission is $6. For information call (814) 466-6263; write to PO Box 160A, Boalsburg 16827; or visit www.pamil museum.org.

Sail on. Sail on. Sail on and on to see relics and heirlooms of Christopher Columbus at the Boal *Mansion and Columbus Chapel,* just off Business Route 322 at 163 Boal Estate Dr. in Boalsburg. The chapel, which was part of the Columbus family castle in Spain, contains the desk of Christopher Columbus and 2 relics said to be pieces of the true cross of Jesus. The Boal family brought the chapel to Boalsburg in 1909. Family scion Pierre Boal was a French flying ace in World War I and later served as a US ambassador. That's why memorabilia from the early days of flight are also collected by the museum. You may visit daily except Mon, May through Oct. Guided tours ($10 per adult) are scheduled from 1:30 to 5 p.m. in the spring and fall and 10 a.m. to 5 p.m. in summer. Call (814) 466-6210, or visit www .boalmuseum.com.

The people who live in Juniata and Mifflin Counties strive to uphold their heritage, their small-town way of life, and a standard of living not usually found in rural areas. Visiting here can be like taking a trip back in time, as you meet descendants of the early German settlers, including many Amish and Mennonite families. Any Wednesday during spring, summer, and fall, drop in on market day in Belleville (on Sale Barn Lane, just off Route 655, due west of Lewistown).

The stellar attraction in Mifflinburg is the Buggy Museum (598 Green St.), commemorating passenger carriages, not mosquitoes and bumblebees. The museum shows you where William A. Heiss manufactured horse-drawn vehicles from the late 19th to the early 20th century, employing painters, blacksmiths, carpenters, and wheelwrights. Abruptly, the family shuttered the shop, and half a century passed before it was reopened, good as new. Visit the museum Thurs through Sat 10 a.m. to 5 p.m. and Sun 1 to 5 p.m., May through Oct. For more information call (570) 966-1355, or visit www.buggy museum.org.

Take a deep breath while driving to *Northumberland,* which has a big spot in history for such a little place. It was the home of Joseph Priestley, who is remembered for his pioneering work in chemistry, most notably the discovery of oxygen. He was also the founder of the Unitarian church. Priestley's philosophic and scientific writings greatly influenced Thomas Jefferson, who based the curriculum of the University of Virginia on Priestley's ideas.

Visit the grand *Joseph Priestley House* (472 Priestley Ave.), which is open for tours Sat and Sun at 1, 2, and 3 p.m. Adult admission: $6. Call (570) 473-9474, or go to www.josephpriestleyhouse.org.

"A school for how to have fun" is how **Camp Woodward** describes itself. Simply put, it's an extreme-sports paradise, outfitted with runs and ramps galore for skateboarders, BMXers, and in-line skaters. Located 25 miles west of State College in **Mifflinburg,** Woodward supplements its kids' summer-camp business with weekend packages Sept through May, and they swear they even get some adult visitors without kids. (If you bring kids, fair warning: The camp requires you to stay and watch their every death-defying move.) Two B&Bs on the property fill quickly, especially during Penn State football season, so always book ahead. For room reservations call (814) 349-5520; for camps, call (814) 349-5633. Or do a double ollie to www.camp woodward.com.

Centralia, a tiny village off Route 61 in Columbia County, has the unique distinction of having been on fire since 1962. That's when an underground blaze erupted in a coal mine under the town. All sorts of engineering marvels were employed to put out the fire; none succeeded, and by 1991 nearly all of the town's residents had been evacuated. The wisps of smoke you see curling up through the ground are evidence that there's still fire down below.

Most people driving along the Susquehanna River between **Sunbury** and Harrisburg take Routes 11 and 15 on the west side for speed; but on the east the less-traveled Route 147 gives you lovely glimpses of the river valley and the interesting towns that dot the banks. In **Millersburg** you can ride the **Millersburg Ferry,** one of the last surviving wooden, double-sternwheel paddleboats in the country. It runs a mile back and forth to Liverpool at one of the river's widest points. A National Historic Landmark, the first ferry began operation in 1825, a big step forward for passengers and freight haulers accustomed to using rowboats and pole boats. At the peak of river commerce, four boats made the trips.

trivia

Lorenzo DaPonte, Mozart's librettist, lived for a time in Sunbury.

Now only the *Falcon* and the *Roaring Bull V* ply the river, which at this spot rarely gets more than 3 feet deep. Each ferry accommodates 4 cars and 50 passengers. To find the pickup point, drive into Millersburg on Route 147 and follow the signs. Generally the ferries run daily from June 1 through Labor Day, Mon through Fri, 11 a.m. to 5 p.m. and weekends 9 a.m. to dusk. In May, Sept, and early Oct, ferries run weekends only. A passenger car or pick-up costs $7 one way. For more information call (717) 692-2442 or visit millersburgferry.org.

Across from the ferry landing, on the west side of the Susquehanna at **Liverpool,** lies **Hunters Valley Winery.** Located on a 150-year-old farm, the winery combines traditional wine-making methods with stainless-steel fermenters and fine filtration. The grapes come from vineyards that were planted in 1982.

In many ways the growing conditions resemble those in parts of France, with full sun, good air circulation, excellent drainage, and temperatures moderated by the river and mountains. You may walk through the vineyards and picnic on the grounds Wed, Thurs, and Sat 11 a.m. to 5 p.m.; Fri 11 a.m. to 7 p.m.; and Sun 1 to 5 p.m. Holiday hours vary. Call (717) 444-7211, or go to www.huntersvalleywines.com.

Southern Border

Head south to *Carlisle,* where I-81 connects with the Pennsylvania Turnpike and Route 15. All that concrete stays, thankfully, on the outskirts of this comfortable Cumberland County seat.

Proud, prosperous, and preservation-conscious, the town's still-inhabited log cabins sport screened windows; the cannonball dents in the courthouse (relics of a pre-Gettysburg skirmish on July 3, 1863) are unrepaired. The colonial street plan is unchanged. The farmers' market has been held weekly for a couple of centuries. And how many towns of 19,000 have their own spacious historical society, complete with research library, gift shop, and guidebooks?

To call the town center the traditional meeting place is an understatement. Five Indian paths converged here before white settlement. The pioneer settlers bent on killing western tribes mustered here in 1756. Constitutional and slave riots followed, a century apart; a hot-air balloon ascended in 1843. Geronimo paraded through in 1905, en route to Teddy Roosevelt's inauguration. And every event was carefully documented. The Historical Society provides a $5 guide for self-guided walking tours. The society is housed in the beautiful redbrick building at 21 N. Pitt St. (717-249-7610), open Mon from 4 to 8 p.m.; Tues through Fri 10 a.m. to 4 p.m.; and Sat 10 a.m. to 2 p.m. As you stroll downtown, look for the illustrated markers that describe three centuries of remarkable events.

The historic district's blocks of stately churches and homes also have a modest hippie vibe, thanks in part to downtown Dickinson College. Instead

trivia

Who knew? The fierce Molly Pitcher, an all-American girl who followed her man (or perhaps men) to Revolutionary War battle and actually got paid for it, is buried in Carlisle, where her statue brandishes a ramrod over the town graveyard.

of costumed interpreters, the streets buzz with skateboarders, guitarists, and pub patrons. And as a college town, Carlisle also boasts plenty of pubs and good restaurants. Two to try: *Courthouse Commons Espresso Bar,* at 2 S. Hanover St. (717-243-8899), and the *Market Cross Pub & Brewery* at 113 N. Hanover St. (717-258-1234; www.marketcrosspub.com), which offers casual alehouse fare and an extensive list of you-know-whats.

Carlisle has been a military town since the first British fort of the 1750s. The *US Army War College* (the site of the famous Carlisle Indian School in the 19th century) is located here, but is not open to the public. Instead, learn about the soldiers who have defended America for 250 years at the *US Army Heritage and Education Center.* AHEC has 2 stories of indoor exhibit and library space at 950 Soldiers Dr.—including the largest collection of Civil War photography in the world. Outside, an outdoor trail (punctuated by an enormous Vietnam-era Huey helicopter) interprets campaigns from the French and Indian War and World War I trenches. Free admission and parking. Hours vary, so call (717) 245-3971 or visit www.usahec.org.

Near Carlisle is some of the best fly-fishing in the world. The Letort Stream runs right through town. Another blue-ribbon favorite, Yellow Breeches Creek, gets its name from the British soldiers who crossed the creek during the American Revolution; their white trousers became stained from the yellow tint of the water. Many outfitters guide on this stream, and because so much of the shoreline belongs to exclusive trout-fishing clubs, it's best to get expert advice on where you can safely throw your line. Contact Tom's Fly-Fishing Service in nearby New Cumberland at (717) 770-0796, or visit www .tomsflyfishing.com.

Boiling Springs, a short drive through the Cumberland Valley from Carlisle, is worth a lunchtime detour. The *Boiling Springs Tavern* has served guests here since 1832, and Yellow Breeches Outfitters, opposite the tavern on First Street, offers angling gear, flies, and expert advice. Contact the tavern (which is closed Sun and Mon) at (717) 258-3614 or www.boilingspringstavern.com; the outfitters at (717) 258-6752 or www.yellowbreeches.com.

Civil War history awaits at *Chambersburg,* 32 miles south of Carlisle on Route 11. The Confederates occupied the city, then an important rail junction, three times during the Civil War. The last time, in 1864, 3,000 Confederate soldiers rode into town demanding $100,000 ransom in gold, which Chambersburg couldn't pay. The Confederates burned the town, putting two-thirds of its citizens out of their homes, then rode off to McConnellsburg. Today, Memorial Square at the center of town honors the Union troops. On the corner of Lincoln Way (Route 30) stands a grand bank designed by architect Frank Furness in 1915. The handsome old structure, complete with a large circular vault, is now the **Chambersburg Heritage Center.** It offers great exhibits about the region's history, from the 1730s, when Indian attacks plagued white settlers, through the 19th century. The center publishes a nice series of themed driving guides. Pick some up to navigate rural Franklin County on your own. Center admission is free Mon through Fri year-round. It adds Sat hours from Apr to Oct. Visit from 8 a.m. to 5 p.m. weekdays and 10 a.m. to 3 p.m. Sat during those warmer months.

South of Chambersburg, two spots illustrate this valley's early history. Mercersburg was the early home of Pennsylvania's only president, James Buchanan. He was also the only bachelor to serve as president, though he served ineptly; in his single term from 1856 to 1860, he was unable to bridge the growing divide between north and south. Remarkably, his childhood home at 15 N. Main St. (Route 16) is now a thriving Cajun restaurant called the **James Buchanan Hotel and Restaurant** (717-328-0011; www.james buchananhotel.com). Across the street is the family home of Harriet Lane. Buchanan's niece, she served as his White House hostess and so was called the first "First Lady."

As homesteaders moved west across Pennsylvania in the mid-18th century, they incurred the wrath of Indians furious at the theft of their lands. Stories of kidnapping and massacres on the frontier are told at the **Conococheague Institute,** headquartered in a homestead that dates from 1752 (12995 Bain Rd., Mercersburg; 717-328-3476; http://conococheague.org). It's part of a network of sites belonging to the Colonel Washington Frontier Forts Association, all dedicated to telling the story of the French and Indian War. It's open mid-Apr through the end of Oct on Tues, Wed, Fri, and Sat from 10 a.m. to 4 p.m., and Sun 1 to 4 p.m.

From McConnellsburg, take Route 522 north 30 miles to the **East Broad Top Railroad,** a National Historic Landmark at Orbisonia. Some railroad buffs believe East Broad Top is the best train attraction in Pennsylvania. It is the last 3-foot-gauge (narrow-gauge) line in the East still operating from its original site. It was built in 1873 to move bituminous coal from the mines to Mt. Union, 11 miles north, where the "black diamonds" were dumped into standard-gauge Pennsylvania Railroad cars. The East Broad Top hauled coal until 1956. Today the 10-mile, hour-long, scenic, fun, and educational trip hauls railroad enthu-siasts, excited kids, grinning grown-ups, photographers—and sound-recording zealots. People show up periodically, lugging audio equipment and stringing microphones along the track, to record the Doppler effect or to commit the train's distinctive chugs and choos to stereo for a film. You can stop for a picnic at the end of the line and come back on a later train. Trains leave at 11 a.m., 1 p.m., and 3 p.m., weekends only, May through Oct and during the holiday season. The fee is $13 per adult. Call (814) 447-3011; or visit www .ebtrr.com.

Shielded from the interstates by the southern Alleghenies, **Bedford** is easy to miss. It's perched alongside the Raystown branch of the Juniata River along Route 30. But don't pass by this classic redbrick county seat, enfolded by deep-forested mountains.

People have been passing through Bedford for centuries, starting with the Shawnee Indians, who blazed the first trail west. The British soldiers who followed hacked their way over the mountains on their way to kicking the French out of Pittsburgh. Bedford's buildings reflect these past transients. Forts and log cabins from the 1750s (a few with aluminum siding additions) still stand alongside Federal-era town houses. George Washington stayed in Bedford, while his troops, farther west, quelled the Whiskey Rebellion in 1794. President James Buchanan received the first transatlantic cable at the Bedford Springs Resort. Since the resort's grand reopening a mile south of town in 2007, Bedford's downtown business district has gotten a boost.

Join the Friday afternoon historical walking tours with Dennis Tice (he's the droll director of the visitors bureau on Juliana Street). The free, easy, 4-block tour includes the 1828 courthouse, the town squares, and the Espy House, where Washington stayed. "This place is operating now as what it was as far back as the 1700s," Tice tells groups at the tour's end at Oralee's **Golden Eagle Inn.** The basement-level tavern used to host muddy boots, smoke, and spurs. Now the 3-story brick hotel and restaurant is beautifully restored, furnished by owner Oralee Kieffer with wit, charm, and lots of antiques. Find it at 131 E. Pitt St., Bedford; call (814) 624-0800; or visit www.bedfordgolden eagle.com.

Also on Pitt Street is the Pitt Theater (showing only 1 movie a night), 3 antiques stores, the Fort Bedford Museum, and Old Bedford Village, a colonial-era re-creation. Another friendly stop is **HeBrews.** Yes, it's a coffee shop, open daily at 103 S. Richard St. (814-623-8600; www.hebrewscoffeecompany.com).

Renfrew and Redware

A 200-year-old farmstead on Route 16 is home to an impressive collection of redware. Local potter John Bell and his family popularized this all-American variety of stoneware pottery during the mid-19th century. Today, authentic redware commands five-figure prices. See the exhibit of original work in the visitors' center at **Renfrew Museum and Park,** 1010 E. Main St., Waynesboro; call (717) 762-4723 or check www.renfrewmuseum.org.

Worth a quiet stroll is Bedford Memorial Park, a nicely restored 200-year-old cemetery.

The *National Museum of the American Coverlet* sounds like a snooze. It's not. Housed in old Bedford Common School, which dates to 1859, the museum showcases examples of fine handwoven folk designs used to adorn colonial beds. The museum shop offers nice replicas of the textiles for your house, too. It's open daily (for $6 per adult) at 322 S. Juliana St.; call (814) 623-1588, or visit www.coverletmuseum.org. Right across the street, retired architect Steve George welcomes guests to the *Chancellor's House,* an Italianate mansion restored as a comfortable B&B (341 S. Juliana St.; 866-535-8414; www .thechancellorshouse.com).

A mile west of town along Route 30, a venerable tavern still serves travelers. The Jean Bonnet Tavern is an authentic 1760s inn, with an authentically dim ground-floor dining room with fireplace, a bright upstairs brewpub, and a few guest rooms. This was a Whiskey Rebellion site—farmers irate with the whiskey tax rallied around a liberty pole here in 1794, as the state historic marker relates. These days, the whiskey flows freely, 7 days a week. Raise a toast to the past at 6048 Lincoln Hwy. Phone (814) 623-2250; www.jeanbonnet tavern.com.

Bedford County has 14 covered bridges, and you can tour them on bike or by car. They are usually named for their original 19th-century builders, and most have been safely rebuilt in recent years. The *Bedford County Visitors Bureau* (800-765-3331; www.bedfordcounty.net) offers a Web link and a printed brochure with distances and details. The bureau is open year-round Mon through Fri 9 a.m. to 5 p.m.; May through Oct, the bureau is also open Sat 9 a.m. to 5 p.m. and Sun noon to 5 p.m. To plan a cycling, paddling, or hiking adventure, see www.thealleghenies.com. Call them at (800) 842-5866.

Breezewood, the self-proclaimed "Town of Motels," is mainly a giant cloverleaf garnished with neon. But for cyclists, it's also a trailhead for a unique thrill ride: the *Pike to Bike Trail.*

The Superhighway Trail, or P2B as it's known hereabouts, became an appendix to the state's main east-west artery in 1968, when the Pennsylvania Turnpike was rerouted through bigger four-lane tunnels. Between the old ones, Sideling Hill and Rays Hill, the discarded stretch of road was relegated to highway researchers and underage boozers. But since the Southern Alleghenies Conservancy took it over in 2001, recreational cyclists—a few hundred each weekend—have reclaimed the roadway. Riding through the pitch-black tunnels (Rays Hill is 0.75 miles, Sideling Hill, 1.3) provides the thrill. In between there's Buchanan State Forest and not much else. Make sure to bring a bike light. Still under development, the 8.5-mile trail is officially closed, but you can

Handmade Along the Highway

Whether you prize hand-woven baskets, art glass, vibrant pieced quilts, hand-painted gourds, or "Scherenschnitte"—old-time German papercutting—you'll find a high-quality selection at the Route 30 stores that sport a red-white-and-blue "Artisan Trail" sign. The state tourism office created the link-up between talented artisans and retailers along the old Lincoln Highway between Gettysburg and Ligonier. Stop, browse, and repeat. See a listing of all participating artists and merchants at www .handmadealongthehighway.org. Look for a list of other Artisan Trails throughout rural Pennsylvania at www.visitpa.com.

get a guided tour from Grouseland Tours; call (814) 784-5000, or check www .grouseland.com.

To paddle the peaceful southern Juniata River, rent a canoe or kayak from **Woy Bridge Campground** (PO Box 102, Bedford 15522; 814-735-2768; www .bedford.net/woybridge), just outside of town. Canoes are $25 for the first 2 days; kayaks are $20. Half-day on-site rates are available, too.

On silent Route 4016 near New Paris, there's a country road that's down-right spooky: **Gravity Hill.** "Stay calm," read the directions in our county-issued brochure. "Keep cool. Put your car in neutral and take your foot off the brake." We did. And then the car began moving. Backwards. Up the hill. On cue, we screamed.

Whatever its explanation, Gravity Hill is one of those certifiably off-the-beaten-path attractions that you can't miss. And once you get there, you'll find a second Gravity Hill three-tenths of a mile past the first. Get the very specific directions from the Bedford County Visitors Bureau.

Seven miles west of Bedford on Route 31 below Route 30 is **Coral Caverns,** the only known coral-reef cavern, formed more than 300 million years ago when the area was covered by the Appalachian Sea. It's open for tours 10 a.m. to 5 p.m., weekends only from mid-May to mid-Oct. Call (814) 623-6882 or visit www.coralcaverns.com for details.

No cappuccino at the **Coffee Pot.** No latte. Not even cream and sugar. Just a way-larger-than-life-sized coffeepot built in 1925, an example of the "pro-grammatic architecture" that dotted the Lincoln Highway, Route 30, aimed at luring tourists and travelers. The pot, located across the street from the entrance to the Bedford County Fairgrounds, has been closed for years. But things may be perking up. The Lincoln Highway Heritage Corridor is trying to preserve the, er, grounds and building for future java lovers. Call (724) 238-9030, or visit www.lhhc.org for more information.

BEST ANNUAL EVENTS IN SOUTH CENTRAL PENNSYLVANIA

JANUARY

Twelfth Day
Joseph Priestley House, Northumberland
(570) 473-9474
In January the Joseph Priestley House in Northumberland celebrates Twelfth Day, ringing in the New Year as English dissenters (like Unitarian scientist Priestley) did at the close of the 18th century.

IceFest
Chambersburg
(717) 264-7101
www.chambersburg.org
Chambersburg celebrates IceFest the last weekend of January, with ice sculptures and entertainment. Merchants around the bustling town square offer late hours and specials.

MAY

Birding Cup
Shaver's Creek Environmental Center
(814) 863-2000
www.shaverscreek.org
The annual Birding Cup at Shaver's Creek Environmental Center is a 24-hour race to count as many different species of birds as possible. Teams of birders compete during the first weekend in May to raise funds for the center's Raptor Center.

Day in Towne
Boalsburg
(814) 466-6311
Memorial Day was born in Boalsburg in 1864 and declared a national holiday a few years later. The village celebrates annually with a Day in Towne on Memorial Day. From 9 a.m. to 5 p.m., it's crafts, food, music, and a reenactment of a Civil War event. At 6 p.m. everybody walks from the square to the cemetery, where cannons boom, a brass band and bagpipes play, scouts raise and lower the flag, and the VFW plays taps. If you're into Memorial Day, this is the real thing.

AUGUST

Vintage Corvette Auto Show
Carlisle
www.carlisleevents.com
The vintage auto shows held at the Carlisle Fairgrounds are a town tradition. The August Corvette show, in particular, is a winner.

OCTOBER

Railfest
Railroaders Memorial Museum, Altoona
(814) 946-0834
www.railroadcity.com
The first weekend in October the Railfest is held at the Railroaders Memorial Museum, Altoona; here's your chance for shorter excursions around Horseshoe Curve and on other rarely used trackage. Call (888) 425-8666 or (814) 946-0834.

Fulton Fall Folk Festival
McConnellsburg
(717) 485-4064
www.fultoncountypa.com
On the third weekend in October, McConnellsburg hosts the Fulton Fall Folk Festival; the annual Grease, Steam & Rust Show (featuring antique machinery); and the Historical Society Open House, all at once.

DECEMBER

Victorian Christmas
Bellefonte
(814) 355-2917
www.bellefonte.com
Bellefonte's Victorian Christmas celebration includes music, theater, and crafts shows. The Santa Express departs from the train station for 1-hour excursions throughout the weekend.

When you hear the name *Road Kill Cafe,* you just have to go. The cafe is 10 miles south of Bedford in Clearville. The bare-bones, cinder block cafe offers home cooking and cabins ($40 for singles, $10 for each additional person, kids stay free) and is run by Barb Snyder, whose homemade pies (as well as T-shirts with tasteful slogans like "You Kill It, We Grill It") have made the place a legend. The cafe (814-784-3257), on Crooked Run Road, is open Mon through Sat 8 a.m. to 7 p.m. and Sun from noon to 3 p.m.

Consider a side trip to Rainsburg on Route 326, a community established so long ago that a 19th-century historian wrote, "the memory of man runneth not to the contrary," regarding its existence. The small borough features the *Rainsburg Male and Female Seminary,* incorporated in 1853 to offer secondary education and train teachers. And while you're in the area, stop in Chaneysville, a small town also on Route 326 that sheltered fugitive slaves before the Civil War. For a wonderful look back in time, read David Bradley's excellent novel *The Chaneysville Incident.*

In New Baltimore, milepost 129 on the Pennsylvania Turnpike, a church sits on the highway. Formally St. John the Baptist, a Catholic sanctuary, the church usually is called the *Church on the Turnpike.* Whether you're traveling eastbound or westbound, you can stop your car right at the church and walk to mass. If you're driving you can take the Bedford or Somerset exit, both about 20 miles away.

Places to Stay in South Central Pennsylvania

BEDFORD

Oralee's Golden Eagle Inn
131 E. Pitt St.
(814) 624-0800
www.bedfordgoldeneagle
.com
An authentic inn with spacious rooms and friendly service.

BELLEFONTE

Reynolds Mansion
101 W. Linn St.
(800) 899-3929
www.reynoldsmansion.com
A grand 1855 home restored as a B&B.

CARLISLE

The Carlisle House
148 S. Hanover St.
(717) 249-0350
www.thecarlislehouse.com
Within walking distance of Dickinson College campus.

DUBOIS

The Inn at Narrows Creek
44 Narrows Creek Ln.
(814) 371-9394
www.narrowscreek.com
Eight rooms and suites in a rural setting, with a country store.

MERCERSBURG

Mercersburg Inn
405 S. Main St.
(717) 328-5231
www.mercersburginn.com
Lavish Greek Revival home near Mercersburg Academy.

STATE COLLEGE

Atherton Hotel
125 S. Atherton St.
(814) 231-2100 or
(800) 832-0132
www.athertonhotel.net
Traditional hotel in the heart
of the Penn State campus.

Places to Eat in South Central Pennsylvania

BEDFORD

Jean Bonnet Tavern
6048 Lincoln Hwy.
(814) 623-2250
www.jeanbonnettavern
.com
Historic 1760s inn.

CARLISLE

Piatto
22 W. Pomfret St.
(717) 249-9580
www.piatto.com
Regional Italian specialties
in a Civil War–era home or
on the porch. BYOB.

NEW BERLIN

Gabriel's Restaurant
321 Market St.
(570) 966-0321 or (800)
797-2350
www.innatnewberlin.com
This Victorian inn serves
dinner Wed, Fri, and Sat.

OSTERBURG

**Slick's Ivy Stone
Restaurant**
8785 William Penn Rd.
(814) 276-3131
www.slicksivystone.com
Hearty family-style meals.
Open Apr through Dec;
closed Mon.

SOUTHWESTERN PENNSYLVANIA →

Golden Triangle

East is Philadelphia, and west is **Pittsburgh,** and never the twain shall meet. You'll be surprised how many folks in the former have only the vaguest idea where the latter is (it's 300 miles to the left). The Allegheny Mountains, it turns out, have been a pretty effective barrier to westward movement ever since the British first hacked their way into the wilderness 250 years ago. But easterners—in fact, any visitors—are bowled over by southwestern Pennsylvania's offerings, from high art to high fives (pro sports are big here), once they arrive.

Downtown Pittsburgh is often called the Golden Triangle, in reference to its location, where the Allegheny and Monongahela Rivers form the Ohio (next stop, via the Mississippi: the Gulf of Mexico). So much water, surrounded by high bluffs with lots of trees, reminds some folks of San Francisco, but with a winter.

All that's gold also glitters. Adding to the scenery is the dazzle of downtown architecture, including Philip Johnson's PPG Place (all glass, of course) and Michael Graves's O'Reilly Theater. Along the waterfront are architect Rafael Viñoly's

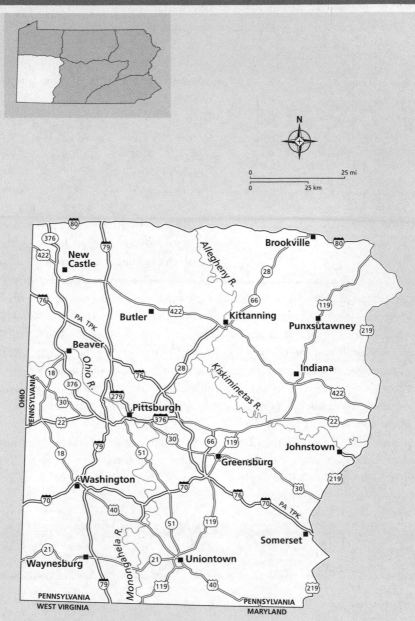

triviatidbits

Between downtown stops, you can ride Pittsburgh's subway train, the T, for no charge.

The identical bridges the city dubs the "Three Sisters" are the Clemente, Warhol, and Carson Bridges across the Allegheny River near downtown. Attribute their lyrical design to John Roebling, who also created the aqueducts in Lackawaxen, Pennsylvania, and the Brooklyn Bridge.

swooping convention center and the contemporary Carnegie Science Center. A hard throw from the business district is PNC Park (named for the PNC Financial Services Group). It's the prettiest retro ballpark in America, next door to Heinz Field, the football stadium. The downtown bridges are painted gold, and the Steelers (football), Penguins (hockey), and Pirates (baseball) all have black-and-gold color schemes (colors that appear on the Pittsburgh city crest).

First, let's look back. From about 1870 to 1970, Pittsburgh led the nation in producing iron, steel, and glass and in mining bituminous coal. Meanwhile, clouds rolled by on skies of black and gray, not blue, and nights sometimes glowed orange. Rivers flowed brown and green. Initial attempts at controlling smoke and floods were hampered by a couple of world wars and by a boom-and-bust economy. In 1941, the year Pittsburgh had the nation's highest rate of pneumonia, the mayor created a commission to eliminate smoke. Now, after decades of civic improvement, Pittsburgh has overcome its industry-induced pollution. And what a transformation: Numerous rankings now call Pittsburgh "America's most livable city." It's a place you've got to see for yourself.

Don't neglect the Cultural District downtown, home to fabulously restored dowager theaters along Penn Avenue. Around the corner, on the side of the Byham Theater, you'll find the inside of an old steel mill—in a fabulous giant

AUTHOR'S TOP 10 FAVORITES IN SOUTHWESTERN PENNSYLVANIA

Confluence	Mattress Factory
Fallingwater	Ohiopyle
Jimmy Stewart Museum	Punxsutawney
Kayak Pittsburgh	St. Anthony's Chapel
Kennywood Park	Vanka murals

Richardson Romanesque

Few architects have an architectural style named after them, but *Henry Hobson Richardson* is one of them. His *Allegheny County Courthouse and Jail,* begun in 1883, is a famous example of the architect's muscular style. Massive stonework, rounded arches, and towers are his signature, shown to great effect in his masterpiece in the heart of Pittsburgh. (Photos show his physique was much like his buildings.) Called Richardson Romanesque because of its similarities to 11th-century European architecture, the architect's style actually draws from a variety of sources.

Richardson stressed theatrical sculptured shapes: deep-set windows, cavernous door openings, and bands of windows. (He devised an arched bridge over Ross Street, between the courthouse and the jail, to allow prisoners to be taken to trial directly from the jail. Hence the local nickname, the Bridge of Sighs.)

Richardson's work can be seen all over the East Coast, and once you see it, you'll always recognize his style. The courthouse is widely considered one of his finest works. He died at age 47 in 1886—just before its completion.

mural by Robert Haas. Next door is a subtle light sculpture by Robert Wilson, which is installed across the top of a building (look for the turning triangles). When you come to the corner of Seventh and Penn, facing a hulking Aztec-style pyramid, you've reached two more public art installations. Temporary ones often join the lineup. They're as much fun as the theatrical performances.

Playwright August Wilson set his famous cycle of dramas in Pittsburgh's Hill District, which overlooks downtown. The *August Wilson Center for African American Culture,* near the Convention Center at 980 Liberty Ave., (www.augustwilsoncenter.org), honors his legacy with exhibits, performances, and other special events.

Around Town

If you ask for directions to "the Carnegie Museum" from downtown, you'll be branded a tourist for sure, because there are four. On the city's North Shore, find the *Carnegie Science Center* (One Allegheny Ave.; 412-237-3400; open daily). Kids love to visit its Earthquake Cafe, which really shakes them up. The museum also salutes Pittsburgh's newest industry with "roboworld," the world's largest robotics exhibit. European visitors—and Pop Art devotees from all over the world—love the nearby *Andy Warhol Museum,* with a cool style that appeals to both kids and adults (117 Sandusky St.; 412-237-8300; closed Mon). The *Carnegie Museum of Art* (4400 Forbes Ave.; 412-622-3131; closed Mon except between the Fourth of July and Labor Day), 2 miles away in the Oakland section, is where old meets new: magnificent casts of architecture and sculpture from antiquity, plus fine impressionist and contemporary art collections. Drop-in tours are offered daily. Look for the bronze Diplodocus, nicknamed Dippy, outside the complex; he'll point you toward the **Carnegie Museum of Natural History** (4400 Forbes Ave.), with its nightmare-inducing *Tyrannosaurus rex* and other fossils. The famous collection is showcased in "Dinosaurs in Their Time" in a vaulting 2-story space. There are wonderful Egyptian mummies and gem collections here, too. For varying admission prices, exhibit information, and hours for all four museums, visit www.carnegiemuseums.org.

The **Pittsburgh Zoo** (One Wild Place; 412-665-3640 or 800-474-4966; www.pittsburghzoo.com) nurtures more than 4,000 animals in habitats as diverse as an African savanna, a reptile house, and a glass-bottomed polar bear pool (where visitors walk underneath the ursine swimmers). The zoo is open daily 9:30 a.m. to 6 p.m. Memorial Day through Labor Day, 9 a.m. to 5 p.m. in the fall and spring, and 9 a.m. to 4 p.m. the rest of the year. Closed Thanksgiving, Christmas, and New Year's Day. Admission for adults is $14, with a reduced rate of $10 in the off-season.

But, hey, you're here to get off the beaten path, so leave time for other stops. Pittsburgh's neighborhoods are the soul of the city. For funky grocery shopping visit **The Strip,** a flat, 20-block stretch along the Allegheny waterfront

eyeballart, anyone?

Go on a scavenger tour of downtown Pittsburgh's great public art with a guide to more than 80 works, from the eyeball benches at Agnes Katz Plaza to the giant mayor on the steps of the City-County Building. They're mapped in a booklet from the Greater Pittsburgh Arts Council. Pick up your free copy at 707 Penn Ave.

Cover the Waterfront

Purposeful Pittsburgh used to use its riverbanks only for work: docks and steel mills. But now the city is celebrating its newly pristine shoreline with the **Three Rivers Heritage Trail,** which connects several paths. Joggers, bicyclers, and in-line skaters glide along the Eliza Furnace Trail (since it passes a county jail, it's usually called the Jail Trail). You can connect to the North Shore and skate to a Pirates game at PNC Park or bike across the Hot Metal Bridge (aka South Twenty-ninth Street; it used to carry buckets of molten steel) and head 10 miles south to connect to the rural Great Allegheny Passage. See the online map at www.friendsoftheriverfront.org.

The Best Front Door in America

Your first words about Pittsburgh are likely to be "Oh, wow!" Called the "Best Front Door in America," the cityscape that bursts upon you as you emerge from the Fort Pitt Tunnel shimmers with rivers and riverboats, skyscrapers, towering hills, and golden bridges. Smoky city? No more.

When planners wanted to raise the guardrails on the Fort Pitt Bridge, local activists raised their voices. They argued that higher barriers would blind incoming motorists to Pittsburgh's signature view. The result: The state highway department bowed to the beautiful and agreed to keep the lower barriers.

above the Convention Center. Start at the handsome **Senator John Heinz History Center** at 1212 Smallman St., a converted 19th-century brick icehouse. It offers a retrospective of three centuries, starting when Pittsburgh was the country's western frontier. The center includes the Western Pennsylvania Sports Museum. This region's especially proud of its great NFL quarterback tradition. Here's where to pay tribute to Pittsburgh greats like Johnny Unitas, Jim Kelly, Dan Marino, Joe Montana, Joe Namath, and more. The museum is open daily 10 a.m. to 5 p.m. except major holidays; adult admission is $10. Call (412) 454-6000 or visit www.heinzhistorycenter.org for more information.

Continue east on Smallman Street, or on parallel Penn Avenue, for a bustling parade of restaurateurs (pinching melons and grabbing gourmet ingredients) and hipsters (browsing the selection of funky furniture shops, like Hot Haute Hot.) The popular Pittsburgh Public Market in the Produce Terminal Market, at 17th and Smallman (pittsburghpublicmarket.org), is open on weekends. The Strip's schizophrenia is part of its charm. Whether you need a whoopee cushion, fresh biscotti, aged cheese, or a full-size inflatable Steeler, this is the place to hit. At **Primanti's** (46 Eighteenth St.; 412-263-2142) get your daily fat quotient in one sitting, with french fries and cole slaw crammed inside your sandwich. For gorgeous gifts try the brick building grandly engraved as the Pennsylvania Railroad Fruit Auction and Sales Building, now the **Society for Contemporary Craft,** 2100 Smallman St. Call (412) 261-7003, or visit www .contemporarycraft.org; closed Sun.

trivia

Novelist Michael Chabon set his *Mysteries of Pittsburgh* and *Wonderboys* here. Like his Pulitzer Prize–winning heroes, Kavalier and Clay, he grew up loving comic books (his favorite hangout was the comic emporium, Eide's Entertainment, on Liberty Avenue).

Mt. Washington is the riverside bluff that looms above the confluence, opposite downtown. A ride to the top on the inclines, the tiny vertical railways that have hauled Pittsburghers up and down the hill for more than a century, is an absolute must for visitors—and cheap, at $4.50 per round-trip.

Start the journey at water level, at **Station Square,** a grand railroad terminus-turned-entertainment center that's an easy subway hop from downtown. (This is also the boarding place for the **Gateway Clipper fleet** of paddleboats, which tour the rivers and ferry fans to Pirates and Steelers games.) Hop the **Monongahela Incline,** built in 1869, here (tip: it's pronounced IN-cline). Its partner, the red-sided **Duquesne Incline,** is a mile up East Carson Street. Both offer a steep and silent 4-minute ride to the top.

The aptly named Grandview Avenue, along the crest of Mt. Washington, encourages gawkers with a promenade and viewing platforms. The street's restaurants are special occasion destinations, mostly for their postcard view, so save your appetite for yet another bustling neighborhood below, the **South Side.**

On the southern bank of the Mon, as locals call the Monongahela River, the South Side boasts that it has "both kinds of blue hair"—on the elderly residents of century-old row houses surrounding former steel mills, and atop youthful loft dwellers and students from Carnegie Mellon University and the University of Pittsburgh. On Saturday evening East Carson Street belongs to the latter, who flood the bars, coffeehouses, and grills.

If you're into magic, don't miss the **Cuckoo's Nest** (2403 1/2 E. Carson St.; 412-481-4411; www.thecuckoosnest.com), a shabby little storefront with juggling clubs, trick cards, wands, scarves, handcuffs—the works. Kids love this place.

Restaurants spring up along the Carson Street sidewalk like crabgrass. One neighborhood secret is the tiny **Dish Osteria and Bar** (128 S. Seventeenth St.; 412-390-2012; www.dishosteria.com), with small appetizers (such as mixed marinated olives), great pasta, and fresh fish. At **SouthSide Works,** a major retail and entertainment complex on the site of the old Jones & Laughlin steel mill, you'll find another dozen choices for casual dining, from the faux-Irish Claddagh pub to the riverside Hofbrauhaus. See all the possibilities at www.southsideworks.com.

Live—and loud—music is offered at the South Side's many bars, especially on weekends. But at **Club Cafe** (56 S. Twelfth St.; 412-431-4950; www .clubcafelive.com), you can find great big-name acts and good local bands on a tiny, starry stage, performing for a hundred folks at cozy tables. It's a sixties coffeehouse with a cyber-vibe.

Above the South Side lie the city's oddest streets: steep vertical steps that no cars could climb. To get to the top of the South Side Slopes, you'll need to bring a walking stick. And maybe a cardiologist. With nearly 700 steps just to the crest of the South Side Slopes, the workout is extreme, but it's the panoramic views that are killer.

The Slopes claim 68 step streets, making this slice of the city feel like a European village: a blend of historic piety, cliffside houses, and quiet corkscrewed streets.

"When I walk the steps, I always get the sense of the mill workers from years ago," local steps historian Bob Regan tells me. "They walked down in the morning, and then, 12 hours later, they walked back up."

Start your climb on Eighteenth Street, pause for a breath at Pius Street, and continue to St. Paul's Monastery, a beautiful Bohemian church at the top. Each fall, the community association sponsors a "Step Trek" tour of the neighborhood; go to www.southsideslopes.org for details.

From the base of the Slopes, follow Carson Street 10 more miles east and you'll arrive at **Kennywood Park** (Route 837 in West Mifflin; 412-461-0500; www .kennywood.com). This charming century-old amusement park is a National Historic Landmark. It's an institution so loved by Pittsburghers that they come back every summer, usually with a crowd: the company picnic, the school picnic, or on Nationality Days, a great local ethnic tradition (Italian Day, Croatian Day, etc.). Nationality Days date back to the immigrant steelworkers who flocked to this bank of the Mon. A few miles downstream is the site of US Steel's Homestead Works, formerly the largest steel mill in the world and now a vast shopping and entertainment center called the Waterfront.

pittsburghfirsts

Radio station, KDKA

Public television station, WQED, home to *Mister Rogers' Neighborhood*

Polio vaccine

The Ferris wheel

Kennywood's claim to fame is its roller coasters: the wooden Thunderbolt, ranked one of the best in the world by enthusiasts; the Phantom's Revenge, a coaster-in-the-dark; and many more. Hold onto the bar! All-day passes are $33.99 for adults, with discounts for shorties (under 46 inches tall) and seniors. Open May through Labor Day.

Rising above I-376 near Monroeville is a sight you might expect along the Ganges River, rather than the Monongahela: a huge, wedding-cake-style temple with Indian flourishes. It's the **Sri Venkataswara Temple,** one of only 10 Hindu temples in the United States. It attracts worshipers from all over the East Coast. Remove your shoes and take a tour; it welcomes anyone who'd like to view the ornate building and appreciate its murals and statuary. It's located at 1230 S. McCully Dr. in Monroeville; call ahead to (412) 373-3380. The website (www.svtemple.org) gives details and directions.

pittsburgh
zombies

One of the most beloved movies ever made in Pittsburgh was George Romero's *Night of the Living Dead*. The 1968 classic has inspired an annual pre-Halloween Zombie Walk, where gruesomely costumed participants stagger with arms outstretched through the Monroeville Mall moaning, "Brains . . . must . . . have . . . brains."

Head back to downtown Pittsburgh to the Point and plunge in. Kayak Pittsburgh, under the Clemente Bridge, offers kayaks and canoes for self-guided tours of the confluence May through Oct. One Federal St.; use the stairway next to the statue of Roberto Clemente at PNC Park on the North Shore. Call (412) 969-9090 or (412) 255-0564, or visit www.kayakpittsburgh.org. Kayak racks at PNC Park and the South Side let you "park" for an afternoon.

The 42-story **Cathedral of Learning,** a Gothic Revival skyscraper, dominates the University of Pittsburgh and the surrounding Oakland neighborhood. The Commons Room, on the first floor, is evocative of a medieval cathedral. Around its perimeter are the **Nationality Rooms** (1209 Cathedral of Learning; 412-624-6000; www.pitt.edu/~natrooms). The classrooms are decorated in the style of 26 different nations. Pittsburghers are proud of them; visitors, especially international ones, are crazy about them. The **Stephen Foster Memorial** next door commemorates the country's first pop music composer (412-624-4100; www.pitt.edu/~amerimus/Museum.htm).

Foster is buried with many other city notables, including Lillian Russell, in **Allegheny Cemetery** (4734 Butler St.; 412-682-1624) in Lawrenceville. Its grand spooky style is echoed in **Homewood Cemetery** (Forbes and Dallas Avenues; 412-421-1822) in Point Breeze. Ghost stories abound; take the tours to hear them.

Around Allegheny Cemetery, one of Pittsburgh's oldest neighborhoods is showing new life. **Lawrenceville,** running from Sixteenth to Sixty-second Streets along the Allegheny River, has turned Civil War–era Butler Street into a district of galleries, cafes, and design boutiques that remind some visitors of Brooklyn's Park Slope.

George Washington Swam Here

Why is it called *Washington's Landing?* Easy. In December 1753 a young George Washington narrowly escaped drowning as he paddled across the Allegheny River where the Washington's Crossing Bridge now stands. Thankfully, he landed safely—in what's now called Lawrenceville.

Washington crisscrossed western Pennsylvania frequently, often in the company of Christopher Gist, a friend and guide. (You'll even find a marker showing his footsteps through Kennywood Park!) In fact, when he first set eyes on Pittsburgh, he made a note to himself: "fine place for a fort."

He was right.

The Butler Street shopping district anchored by the World War I doughboy statue has plenty of antiques shops; try Scavengers at 3533 (412-682-6781). For women's apparel, it's Sugar at 3703 (412-681-5100) and Pavement Shoes at 3629 (412-621-6400). This laid-back group of friendly shop owners sponsors fun come-ons like an annual Christmas cookie tour and Easter egg hunts. Check out the Thunderbird Cafe at 4023 (412-682-0177) for nightlife and Piccolo Forno at 3801 (412-622-0111) for chic Italian eats. The daytime Coca Cafe at 3811 (412-621-3171) is located directly across from a historic landmark: The Arsenal School is named for the site where 78 young workers, mainly women, were killed in an explosion at a Union munitions plant in 1862.

Schenley Park, behind the universities in Oakland, has amenities galore. A student favorite is the city's popular disc-golf course (where 18 holes means tossing a Frisbee into 18 baskets). The park's newest attraction is the shiny carousel at Schenley Plaza, a great public space with outdoor cafes, performances, and a sleek new restaurant called the Porch at Schenley. It's just off Forbes Avenue. The glass onion just over the hill is the **Phipps Conservatory,** a Victorian wonderland of exotic flowers and fountains. The indoor tropical forest overlooks a dramatic ravine. All exhibits are wheelchair accessible. Admission ranges from $12 for adults to $9 for children aged 2 to 18. Open daily from 9:30 a.m. to 5 p.m., till 10 p.m. Fri, at 700 Frank Curto Dr.; call (412) 622-6914 or check www.phipps.conservatory.org. Overlooking the Steve Faloon Trail (voted one of America's top 20 urban running trails by *Runner's World* magazine) is the park's visitor center, a charmingly restored cottage that's now a coffeehouse with a balcony. Get details and directions at www.pittsburghparks.org or (412) 682-PARK.

Nearby **Clayton** (7227 Reynolds St.; 412-371-0600; www.thefrickpittsburgh.org) is the grand former home of Henry Clay Frick, where you can see how

Pittsburgh's millionaires lived at the dawn of the 20th century. Don't miss the working orchestrion, a room-size mechanical orchestra that was the home theater of its day. The greenhouse, art museum, and car museum are free. The cafe is award-winning gourmet; its afternoon teas are white-glove. House tours cost $12; open 10 a.m. to 5 p.m. except Mon.

trivia

"Pittsburgh is undoubtedly the cockeyedest city in the United States," complained journalist Ernie Pyle in 1937. "Physically, it is absolutely irrational. It must have been laid out by a mountain goat. . . . And then the steps—oh, Lord, the steps!"

In the historic Mexican War Streets section of the North Side is the **Mattress Factory** (500 Sampsonia Way; 412-231-3169; www.mattress.org), a fascinating display of contemporary art. The factory, which is, indeed, a converted factory, commissions, exhibits, and collects site-specific installations; it also provides living and working space for artists from around the world. Visionary contemporary artists such as James Turrell, Ann Hamilton, and Damien Hirst have exhibited here; your fellow visitors are likely to be overseas art lovers who've come to Pittsburgh expressly because of the Mattress Factory's world-class reputation for cutting-edge programming. (Check out the basement.) Hours are Tues through Sat 10 a.m. to 5 p.m. and Sunday 1 to 5 p.m. Admission is $10 for adults.

The motto of the **Pittsburgh Children's Museum** is "play with real stuff." So go ahead. Squirt water. Take things apart in The Garage. Get muddy in The Backyard. The award-winning renovation of this combination of two grand old buildings is a treat. It's at 10 Children's Way; call (412) 322-5058 or visit www.pittsburghkids.org. Make a play date Mon through Sat 10 a.m. to 5 p.m., Sun noon to 5 p.m. Admission is $12 for adults, $11 for seniors and children. Just a few steps away, in the Victorian park called Allegheny Commons, are the kid-friendly **National Aviary and Lake Elizabeth.** The Aviary gives a perch to more than 600 species in a lovely old-fashioned glass conservatory; it's open daily except Christmas. Adult admission is $13. In the summer, Lake Elizabeth offers a chance to try kayaking and wall-climbing. Call Venture Outdoors at (412) 969-9090 for details.

Other North Side gems: **Photo Antiquities** (531 E. Ohio St.; 412-231-7881; www.photoantiquities.org), a collection of rarities from the 19th century, including fine Civil War–era images (soldiers loved the newfangled invention). Closed Tues and Sun. Open 10 a.m to 4 p.m. every other day of the week. Admission is $10. And don't miss **St. Anthony's Chapel,** with its collection of 4,200 Catholic relics from saints and popes. In the 1890s St. Anthony's was a

They Came from Pittsburgh

- Stephen Foster, composer

- Billy Eckstine, musician

- Rachel Carson, conservationist

- George S. Kaufman and August Wilson, playwrights

- Gene Kelly, actor and dancer

- Willa Cather, author

- Gertrude Stein, author

- Shirley Jones, actress

- Mary Cassatt, artist

- Henry Mancini, composer

- Perry Como, singer

- Michael Keaton, actor

- Wiz Khalifa, rapper

- Christina Aguilera, singer

sort of mini-Lourdes, where the faithful flocked to be blessed and healed by the church's pastor (who collected most of the bones, skulls, and other relics). Even in a city of churches, this one is completely unique. The ornate European-style chapel, at 1704 Harpster St. in Troy Hill, is open afternoons for tours Thurs through Sat (knock at the rectory next door). Call (412) 231-2994 for details.

Allegheny River Valley

Heading north from Pittsburgh on Route 28, the gritty post-industrial town of **Millvale** appears to have spent all its treasures. In fact, the hillside church of St. Nicholas hosts one of the most unusual mural collections in the country.

Between 1937 and 1941, Croatian artist **Maxo Vanka** created a searing series of religious murals in the interior of the Catholic church. Depicting the struggles of Croatians and other ethnic groups then arriving in southwestern Pennsylvania, the images combine social realism with elements of Byzantine church decoration and Croatian folk art. As the church raises funds to protect and restore the murals, it welcomes visitors. Parishioner Mary Petrich, who remembers seeing Vanka's scaffolding while a pupil here, gives wonderful

Pittsburgh Rocks

The view from the choir loft is impressive: a huge nave swelling with music, with wisps of smoke wafting from the sanctuary. The upturned faces of the young congregation seem transported. But then a snarling guitar chord rips rudely through the congregation, and the crowd at the former St. Ann's Church erupts. The liturgy being celebrated in this century-old house of worship isn't High Mass, but a gig at Pittsburgh's church of rock 'n' roll.

Let us play.

Clubs like *Mr. Small's*—the desanctified Catholic church a few miles upriver from downtown in Millvale—the *Brillo Box* and *Arsenal Lanes* (yes, it's a bowling alley) in Lawrenceville, the *Smiling Moose* on the South Side, *Gooski's* on Polish Hill, and the *Quiet Storm* in Garfield attract the city's best local bands.

Rock comes downtown too. Check *Stage AE,* an indoor/outdoor venue on the North Shore, and the *Byham Theater.* The *Three Rivers Arts Festival* also offers free outdoor concerts each June.

tours. One-hour tours are offered Sat and Sun from 1 to 4 p.m. For weekday tours and special arrangements, call Mary at (412) 681-0905 or Diane Novosel at (724) 845-2907. The church is located at 24 Maryland Ave. Visit www.vanka murals.org

It's easy to miss *Aspinwall*—but don't. This old-fashioned cutie of a riverside town has a real five-and-ten store (J&W Variety, 12 Brilliant Ave.; 412-782-2993), bookstores, gift shops, and great architecture.

Audubon at Beechwood, a property of the Western Pennsylvania Conservancy, has varied walking trails. Stop by the Audubon Society; the reserve is great for wildflowers, birds, and photography. Eight marked, named footpaths range in length and ease of terrain. The Pine Hollow path smells best. Weekly guided nature walks are scheduled year-round. To get to the reserve from Route 28, take the Fox Chapel Road exit north and go about a mile. Turn left on Squaw Run Road, then right on Dorseyville Road. Beechwood Farms is almost 2 miles on the left. For more information write 614 Dorseyville Rd., Pittsburgh 15238; phone (412) 963-6100; or go to www.aswp.org.

On a warm evening there's no hotter ticket than the free concerts at *Hartwood Acres* (215 Saxonburg Blvd.). This county park cradles a band shell at the bottom of a 10-acre meadow and hosts summer concerts with national names. In the winter there are hayrides. Year-round there are tours of the original manor house. Call (412) 767-9200, or visit www.alleghenycounty.us/parks for more information.

Talk about the sound of music: The ***Bayernhof Museum*** in Pittsburgh's North Hills turns up the volume. This suburban home, with a bizarre rococo-Bavarian theme that includes gnome statues and an indoor pool and grotto, houses a large collection of music boxes and other kitschy contraptions. Check out the serinettes (musical bird boxes), Wurlitzer band organs, player pianos, and more. It's at 225 St. Charles Place in a quiet residential neighborhood overlooking the Allegheny River. Tours (for those over the age of 5) are available by appointment for groups of no more than 12 people; call ahead—at least a week in advance if possible. Admission is $10. The phone number is (412) 782-4231; the web address, www.bayernhof museum.com.

trivia

The nickelodeon, the earliest form of public film exhibition, opened on Smithfield Street in Pittsburgh in 1905. The Harris Theater, which screens films around the corner, is named for the nickelodeon's inventor.

In nearby Gibsonia lies one of southwestern Pennsylvania's best restaurants, the ***Pines Tavern and Restaurant*** (5018 Bakerstown Rd.; 724-625-3252; www.thepinestavern.com). This is a 5-star treat, well worth a drive from downtown.

Allegheny anthracite lies under most of the mountains in western Pennsylvania. To get an up-close look at the history of coal mining, go underground at Tarentum's ***Tour-Ed Mine*** (748 Bull Creek Rd.; 724-224-4720; www.tour-ed mine.com). Take a tour 150 feet below the surface on a specially modified train. Don't worry; it's perfectly safe. The mine is just off exit 48 (old exit 5, Allegheny Valley) of the Pennsylvania Turnpike. It's open Memorial Day through Labor Day; limited hours through Oct. Admission is $9 for adults and $8 for children 12 and under.

trivia

The Pittsburgh Pirates are the second-oldest professional athletic team in the country. Originally called the Alleghenies, they changed their name when other teams accused them of "pirating" players from their rosters.

Above ground, the Tour-Ed Mine and the Allegheny-Kiski Historical Society get support from the ***Fleatique,*** a popular seasonal flea market. A $3-per-car charge supports the nonprofits, and shoppers and swappers get to browse several acres of Hawaiian shirts, vintage glassware, and other finds. The outdoor Sunday market is held monthly May through Oct. See the schedule at www.akvhs.org.

You can appreciate history on a trip to ***Old Economy Village.*** at ***Ambridge,*** less than an hour northwest of Pittsburgh. Old Economy is the

Ride 'em Shovelers!

The annual **Beaver County Snow Shovel Riding Championship** in Ambridge is a classic community event, with minimal equipment required. "The key to winning," says organizer Jack Hilfinger, "is to remember that the shovel doesn't have to touch the ground." That means you can customize your ride with a snow tube, skis, or anything else that slides. The fun takes place the third Saturday of January, snow permitting.

preserved third and final home of the Old Harmony Society. One of the many pious and industrious German sects to settle in Pennsylvania, they arrived in 1804. Because they expected the Second Coming of Christ to happen at any moment, they adopted celibacy to purify themselves for Christ's thousand-year reign on earth. Religion came first in their lives—they celebrated the Last Supper six times a year—but their communal lifestyle was not austere. Harmonites ate well, adorned their furniture, played music, planted flower gardens, and made money for the community. By 1825 they had built cotton and wool factories powered and heated by steam engines, a steam laundry, and a dairy. They constructed shops for blacksmiths, hatters, wagonmakers, and linen weavers. Their canny business sense produced fine furniture, sturdy buildings, beautiful grounds, and many beneficial investments in the nearby towns. The community lasted until 1905.

Your hour-long tour takes in the community kitchen, the cabinet and blacksmith shops, granary, wine cellar, tailor shop, store, great house, and gardens. The village and its gift shop are open mid-March through December. Hours are Tues and Wed 10 a.m. to 4 p.m., Thurs through Sat 10 a.m. to 5 p.m., and Sun noon to 5 p.m. The village is closed Mon. Admission is $10 for adults, $9 for seniors, and $6 for youth. For information about daily tours and special events, write Friends of Old Economy Village, 270 Sixteenth St., Ambridge 15003; call (724) 266-4500; or visit www.oldeconomyvillage.org. To get there follow I-79 to Sewickley, then go north on Route 65 along the Ohio River until you see the white picket fence.

If you're looking for a gentle adventure, consider hot-air ballooning over western Pennsylvania. Balloonist Tim Meteny flies daily in warm weather at dawn and dusk. You'll lift off from the tiny **Beaver County Airport** off Route 51 at the speed of the wind. That means the experience is gentle; the gondola barely sways as the green hills pass smoothly, 1,000 feet below. Schedule your adventure ($200 per person) in advance, but remember that weather conditions can rearrange your plans. Call (724) 336-2300 or visit www.balloonpa-ohio.com.

As you head south from New Brighton, you're entering Whiskey Rebellion country. The *Oliver Miller Homestead,* in Allegheny County's South Park, is the home of one of the instigators, shot in August 1794 when he joined an angry mob that surrounded nearby *Woodville Plantation,* the home of General John Neville. Both sites, though modest, are open to the public. The Miller Homestead (412-835-1554; olivermiller.org), located on Corrigan Drive, South Park, is open Sun afternoons from the beginning of May until the second Sunday in Dec; admission is $1 ($2 for special events). Woodville Plantation (412-221-0348; www.woodvilleplantation.org) is located on Route 50, Bridgeville, and is open year round. The grounds are open at no cost for self-guided tours Wed through Sat from 10 a.m. to 6 p.m. House tours are offered Sun from 1 to 4 p.m.; admission is $5 per person, $10 per family.

trivia

Dancer Gene Kelly and composer Billy Strayhorn grew up in Pittsburgh's East Liberty neighborhood. They are remembered there at the Kelly-Strayhorn Theater, 5941 Penn Ave.

Westsylvania

Passionate collectors create great museums. One little gem in Butler, easily reached from I-79 or Route 8, is the *Maridon Museum.* Named for its founders, Mary and Donald Phillips, it's the only museum in the region devoted to Asian art. Jade, ivory, and Meissen figurines are specialties in this collection of pieces from Japan and China. It's open Wed through Sat from 11 a.m. to 4 p.m. or by special appointment at 322 N. McKean St.; admission for adults is $4 (724-282-0123; www.maridon.org).

Slightly farther north you'll find *McConnell's Mill State Park,* which appeals to historians, geologists, rock climbers, birders, botanists, hunters, anglers, rafters, and, of course, picnickers. The park gets its name from a restored gristmill, open seasonally, which you can reach by parking in a lot near the top of the hill and following a footpath down. You may take a free guided tour of the mill in the summer or visit on your own. Through the park runs Slippery Rock Creek and its adjacent walking trail. Be sure to venture toward *Slippery Rock Gorge,* 20,000 years old and 400 feet deep. For details about tours, hunting, and fishing, phone (724) 368-8091. Take I-79 to the Route 422 exit, and go almost 2 miles west on Route 422. A sign indicates a left turn for the park.

Want your own fishing cabin on a peaceful lake? At *Moraine State Park,* on the opposite (eastern) side of I-79 from McConnell's Mill, rent a nice one for

trivia

Zelienople, in Butler County, has a sweet, old-fashioned Main Street and a peaceful stream alongside. But what's with the grandiose name? The town is named for Zelie Basse Passavant, wife of the town's founder. The locals affectionately call it Zelie.

a week (for $421 during peak season, if you're a state resident), and fish Lake Arthur to your heart's content. The only powerboats allowed on the 3,200-acre lake are the putt-putt pontoon type, so it's blissfully quiet. Off Lakeview Beach, one of two sandy swimming areas, windsurfers abound. To windsurf you'll need a state park launching permit from the Crescent Bay boat rental office on the south shore, which offers canoes and paddleboats (get details at 724-368-9955 or www.moraineboatrentals.com). A 7-mile paved bike path winds along the lake. It's easy enough for youngsters and there's a rental concession in the northwest corner of the park. For more information visit www. www.dcnr.state.pa.us/stateparks/findapark/moraine/index.htm .

The town of *Slippery Rock*—home of the former Slippery Rock State Teachers College, now *Slippery Rock University*—resembles most college towns, with music stores and coffee shops. One resident said the addition of a McDonald's made the place "big time." Then came Burger King. If the town's name sounds familiar, it's because many football stadiums in the country announce the Slippery Rock scores at the end of their games. Enough people have been titillated by the name to generate some funny stories about its origin.

Between Erie and Pittsburgh, I-79 is largely rural, scenic, and lightly traveled. Roughly halfway between these cities, it's worth taking some time to go both east and west on Route 208. Near the intersection of I-79 and I-80, the easterly road goes to Grove City, where signs direct you to *Wendell August Forge* (1605 S. Center St.). The forge is a self-contained industry in the middle of a quiet community, one of the few remaining forges in the country that still fabricates aluminum, pewter, bronze, and sterling-silver pieces by hand, without any production machinery.

Today the forge is operated by the Knecht family, who bought it in 1978. You can walk through part of the forge to witness the entire process and ask the craftspeople questions. All items produced at the forge are for sale in the showroom for prices ranging from a few dollars to a few thousand. No two pieces are alike. Call (724) 458-8360 or (800) 923-4438, or visit www.wendellaugust.com.

Going west on Route 208 from I-79 takes you to *Volant,* about 10 miles from Grove City, and, 4 miles farther, to *New Wilmington,* the historic home of Westminster College. This is the heart of a refreshingly noncommercial

Amish area. The handsome college overlooks Brittan Lake, and the carillon in Old Main peals for special town events. Amish craftsmen bring their buggies to Wilson's Lumber to pick up supplies, so there are often as many horses on the street as there are cars. Stop for a cup of coffee at Mugsies (that's all that's served here; the town is dry), and drink in the quiet.

As you pass the giant Prime Outlets at Grove City, where I-80 meets I-79, you'll swear the mall is being invaded by paratroopers. Wrong. Those parachutists are landing at an airfield just behind the shops, at **Skydive PA** (496 Old Ash Rd., Mercer; 800-909-JUMP; www.skydivepa.com). Experienced instructors there, with a perfect safety record, will get you up and back to earth in just a day. Your jumping companions might be fraternity brothers, members of a wedding party, or an 80-year-old grandma. Says owner Jeff Reckard, "The goal is to land safely with an open parachute over your head." (Duh.) Or stop for an hour, stretch out on the patio, and watch others land.

trivia

Chipped ham, short for chip-chopped ham, is a local delicacy. It's pressed ham, sliced so thin you can see through it. Any self-respecting deli or grocery store in the Pittsburgh area carries it

Golf, anyone? You might think that Atlanta and Palm Springs have the best golf courses. And, indeed, they might. But the nation's *first* golf course, or at least the oldest course in continuous use, is near where you are at this very moment: in Foxburg. One Joseph Mickle Fox learned the game of golf from a pro at St. Andrews, Scotland. He returned to his estate in Foxburg with golf clubs and balls made of gutta-percha. In 1887 Fox built a five-hole course for the enjoyment of his neighbors, with greens of sand and one-quart tomato cans serving as cups. Three holes were added, then one more, bringing the modern total to nine. Since its inception the course has seen continuous play and is now the **Foxburg Country Club.** Midweek fees are $25 for 18 holes with a cart; weekends and holidays, prices go up to $30. Fore!

The nostalgic log clubhouse contains the **American Golf Hall of Fame** and the Tri-State P.G.A. Hall of Fame. The museum and library chronicle 400 years of golf. The museum, golf course, and clubhouse are open daily, Apr through Oct. For more information and tee times, call (724) 659-3196 during the season. The Foxburg Country Club is located just minutes south of I-80 (exit 45) just off Route 58 in Foxburg, and the Allegheny Grille (40 Main St.; 724-659-5701 or www.visitfoxburg.com) offers waterfront dining.

Three miles from Foxburg, the wild and scenic Allegheny River runs through a spectacular and densely forested valley. Quaint Victorian homes lie just across the river in Emlenton (near I-80 exits 5 and 6). At the corner of

Main and Second Streets stands America's first steam-powered gristmill. Built in 1875, the refurbished *Old Emlenton Mill* serves as a central point for the annual Christmas in Oil Country celebration.

Southwest Corner

Southwest of Pittsburgh, where the state borders West Virginia, Pennsylvania presents many winning, off-the-beaten-path discoveries. At the intersection of I-70 and I-79 is the town of *Washington,* where you can visit the *LeMoyne House Historical Museum* (49 E. Maiden St.), Pennsylvania's first National Historic Landmark of the Underground Railroad. In the house, built in 1812, you can learn about life before the Civil War. A 19th-century apothecary exhibit fills one room, and exhibits on local history change regularly. You might find a display on Victorians at home, for example, or 19th-century wedding gowns. Another interesting feature, way off the path most people want to follow, is the crematory LeMoyne built, the first in the Western Hemisphere; you can tour it the second Sat of each month, May through Sept, 2 to 4 p.m.

Just outside, the garden contains medicinal herbs that LeMoyne used in his medical practice, plus culinary herbs and fragrant and flowering herbs for pleasure. Volunteers tend the garden, changing plants and shrubs frequently. You can take a self-guided tour of the garden and see, in addition to mint, foxglove, and brown-eyed susans, a Native American grinding stone and mile markers from the old National Highway. Tours run year-round Tues through Fri 11 a.m. to 4 p.m.; group tours only on Sat. Admission is $5 per adult. Call

Albert Who?

At the three forks of the Missouri River, Lewis and Clark came to an agreement about names for them. They were to be the Jefferson, Madison, and Gallatin Rivers. Uh—Gallatin?

Albert Gallatin—the statesman, diplomat, financier, historian, ethnologist, industrialist, and farmer—is remembered today, at least by a few, at *Friendship Hill,* his frontier home near Point Marion (223 New Geneva Rd.; 724-725-9190; www.nps.gov/archive/frhi/home.htm). Overlooking the Monongahela, the estate (which Gallatin left in 1825) is a monument to the savvy financier, who paid for the Louisiana Purchase and oversaw the beginnings of a national transportation system. The next time you hear his name on *Jeopardy*, you'll be an expert. Check out the house, and stay till sunset to wander the trails. Open daily 9 a.m. to 5 p.m., except federal holidays; free admission.

(724) 225-6740, or visit www.wchspa.org for details. While you're at LeMoyne House, peek at the guns and uniforms in the **Southwest Pennsylvania Military Museum,** a repository of memorabilia from all of America's wars. The book and gift shop offers an array of history-inspired products. Appropriately, the Washington County Historical Society also operates from the LeMoyne House.

Also in Washington, tour **Bradford House** (175 S. Main St.), once the home of David Bradford, a leader in the Whiskey Rebellion of 1794. The home is furnished in period antiques and is open for tours May through Dec from 11 a.m. to 5 p.m., and other times by appointment; call (724) 222-3604, or visit www.bradfordhouse.org.

A great place to take children is the **Meadowcroft Museum of Rural Life,** about 20 miles northwest of Washington. (Go north on Route 844, then west on Route 50.) People have lived and worked on the land at Meadowcroft for 14,000 years—longer than at any other documented site in North America. Archaeologists continue to excavate the Meadowcroft rock shelter, but it's also open to the public. Here you can see how Native Americans, frontier settlers, farmers, lumbermen, and coal miners shaped the history of western Pennsylvania. Step back in time and spin wool from the museum's flock of sheep, or watch a blacksmith forge red-hot iron. Meadowcroft is open Memorial Day through Labor Day, Wed through Sat noon to 5 p.m. and Sun 1 to 5 p.m.; special hours in May, Sept, and Oct. Adult admission is $12. For information call (724) 587-3412; write to 401 Meadowcroft Rd., Avella 15312; or visit www.meadowcroftmuseum.org.

Here in Greene County, a soggy summer day is always a cause for celebration. Back in 1978, locals noticed that it always seemed to rain on July 29. So, ever since then, the town has thrown an annual party on High Street, with food, music, crafts, and umbrellas. Get details on the **Waynesburg Rain Day** celebration at www.waynesburgchamber.com, or call the borough office at (724) 627-5926.

Three miles east of Waynesburg (take exit 3 off I-79) the **Greene County Historical Museum,** a mid-Victorian mansion, features period antiques, a country store, and collections of pottery, glass, quilts, and Indian and early-American artifacts—more than 10,000 items in all. The site, at 918 Rolling Meadows Rd., once housed the county poor farm. Little is known about the operation of the poor farm except that after an extremely unfavorable review of the home by the *Atlantic Monthly* in 1886, a reform campaign was launched to improve the conditions. The museum is open Tues through Sat from 10 a.m. to 3 p.m. and Sun by appointment only. Adult admission is $5. Call (724) 627-3204 or visit www.greenecountyhistory.com.

A sculpted Mingo Indian seems ready to pounce at **Busby Run Battle-field** (Route 993, Jeannette; 724-527-5584; www.bushyrunbattlefield.com). The statue stands in a museum that marks the site of a fierce battle where Chief Pontiac's warriors fought 400 British soldiers at the end of the French and Indian War in August 1763. If the British hadn't won that crucial battle, we wouldn't need English. Check out the site's visitor center, open Apr through Oct, Wed through Sun, 9 a.m. to 5 p.m. Admission is $5 for adults.

Five miles east lie the crossroads of **Hanna's Town.** Homesteaders built a thriving village here between 1758 and 1773, when it became the county seat. When word of the battles of Lexington and Concord reached these western settlers two years later, they protested British authority by issuing the Hanna's Town Resolves, which foreshadowed the Declaration of Independence. They even created their own flag, with a rattlesnake and the "don't tread on me" motto. An interpretive center is planned for the hilltop overlooking the settlement. Visit the site at 809 Forbes Trail Rd., Hempfield Township, Westmoreland County, or check (724) 836-1800; www.starofthewest.org.

The 104-mile Western Division of the Pennsylvania Mainline Canal ran through Saltsburg before connecting with Johnstown and Pittsburgh. Beginning in 1829, it was the town's lifeblood for nearly 30 years. Nearly two centuries later the village on the Kiskiminetas River remains mostly unchanged. To see it, shoot for Canal Days, held the first weekend of every June. Or paddle the local waterways in a kayak or canoe. And be sure to visit the **Rebecca B. Hadden Stone House Museum** (105 Point St., Saltsburg; 724-639-9003; www .visitsaltsburg.com/recreation.html). Hours are Wed from 10 a.m. to 2 p.m. and Sun from 1 to 4:30 p.m. Call for tour information.

Punxsutawney

Remember the movie *Groundhog Day,* in which Bill Murray plays a grumpy TV weatherman who has a really bad day—over and over and over again? Murray tries to learn from his mistakes—and turn the page on the calendar. Check out the scene for yourself in **Punxsutawney.**

In Punxsutawney (rhymes with chunks-a-SAW-me), Punxsutawney Phil, the groundhog, officially does or does not see his shadow at dawn on February 2, determining whether we will or will not have six more weeks of winter.

The televised event takes place on **Gobbler's Knob,** a mythical, magical area, before an audience of media and more than 35,000 people. The town sits where Route 119 crosses Route 36. For more information call (814) 938-7700 or (800) 752-7445, or go to www.punxsutawney.com.

The groundhog tradition stems from beliefs associated with Candlemas Day and the days of early Christians in Europe. According to an old English song:

> *If Candlemas be fair and bright,*
> *Come, Winter, have another flight;*
> *If Candlemas brings clouds and rain,*
> *Go, Winter, and come not again.*

In Europe hedgehogs emerged in spring; in western Pennsylvania a groundhog had to do.

There's only one way to see Phil up close and personal on his big day: Get there early, around 2:30 a.m. That's when shuttle buses depart from six downtown locations for the music, fireworks, food, and mindless hilarity until 7:25 a.m., when Phil usually debuts. Visitors can't drive to the Knob and can't bring alcohol or illegal substances. But they can and do wear groundhog hats, suits, and T-shirts; carry banners ("Free Phil"); and cheer insanely when the Seer of Seers finally appears.

This is a once-in-a-lifetime must-do. But since the town has only one hotel, accommodations are scarce. The town sponsors overnight "crash pads" in public buildings, and there are a handful of motels within a half-hour drive. (One solution for partiers: Bring your own RV, park at the town campsite, and shuttle to the Knob.) At the conclusion of the festivities, linger to enjoy church-sponsored pancake breakfasts and small-town charm.

Many of Punxsutawney's nostalgic Main Street building facades have been renovated, and beautiful tree-lined West Mahoning Street features Millionaires'

Up Close & Personal with Phil

My sons will never forget their first Groundhog Day in Punxsutawney. Unprepared for the crowds, we didn't reach the Knob in time for Phil's official pronouncement. But when we finally arrived, the mob had thinned out to reveal Phil himself—fat, sleek, and toothy. His top-hatted handler kindly let James and Bill pet the 15-pound prognosticator—a thrill they remember fondly each February 2. They also remember that we found a five-dollar bill lying in the snow.

Row, preserved from the days when Punxsutawney was a thriving coal, oil, and lumber town.

In the children's library of the Mahoning East Civic Center, downtown Punxsutawney, a window lets kids watch Punxsutawney Phil between his on-duty days. Who knows what Phil will predict next year? The shadow knows.

Even if groundhogs are the animals with the biggest reputation in metropolitan Punxsutawney, they're not the biggest animals. Bison are. At **Nature's Comeback Bison Ranch,** the Hineman family raises the large mammals. They may end up on your table, but they're happy, well-fed, free-range bison during their lifetime. "Many people are amazed at how playful bison actually are," says owner Brian Hineman. "They have been seen throwing logs that weigh over 500 pounds several feet in the air and bouncing around like little lambs. Bison can run up to 45 miles an hour—amazingly fast for their massive size." The breeder bull, who weighs over a ton, is called Hercules. To produce more healthful meat with lower fat content, Nature's Comeback feeds the bison only hay and grass. The meat, says Hineman, "tastes like your best cuts of beef without the waste of trimming the fat." The ranch, which has been in the family for over 150 years, will give you a warm-weather tour or sell you some tasty meat; call ahead (814) 590-6965 to make a tour reservation at this off-the-beaten-path attraction. (Watch where you step as you get up close and personal with large animals.) You can write to Nature's Comeback Bison Ranch at 1436 Bower's Rd., Punxsutawney 15767, or visit http://buffalobrian.tripod.com. Take I-80, exit 97, 1 mile off Route 119 south.

trivia

In 1868, in the Jacks (Oak Hall) School in Porter Township, Clarion County became the home of the Anti-Horse Thief Association. Although there is no record of a horse's being stolen for several decades, the association holds an annual dinner. In 1956, when Dwight D. Eisenhower and Arthur Godfrey belonged, it cost $1 to become a life member.

A trip to nearby **Smicksburg** is an enjoyable drive, particularly at harvest time. Home of the largest Amish settlement in western Pennsylvania, Smicksburg has a lovely rolling landscape freckled with farms. Motorized vehicles share the winding roads with horses and buggies, and you find fine craftsmanship and craft shops at every turn. Because of the strong religious faith, many shops close on Sunday.

Off Route 219, 4 miles north of Grampian, you will find **Bilger's Rocks,** a phenomenon of massive, ancient sandstone formations, called "rock city," covering some 20 acres. One 500-ton boulder rests on a smaller one in perfect balance. Visited for centuries, these giant sandstone formations tower 30 to 50 feet.

From groundhogs to bison to rabbits. Or at least invisible rabbits. Okay, one invisible rabbit. You know, Harvey, the bunny only Jimmy Stewart could see in the movie *Harvey*. Stewart's life and films are alive and well and entertaining everyone at the ***Jimmy Stewart Museum*** in Indiana, Pennsylvania. Sit back in a 1930s-style movie theater and watch *Mr. Smith Goes to Washington* and *It's a Wonderful Life*. The small museum occupies the third floor of the public library, and it's dedicated to the homeboy who catapulted from his family's hardware store to the heart of Tinseltown. Admission costs $7 per adult, and the museum is open from 10 a.m. to 4 p.m. Mon through Sat and noon to 4 p.m. Sun and holidays. The library is at 845 Philadelphia St., and the mailing address is Box One, Indiana 15701. Call (724) 349-6112 or (800) 83-JIMMY (that's really 800-835-4669), or visit Harvey and the gang at www.jimmy.org.

coalinthem tharhills

As you pedal the Ghost Town Trail, look beside you: Near Vintondale you'll spy an exposed anthracite seam in a rock face alongside the trail, shining like dark icing in a stone layer cake. That's why Cambria County is still coal-mining country.

The ***Ghost Town Trail*** threads through 16 miles of abandoned mining towns along the Black Lick Creek. At the midpoint of its run from Dilltown in Indiana County to Nanty Glo in Cambria County is ***Eliza Furnace,*** one of the best-preserved iron furnaces in the United States—and the source of haunted tales. Some say that owner David Ritter's wife ran off with a man named George Rodgers, or that Ritter's son fell into the furnace and was killed. Either way, he was so distraught that he hanged himself. His ghost can supposedly be seen hanging in the furnace's entrance.

But don't let the tall tales keep you away. The Ghost Town bike trail features masses of rhododendrons in the spring (and some wild water colors where mine subsidence still fouls the creek). For directions call the Cambria County Conservation and Recreation Authority at (814) 472-2110; for details go to www.indianacountyparks.org.

Noah weathered a flood, but he heeded the warning. The town of ***Johnstown*** did not. Late in May 1889 it started raining. The neglected South Fork Dam, upriver from Johnstown, gave way May 31, and a wall of water moved 14 miles downstream, plucking chairs, doors, walls, and complete houses out of their rightful places. The water immersed and erased the industrialized city in 10 minutes, killing more than 2,200 people. The ***Johnstown Flood Museum*** (304 Washington St.) re-creates this shocking episode—the catastrophe of death and homelessness, followed by the triumph of human spirit that allowed the town to rebuild. Every hour the museum shows *The Johnstown Flood*, which won the 1989 Academy Award for best short-subject documentary. One survivor expresses the drama: "My boyhood home was crushed like an eggshell before my eyes, and I saw it disappear." See the flood in 3-D, in books, and in souvenirs at the museum.

Around the time of the flood, thousands of immigrants from southern and eastern Europe, lured by ready jobs in its steel mills, came to Johnstown to build a better life. Experience their stories firsthand at the Frank & Sylvia Pasquerilla **Heritage Discovery Center** at 201 Sixth Ave. You'll be handed an immigrant "identity card" that allows you to assume the role of one of eight characters, from a Bohemian farmhand to a Russian peasant, in the interactive exhibits.

Combined admission to the Heritage Discovery Center and the Flood Museum is $6. They're located about a mile apart but are online together at www.jaha.org. Hours are Tues through Sun, year-round, 10 a.m. to 5 p.m.

Two years after the flood, the Cambria Iron Company (a predecessor of Bethlehem Steel Corporation) began building houses in the community of Westmont, 500 feet up Yoder Hill from downtown Johnstown. Since no roads existed, the company assembled a vertical commuter system, which remains today as the **Inclined Plane,** rising at a grade of 71 percent. The *Guinness Book of World Records* ranked it the steepest vehicular inclined plane in the world. Originally designed to carry people and their horses and wagons, it now accommodates people and their cars. In 1935 Bethlehem Steel sold the railway for $1 to Westmont Borough, which now leases it to the Cambria County Tourist Council for $10 a year. The wheels, rails, and other parts came from standard railway equipment (and, in fact, the cars are duplicates of those that hauled cargo boats over the Allegheny Portage railroad). The Inclined Plane is composed of 2 sets of tracks implanted in the side of the hill; 2 cars run simultaneously, 1 going up and the other going down. The cables, 3 on each side, are 2 inches in diameter and 1,130 feet long. They can safely carry 337,000 pounds, or 167 tons. Here's the fun part: You may ride it. You can access the top from Route 271 and the bottom from Route 56. Above the funicular hangs an American flag that measures 30 feet by 60 feet. The plane operates from 11 a.m. to 11 p.m. during the winter and from 9 a.m. to 11 p.m. May through Oct. Round-trip tickets are $4 for adults and $2.50 for kids ages 2 to 12. Hours vary depending on the season and day of the week. For more information call (814) 536-1816 or (814) 535-5526, visit www.inclinedplane.org. The address is 711 Edgehill Dr., Johnstown.

At the top of the Inclined Plane is **Westmont,** originally called Tiptop. Take time to explore this appealing Victorian enclave, a bit of small-town America where you might wish you grew up. Locals say the town has always been divided in two parts: the more affluent southern section with single-family homes, called the "dinner" side, and the less affluent northern section with twin homes and smaller singles, called the "supper" section. Westmont attracts naturalists, too: Lucerne Street contains the longest municipally owned stand of American elm trees east of the Mississippi (even small towns like a claim to fame). Although half of all American elms were killed by Dutch elm disease, this beautiful, stately "cathedral arch" of elms is maintained. The borough now has nine trees that qualify as historic elms, which means they measure at least 10 feet in circumference at chest height.

If you have a pioneer spirit, follow Route 219 south to **Somerset** and visit the **Somerset Historical Center,** which portrays rural life in southwestern Pennsylvania from the rugged pioneer struggles of the 18th century through the commercial agrarian enterprises of the mid-20th. At the center you can see utensils, machinery, and restored buildings from different periods of Pennsylvania history. From May through Oct, guided tours take place from 9 a.m. to 5 p.m. Tues through Sat and from noon to 5 p.m. Sun. From Nov through Apr, guided tours and Sunday hours are not available, so it's best to call ahead at (814) 445-6077. The center closes on holidays and Monday, except Memorial Day and Independence Day. Write to the historical center at 10649 Somerset Pike, Somerset 15501, or visit www.somersetcountychamber.com.

Shanksville, 6 miles from Somerset, will forever be remembered in world history as the first resistance to the war on terrorism. On September 11, 2001, United Airlines Flight 93 crashed here after passengers attempted to wrest the plane away from terrorists. Forty innocent people lost their lives. The formal memorial opened here in 2011. To get to the site from Route 30, take Lambertville Road south for 1.7 miles to Skyline Drive and follow it 0.8 mile to the parking area. There's also a memorial website at www.nps.gov/flni.

To experience a different era of history, you can raft through the past on **Wilderness Voyageurs** historic float trips down the Youghiogheny River. In warm-weather months groups of 6 or more embark from Connellsville with guides clad in 1750s gear (you can wear a sweatshirt and sneakers—you won't get wet). On the 2.5-hour float trip to tiny Dawson, the guides do all the work and offer fascinating lore about the river's role in the French and Indian War, the Whiskey Rebellion, and the coal and coke industries. Reservations are required; cost is $32 per person. Call Wilderness Voyageurs at (800) 272-4141, or visit www.wilderness-voyageurs.com.

Laurel Highlands

Everyone who visits—or lives in—Pennsylvania should see **Fallingwater,** the summer retreat that architect Frank Lloyd Wright designed for the Pittsburgh department-store owner Edgar J. Kaufmann. The house, completed in 1939, was constructed of sandstone quarried on the property and built by local craftsmen. It's the only remaining Wright house where the original setting, furnishings, and artwork remain intact. Fallingwater reflects Wright's genius, which allows the house to merge with its environment outside and to echo nature in its stone and wood interior. The house, appearing to grow out of the boulders and rocks, extends over a natural waterfall of Bear Run. You can't see or hear the water from inside, but you can do both from any balcony or from a stairwell down from the living room. A gray sandstone four-story chimney at the core of the house anchors it into the stone cliff. Wright built a desk in every bedroom and placed all headboards on eastern walls so that no one would be awakened by the sun. Genius. The home retains a feeling of seclusion and oneness with the natural environment, even though many people visit. It's open for guided tours (no wandering on your own) from mid-March through November, daily except Mon, 10 a.m. to 4 p.m. In December and early March it's open only weekends, and it's closed January and February. Reservations are required, especially during July, Aug, and Oct, the busiest months. Try to visit midweek, and bring comfortable walking shoes. For more information write PO Box R, Mill Run 15464; call (724) 329-8501; or visit www .fallingwater.org.

Fallingwater is on Route 381 between the villages of Mill Run and Ohiopyle (pronounce it Ohio-PILE) about 90 minutes southeast of Pittsburgh. Children under age 6 may not tour Fallingwater, but they can play at its Family Room, and there's a nice little cafe on-site. One-hour tours cost $20; they are scheduled from 10 a.m. to 4 p.m. For an in-depth 2-hour tour, scheduled each morning at 8:30, the cost is $65.

Two other Wright-designed homes are close by. West of Ohiopyle, 7 miles along a scenic mountain road, lies *Kentuck Knob,* a smaller, simpler 1950s home that Wright designed for the Hagan family of Uniontown. (It was originally known as the I. N. Hagan House.) The house is hexagonal, with hexagonal accents, all made of native fieldstone and tidewater red cypress. It hides in—rather than sits on—the mountain it occupies, so you're practically at the front door before you see it. On the grounds behind the visitor center is an oversize apple core by artist Claes Oldenburg and other large-scale contemporary sculpture. In Jan and Feb you're invited to cross-country ski the grounds after your house tour. The house is open for tours on weekends in early March and most of December; from April to November, it's open 10 a.m. to 4 p.m., except Wed. Admission is $18 for adults if you reserve early. Book tickets online through the Fallingwater website. Visit www.kentuckknob.com for more information.

If you've ever wanted to spend the night in a Wright creation, here's your chance. North of the Pennsylvania Turnpike in Acme—no relation to Wile E. Coyote's famous products—is Polymath Park. One of Wright's ultra-practical Usonian homes was moved to this property in 2007. Called the **Duncan House,** it flanks two similar homes designed by Wright disciple Peter Berndtson. Treetops Restaurant on the property offers BYOB dining Thurs through Sat evenings. On Sun—the only day when Duncan House is open for public tours—the restaurant is open from 11 a.m. to 6 p.m. Make sure to call (877) 833-7829 for dining reservations, especially during the winter months when hours can vary. Get all the other details at www.polymathpark.com.

South on Route 40 in Markleysburg you'll find a trucker's secret: the home cooking at Glisan's (4625 National Pike; 724-329-4636). With country ham, fresh bread, and 15 varieties of pies baked daily, it's worth a stop.

Now is a perfect time to stop for a walk or a picnic along the Youghiogheny River at **Ohiopyle State Park,** almost 18,500 acres of wilderness delight. The Youghiogheny Gorge, carved 1,700 feet into the Laurel Ridge by the river, takes your breath away. Totally contained within the state park is the borough of Ohiopyle, almost 2 whole blocks long. Eighty-three people live here, and commercial establishments include a grocery store with a few small cafes, a gas station, and, in season, a Dairy Queen and a pizza parlor. One ultra-casual spot, perfect for beer-drinking in soggy post-river attire, is the **Falls City Restaurant and Pub** (112 Garrett St.; 724-329-3000; www.fallscitypub.com). Owner Eric Martin also owns Wilderness Voyageurs next door. The tavern's hours vary seasonally, so call ahead.

"The name of the town, Ohiopyle, is subject to fact and fiction depending on who you're talking to," says Mark McCarty, mayor and manager of an outfitter. The state park's interpretation is something like "white frothing water," but if you study the early settlers' writings, it's more like "peaceful river." The water in this case is the Yough, Youghiogheny being an Indian word for "flowing in a roundabout course." Yes, it's off the beaten path, says Jim Greenbaum, manager of **White Water Adventurers.** "On the other hand,

The Slides

I love the scenic waterfalls at Ohiopyle State Park—especially the Slides, where our family always ends the day with a ride down the slick limestone boulders. The stream varies from gentle to intense, depending on recent rainfall. If it's early in the summer, or there have been lots of recent showers, you'll move at top speed (and the water will be colder). Watch your step—Band-Aids may be required.

there are two interstate highways within a half hour of here." Ohiopyle has lured tourists since the early 1900s, when people came by train from Pittsburgh and Washington to swim in the river and hike on Fern Cliff. Once three large hotels dominated the borough. Then "the railroads went away," as Greenbaum puts it. In the early 1960s a new industry—white-water rafting—was born. The season for rafting runs Mar through Oct, with the bulk of tours scheduled from mid-May until mid-Sept.

The Middle Yough, says Greenbaum, is the easy section, great for kids over 5 or first-time adult rafters. The Lower Yough is rated intermediate, recommended for people age 12 and older. The Yough sections called Pure Screaming Hell, Bastard, and Double Pencil Sharpener are recommended for rafters with the most technical expertise—but then, so is Cheeseburger Falls. If you'd like to try a rafting trip, call one of the four outfitters with state concessions:

White Water Adventurers, PO Box 31, Ohiopyle 15470. Phone (724) 329-8850 or (800) 992-7238; www.wwaraft.com.

Laurel Highlands River Tours, PO Box 107, Ohiopyle 15470. Phone (724) 329-8531 or (800) 472-3846; www.laurelhighlands.com.

Ohiopyle Trading Post, 4 Negley St., Ohiopyle 15470. Phone (724) 329-1450 or (888) 644-6795; www.ohiopyletradingpost.com.

Wilderness Voyageurs, 103 Garrett St., Ohiopyle 15470. Phone (724) 329-1000 or (800) 272-4141; www.wilderness-voyageurs.com.

The Great Allegheny Passage is a 150-mile trail from Pittsburgh to Cumberland, Maryland. Biking fanatics have worked for two decades to clear this gorgeous path along the Youghiogheny and Casselman Rivers. The result is a flat, scenic route right through to the 185-mile Chesapeake and Ohio Canal

Yurt, Anyone?

Pennsylvania has 11 state parks that offer Mongolian-style accommodations in addition to cabins, and Ohiopyle has more yurts than any other park. The round-framed, fabric-covered structures have floors and even decks (but in typical nomadic fashion, no indoor plumbing).

The cost for Pennsylvania residents for a 4- to 5-person yurt is $33 per night Sun through Thurs; $55 per night Fri and Sat in the off-season ($39 and $73 for nonresidents); and $238 per week in summer ($350 for nonresidents). Larger 6-person yurts are available too. If you're not a Pennsylvania resident, rates are higher (one perk of being a citizen of the Commonwealth). Otherwise, Western-style cabin rules apply: no pets, no alcohol, check in at 3 p.m., check out at 10 a.m. To reserve, go to www.visitPAparks.com or call (888) 727-2757.

towpath, which travels on Washington, D.C. The trail uses Big Savage tunnel, a spooky passage through a mountain on the Pennsylvania-Maryland border. (The Western Maryland Railroad used to travel this right-of-way, hence the name rails-to-trails.) Meanwhile, you can explore as much or as little as you like.

If you like to recline while you reconnoiter, consider renting bikes from *Allegheny Recumbent Tours* in Confluence. Because the passage follows the level rail bed, it's hill-free and easy to pedal. That makes these bikes with seat backs and low centers of gravity an ideal choice. Owner Jay Duchesne says they're safe for all ages and abilities. Get details at www.alleghenyrecumbentours .com or (888) 395-9380.

In addition to Ohiopyle, where the river outfitters also offer cheap bike rentals, seek out the other charming villages along the trail. Confluence, some 12 miles south of Ohiopyle, has a great breakfast spot—*Sisters Cafe* ("sisterly advice free of charge"; 482 Hughart St.; 814-395-5252; www.sisters-cafe.com). It's right next to Confluence Hardware, owned by the brothers-in-law. The *River's Edge Cafe* (203 Yough St.; 814-395-5059; www.riversedgecafebnb .com) has a comfy Victorian porch for lingering in the twilight. Next door is the *Parker House* (213 Yough St.; 814-395-9616, www.theparkerhousecountry inn.com), a beautifully restored guest house, great for groups. In Rockwood, another 18 miles south, you'll find a few more B&Bs, a real opera house (now shops and a cafe), and the Rock City Cafe, a beer 'n' wings spot.

As you pedal along, you'll see a few anglers (trout fishing is big here), maybe a few black bears way down in the ravines, and lots of families also pedaling around Ohiopyle, especially on the weekends. Other than that, you'll have the Laurel Highlands to yourself—on the level.

For super-easy, one-click planning, including accommodations and meals, log on to www.gaptrail.org, or contact the Great Allegheny Passage, PO Box 501, Latrobe 15650; (888) 282-2453.

If the sophistication of Frank Lloyd Wright's Fallingwater home makes you pine for an upscale night or two, consider *Nemacolin Woodlands Resort and Spa* in Farmington. With French food, French paintings, and a par-72 golf course, its motto could be "extravagance R us." Elegantly appointed guest rooms include marble baths and plush terry-cloth robes. Entertainment for kids, a shopping mall, a ski slope, a wild animal park, a golf course, skeet shooting, stables, and a climbing wall are on the premises. Dining? Choose among 4 elegant restaurants, including Lautrec, the only western Pennsylvania recipient of AAA's Five Diamond rating. The place is named for a western Delaware Indian named Nemacolin who, in 1740, carved a trail through the Laurel Mountains between what is now Cumberland, Maryland, and Brownsville, Pennsylvania.

BEST ANNUAL EVENTS IN SOUTHWESTERN PENNSYLVANIA

JANUARY

Beaver County Snow Shovel Riding Championship
Economy Park
(724) 846-5600
This annual race is held in Economy Park on the third Saturday in January, unless there's too little snow. Call (724) 846-5600 or (800) 342-8192 for more information.

FEBRUARY

Groundhog Day
Punxsutawney
There's only one place to be on February 2: Punxsutawney. The savvy little town has turned Groundhog Day into a multiday extravaganza with food fests, weddings performed by the mayor, music, and hilarity (when the holiday falls next to a weekend, look out).

Frostburn
Cooper's Lake Campground
http://frostburnpgh.com
Frostburn is Pittsburgh's answer to Burning Man, a groovy participatory art event held at chilly Cooper's Lake Campground in Slippery Rock each February.

MAY

National Road Festival
National Road Heritage Park
(724) 437-9877
www.nationalroadpa.org
In mid-May the National Road Festival celebrates the historic national road, US Route 40. Food, fun, and entertainment stretch for 90 miles along the National Road Heritage Park.

JULY

Big Butler Fair
(724) 865-2400
The Big Butler Fair is a 150-year-old institution with plenty of noise—demolition derbies, tractor pulls, and more. It's held over the Fourth of July.

AUGUST

Antique Flea Market
Somerset
(814) 445-6431
The Antique Flea Market is held in Somerset the second Saturday in August.

North Washington Rodeo
(724) 894-2064
http://nwfd.com/rodeo
Saddle up yer bronco, or at least your sport-utility vehicle, and head to the North Washington Rodeo, on Route 38, 16 miles north of Butler, during the third week in August. Daily performances at 8 p.m. feature men doing saddle bronc, bareback, and calf roping, and women running barrel races. There's always something at intermission for the kids and raffles for the grown-ups. You might win a registered colt or a steer that the rodeo organizers have purchased from the local 4-H group.

Flood City Music Festival
(814) 539-1889
www.jaha.org
Accordions. Trombones. Blues. Balkan bop. It's all at the Flood City Music Festival, held each August. More than 70 hours of nationally known acts are programmed each year. Everything takes place at the downtown festival park, bordering the stone bridge made famous by the infamous 1889 flood.

SEPTEMBER

Flax Scutching Festival
Monticue's Grove, Stahlstown
(724) 238-9244
During the second weekend in September, there's a Flax Scutching Festival at Monticue's Grove in Stahlstown. If the town's not off the beaten path enough for you, the event surely is. Here you can see how craftspeople used to take the flax plant and scutch it—in other words, break down the tough fibers to make linen. To learn more about scutching or the second-oldest flax-scutching festival in the world, call (724) 238-9244.

Peanut Butter Festival
Gumtown Memorial Park,
New Bethlehem
(814) 275-3929
New Bethlehem initiated its annual Peanut Butter Festival in 1996 to promote the Smucker's peanut butter plant. If you think toast and jelly are naked without p.b., visit Gumtown Memorial Park on Water Street on a weekend in mid-September.

OCTOBER

Step Trek
Pittsburgh
(412) 488-0486
www.steptrek.org
Get a cardio workout and a great view of downtown Pittsburgh during Step Trek, the South Side Slopes Association's open house along the steepest step streets in Pittsburgh. The October event benefits the neighborhood association.

VIA Music & New Media Festival
Pittsburgh
www.via-pgh.com
The reputation of the VIA Music & New Media Festival, founded in 2010, is growing. It brings bands, visual artists, DJs, and other experimental types together in tremendously entertaining ways. The 5-day event happens each October in Pittsburgh; check www.via-pgh.com.

Pumpkinfest
Confluence
www.visitconfluence.org
The tiny Youghiogheny River town of Confluence proves it has more gourds than people each October at Pumpkinfest. There's a Pumpkinfest Queen, a tough-guy tractor pull, live bands, and more.

DECEMBER

First Night
Pittsburgh
(412) 471-6070
www.firstnightpgh.com
December 31, celebrate First Night (it's really Last Night, isn't it?) throughout downtown Pittsburgh.

When Congress established the National Highway in the mid-1800s, the highway incorporated Nemacolin's trail. For resort reservations log on to www .nemacolin.com, or call (724) 329-8555 or (866) 344-6957.

Near the popular ski resorts of Seven Springs and Hidden Valley lies the old-money charm of *Ligonier,* founded as a British fort in 1758. The *Fort Ligonier Museum* has re-created the redcoats' armaments, used against the French and the Indians, in authentic detail. Its treasures include jaw-dropping portraits of the British leaders of the 1750s by Joshua Reynolds, Allan Ramsay, and others. There's also a comprehensive, 300-artifact exhibit on the Seven Years' War, the worldwide European conflict that touched North America as the French and Indian War. It's open seasonally at 200 S. Market St. Call (724) 238-9701 or visit www.fortligonier.org.

Ligonier's central "diamond" has a Victorian bandstand and pleasant shopping—good restaurants, too. And just on the edge of town lies *Idlewild,* an amusement park with low prices, low temperatures, and a laid-back feel. Its biggest coaster isn't the Mauler, but the Wild Mouse. Even the shyest toddlers will love Idlewild's Storybook Forest, where they can meet the Billy Goats Gruff (played by real billies, but minus the trolls). Older kids can holler on the Tarzan vines and water chutes. A miniature railway runs over Loyalhanna Creek, and the towering trees keep pathways cool. Don't miss the restored pastel merry-go-round. Idlewild is open from Memorial Day weekend through Labor Day on Route 30, Ligonier. Admission prices vary. Call (724) 238-3666, or visit www .idlewild.com for details.

On Route 381 in nearby Cook Township lies *Powdermill Nature Reserve,* a field research station of the Carnegie Museum of Natural History. Here kids and adults can spy on wildflowers, trees, songbirds, butterflies, and salamanders with eyes and ears, magnifying glass, or camera. Youngsters can sign up for weeklong nature classes during the summer, and individuals and families can attend other free programs. The nature reserve is open year-round Wed through Sat 9 a.m. to 4:30 p.m. and Sun noon to 4:30 p.m. It is also open Tues 9 a.m. to 4:30 p.m. from April through mid-November. For hours and program information, call (724) 593-6105, or visit www.powdermill.org.

All these hills, all these valleys: Sounds like a perfect place for mountain biking, and there are some gnarly opportunities on the *PW&S Trails* in Forbes State Forest. "When I ride here in the evening, I see grouse, deer, and bear," says Gates Watson, a local enthusiast. There are 5 loops here, carved from an old logging railroad; like ski trails, they vary in length and difficulty. For details call (724) 238-7560, or pick up a map at the Forbes State Forest office on Route 30 outside Laughlintown.

Route 669 leads you straight to (well, not really straight, but toward) *Mt.*

Davis in the Forbes State Forest—at 3,213 feet above sea level, the highest elevation in the state.

If you're into gallows humor, pop up Route 281, nearly to I-70, and go to the courthouse in Somerset. The building served as the county jail from 1856 to 1981, and the double hanging gallows is still intact: a warning, perhaps, to tardy employees.

Places to Stay in Southwestern Pennsylvania

BEAVER FALLS

Beaver Valley Motel
Route 18
(724) 843-0630 or
(800) 400-8312
www.bvmotel.com
Old-fashioned drive-up motor inn.

FARMINGTON

Stone House Inn
3023 National Pike
(724) 329-8876
www.stonehouseinn.com
Serving travelers since 1882. Near Fallingwater and Ohiopyle State Park.

HOLBROOK

Cole's Country Cabin Bed and Breakfast
544 Hoovers Run Rd.
(724) 451-8521
Quiet rural inn west of Waynesburg, Greene County.

INDUSTRY

Willows Inn
1830 Midland Beaver Rd.
(724) 643-4500
www.willowsinnpa.com
Just off Route 60, a short drive from Beaver business district.

PITTSBURGH

The Priory Hotel
614 Pressley St.
(412) 231-3338
www.thepriory.com
Formerly a monastery, now a popular North Shore boutique hotel.

Sunnyledge Boutique Hotel
5124 Fifth Ave.
(412) 683-5014
www.sunnyledge.com
Sophisticated spot near the universities. Try the martini bar.

PUNXSUTAWNEY

Jackson Run Bed and Breakfast
363 Jackson Run Rd.
(814) 938-2315
www.jacksonrun.com
Farmhouse accommodations in an apple orchard.

Pantall Hotel
135 E. Mahoning St.
(800) 872-6825
www.pantallhotel.com
Renovated historic hotel.

SLIPPERY ROCK

Applebutter Inn
666 Centreville Pike
(724) 794-1844
www.applebutterinnpa.com
Country lodgings a mile from the university campus.

SOMERSET

Bayberry Inn
611 N. Center Ave.
(814) 445-8471
Downtown B&B in the county seat, near the turnpike exit.

VOLANT

Candleford Inn Bed and Breakfast
Mercer Street
(724) 533-4497
www.candlefordinn.com
Open year-round in Mercer County's Amish country.

Places to Eat in Southwestern Pennsylvania

BEAVER

Cafe Kolache
402 Third St.
(724) 775-8102
www.cafekolache.com
A friendly Main Street coffeehouse with delicious filled Czech pastries. Closed Sun.

Wooden Angel
308 Leopard Ln.
(724) 774-7880
www.wooden-angel.com
Award-winning American wine cellar.

BROOKVILLE

Courthouse Grill and Pub
209 Main St.
(814) 849-2557
Open daily for casual lunches and dinners.

CORAOPOLIS

Hyeholde Restaurant
1516 Coraopolis Heights Rd.
(412) 264-3116
www.hyeholde.com
Elegant 5-star dining in a faux chateau.

FARMINGTON

Stone House Inn
3023 National Pike
(724) 329-8876
www.stonehouseinn.com
Casual fine dining year-round.

MERCER

Iron Bridge Inn
1438 Perry Hwy.
(724) 748-3626
www.springfields.com
Famous for prime rib and Sunday brunch.

PITTSBURGH

Church Brew Works
3525 Liberty Ave.
(412) 688-8200
www.churchbrew.com
Microbrewpub in the former St. John the Baptist Church in Lawrenceville.

Harris Grill
5747 Ellsworth Ave.
Shadyside
(412) 362-5273
www.harrisgrill.com
A youthful Shadyside bar. Tuesday is the wildly popular bacon night.

Isabella on Grandview
1318 Grandview Ave.
Mt. Washington
(412) 431-5882
www.isabelaongrandview.com
Eclectic fine dining with a view in a converted cliffside Victorian.

Kaya
2000 Smallman St.
Strip District
(412) 261-6565
www.bigburrito.com
Upscale casual with tapas, alligator on a stick, and veggie dishes.

The Warhol Cafe
Andy Warhol Museum
117 Sandusky St.
(412) 237-8300
www.warhol.org
Open Tues through Sun 10 a.m. to 4 p.m. (Fri to 9 p.m.). Seasonal light meals, wines, and microbrews.

SCENERY HILL

Century Inn
2175 National Rd. East
(724) 945-6600
www.centuryinn.com
Casual dining in a 1794 landmark.

NORTHWESTERN PENNSYLVANIA →

The Lake District

The Erie area is Pennsylvania's beach. Ohio, Lake Erie, and New York State form the western, northern, and eastern borders of Erie County, respectively, and getting to **Erie** from anywhere in Pennsylvania means driving through miles and miles and miles of scenic woodland and uninhabited terrain.

People here are fiercely proud of the pristine natural environment, from wildlife refuges to forest wilderness to rushing streams to the lake.

A few decades ago, Lake Erie was pronounced dead. But it wasn't really dead—the problem was actually too much of the wrong kinds of life. Nutrients such as phosphates and nitrates, especially plentiful in agricultural runoff, encouraged excessive growth of algae, which grew so fast that it choked out other forms of plants and fish. The process is called eutrophication. In water where no oxygen can reach the bottom, the only fish that can live are small panfish. As Lake Erie deteriorated, only the panfish survived. A massive combined effort by area manufacturing companies, local colleges, state and federal governments, and concerned citizens turned things

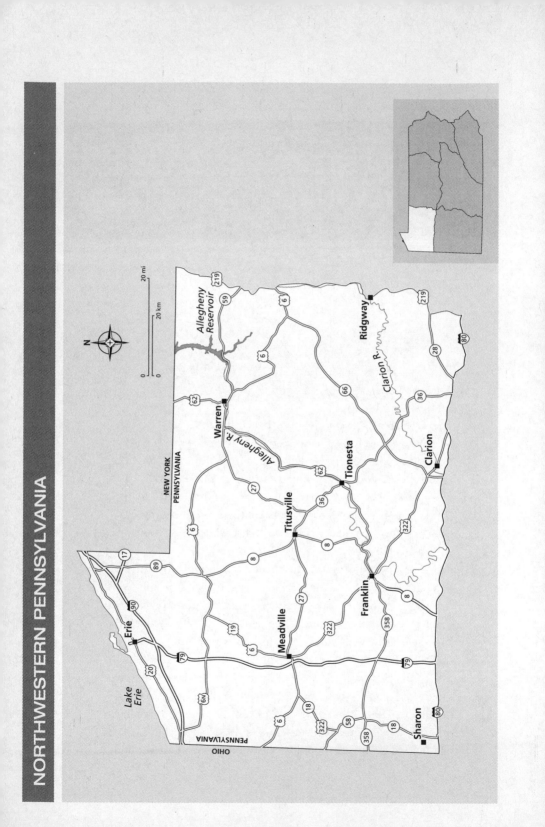

NORTHWESTERN PENNSYLVANIA

around. The City of Erie improved its sewage disposal system. The Department of Health now tests regularly for harmful bacteria. Industries treat their wastes so that they won't hurt the lake. Colleges run ecology projects, continuously monitoring the state of the water. At least one Erie councilman pilots his boat, at cost, for the monitoring teams. Game fish have returned. In fact, the city celebrated when the first coho salmon was caught after a long dry spell.

The resurgence of other species is no fish story. Every fall, hundreds of Pennsylvania anglers descend on the Lake Erie tributaries—Elk and Walnut Creeks and the mouths of Trout and Godfrey Runs—for the annual steelhead spawning runs. These whoppers are reputed to swim right up to the boat and can almost be scooped up by hand. They're most plentiful when the water temperature hovers around 55 degrees.

Part of the success story comes from the central role that Lake Erie plays in the lives of the people who live here. Hundreds of people go to the public dock in the city every day, if not to fish, at least to check out conditions. Adults who've lived here all their lives talk about having gone out fishing every morning before school or every evening after school. These stories help explain the spirit of the lakeshore. The passion is contagious. Among the most ardent anglers are the Erie Benedictine Sisters, whose main house is on East Lake Road. The sisters live a life of prayer, promoting peace and justice—but they're also avid anglers.

The best place to learn about Erie and the lake is *Presque Isle State Park* (rhymes with press-TILE). One of the most remarkable places in Pennsylvania, it offers enough outdoor recreation to keep you busy for weeks. It's a 3,200-acre peninsula extending from the City of Erie (just 4 miles west of downtown) into Lake Erie. Although in French Presque Isle means "almost an island," this area has been a real island several times. Storm waves have broken

AUTHOR'S TOP 10 FAVORITES IN NORTHWESTERN PENNSYLVANIA

Dan Rice Days in Girard	Park Dinor
French Creek	Pithole
Glass Growers Gallery	Presque Isle State Park
Hickory Creek Wilderness	Quaker Steak and Lube
Indian God Rock	Flagship *Niagara*

through the neck of land, isolating the distant portion at least four times since 1819. One gap remained open for 32 years. Interestingly, the combined effects of erosion on one side and sand deposits on the other change the peninsula's shape and location noticeably, not in thousands of years, but in just a few. Geologists call it a recurving sand spit and estimate that the peninsula has moved about 0.5 mile east in the past hundred years. The Stull Interpretive Center, located at the beginning of the park near Barracks Beach, displays maps showing the changes. If you avoid the peak summer swimming season, it's possible to walk for hours along the beaches and in the woods without seeing another human being.

The diverse nature of Presque Isle is astounding. It has 6 distinct ecological zones, each with a unique plant and animal community. Due to the peninsula's location along the Atlantic flyway (that's the celestial interstate system for migratory birds), more than 320 species of birds have been recorded here. They usually visit in April, while heading north, and again in November, because Presque Isle offers one of the best avian bed-and-breakfast systems around. At the tip of the peninsula, Gull Point is designated a restricted, protected, fragile ecosystem. You may not enter this area between April 1 and November 30.

The big glass lighthouse shape just outside the park entrance is the ***Tom Ridge Environmental Center,*** named for the Erie native son who served as Pennsylvania's governor and the first director of the US Office of Homeland Security. Admission to its exhibits about the wonders of Presque Isle is free. Tickets to the Big Green Screen, a large-format movie theater for family-friendly nature films, are $7.50 for adults. (Get a bargain by arriving after 3 p.m., when 2 tickets cost $10.) The center is open daily except Thanksgiving, Christmas, and New Year's Day at 301 Peninsula Dr. Call (814) 833-7424 or check www.trecpi.org.

Children will probably want to skip the center and head for the beaches, where the surf is usually high enough to be interesting without getting rough

Discoveries on Presque Isle

Jerry McWilliams has been birding on Presque Isle since he was 5. As we hiked the secluded 1-mile trail to Gull Point, he talked excitedly about recent rare sightings: a white-morphed gyrfalcon from Greenland, the first ever seen at Presque Isle, and a boreal owl, a northern Canadian native not seen here since 1893. "They live in forests so deep that if they saw a human, they'd allow you to touch them. They don't know fear," explains McWilliams. For all things Presque Isle State Park call (814) 833-7424 or surf to www.dcnr.state.pa.us/stateparks/parks/presqueisle.aspx.

enough to be dangerous. Sadly, some beaches are closed when water contaminants rise, so call ahead: (814) 833-7424. Near Grave Yard Pond you can rent rowboats, canoes, and motorboats, but stay tuned to Channel 16 for boating conditions.

Presque Isle also offers bliss for bladers: a superb 13.5-mile recreation trail, beautifully leveled and paved, along the shoreline loop. Park at the first lot inside the park entrance off Route 832, strap on your in-line skates, and go.

Kids will also love **Waldameer Park and Water World,** the kind of old-fashioned amusement park that summer vacations are all about. Its wooden Ravine Flyer coaster swoops over the park's entrance road. It's located at 220 Peninsula Dr., the road into the park (814-838-3591; www.waldameer.com). Waldameer's competition is **Splash Lagoon,** a year-round indoor water park with laser tag, located off I-90, exit 24 (old exit 6); call (866) 3-SPLASH or visit www.splashlagoon.com.

Another way to cover the waterfront is aboard the **Lady Kate.** The 110-passenger cruiser makes frequent trips around Presque Isle from its moorings by the Perry Monument (on East Fisher Drive). From mid-June through Labor Day, there are 5 90-minute narrated tours each day, from 11 a.m. to sunset. From mid-May to mid-June and again from Labor Day through the end of September, there are 3 sailings a day on weekends only. Reservations are suggested. Fares for adults are $16; $9 for children 5 through 12; children under 5 are free. Call (814) 836-0201 or (800) 988-5780, or visit www.tinytims fishing.com.

For boating on a grander scale, visit the restored **Flagship** Niagara in Erie. The ship, captained by Oliver Hazard Perry during the War of 1812, commemorates the victory on September 10, 1813, when nine American ships triumphed over the British fleet on Lake Erie—the first time in naval history that a British squadron was defeated and captured. The *Niagara* and Perry gave the world the famous line: "We have met the enemy, and they are ours." (See the *Niagara* on special Pennsylvania license tags with a retro, sepia image.) The beautifully restored *Niagara* is one of only four remaining ships in the world from that era; the *USS Constitution* and *Constellation* and Britain's *HMS Victory,* all built at the end of the 18th century, are the others. But the *Niagara* is the only one seaworthy enough for regular cruises (usually through the Great Lakes, but every 4 years, along the Atlantic Coast). During warm-weather months lucky landlubbers are welcome aboard for day cruises—but you must apply in advance for this thrill. Demand far exceeds available space on the summer weekends the *Niagara* boards guests. Schedules change each season. All the requirements for being an able-bodied seaman are online, where you can download the day sail application form: go to www.flagshipniagara.org. You can also call (814)

Three Erie Lighthouses

- **Presque Isle,** residence of park superintendent. Exterior viewing daily 8 a.m. to sunset.

- **Erie Land Lighthouse,** first built in 1818, replaced in 1856; no light since Christmas Eve 1899. Exterior viewing daily.

- **North Pier,** located at the south entrance of the channel. Viewing daily.

452-2744, extension 223, or write to Erie Maritime Museum, Homeport, Attn: Sailing Program Coordinator, 150 E. Front St., Suite 100, Erie 16507.

When the *Niagara* is berthed dockside at the Erie Maritime Museum, you can take 1-hour tours (make reservations) above and below deck. In the days when its crew numbered 140, quarters on board were extremely tight, what with all those cannon, furled sails, and the manger of live animals. Watch your head below deck—the ceiling is 5 feet tall. By contrast, the tops of the masts tower 12 and 10 stories above deck.

Even if the *Niagara* has left port, the **Erie Maritime Museum** (the Commonwealth's newest) is well worth a visit. Inside a former power-generating plant, its creative exhibits give an overview of the War of 1812 and a glimpse of the human side of the conflict and its heroes. Did you know that a quarter of Commodore Perry's men were African Americans? A short video takes you through the famous battle of September 10, 1813. It's open Apr through Oct, Mon through Sat 9 a.m. to 5 p.m. and Sun noon to 5 p.m. Winter hours are Thurs through Sat 9 a.m. to 5 p.m. Closed most holidays and Christmas week. Admission is $8 for adults. Call (814) 452-2744, extension 223, or visit www .flagshipniagara.org.

But naval brigs aren't the only way around the Bayfront District. Buy an $8 round-trip pass for the **Presque Isle Water Taxi,** and you (and a bike or wheelchair) can hop from Dobbins Landing to Liberty Park and Presque Isle. The "taxis" run hourly during warm-weather months, with extra service on weekends. Call (814) 881-2502 for details.

For an action-oriented display visit the **Firefighters Historical Museum** (428 Chestnut St.), which is in the old #4 Erie Firehouse. It contains more than 1,300 items of fire department memorabilia, including old uniforms and equipment and an 1830 hand pump. The museum is open in June and July from 11 a.m. to 4 p.m. Sat and 1 to 4 p.m. Sun. In Sept and Oct, the museum is open from 1 to 4 p.m. Sat and Sun. Admission costs vary. Call (814) 456-5969 or visit www.firefightershistoricalmuseum.com for more information.

The ***Watson-Curtze Mansion and Erie Planetarium*** (356 W. Sixth St.), housed in a 24-room mansion from the late 1800s, has exhibits on regional and maritime history, including the Battle of Lake Erie. Other rooms contain decorative arts and period decor with outstanding woodwork and stained glass. The planetarium, in the carriage house, re-creates the movements of the sun, planets, and stars. The museum is open Wed through Sat 11 a.m. to 4 p.m. and Sun 1 to 4 p.m., and the planetarium has shows Thurs at 11 a.m. and 1:30 p.m. and Sat at 1:30 and 3 p.m.; call (814) 871-5790 for details.

Kids in Erie love the ***ExpERIEnce Children's Museum*** (420 French St., 2 blocks from the waterfront), where they can paint their faces, dance on a stage, and learn what owls eat for dinner. Kids age 1 and under enter free, and others pay $6. The museum is open Tues through Sat 10 a.m. to 4 p.m. and Sun 1 to 4 p.m. Call (814) 453-3743 or visit www.eriechildrensmuseum.org.

In the same complex, called Discovery Square, are two other museums. The ***Erie County History Center*** (419 State St.) focuses on county history. Phone the center at (814) 454-1813; fax (814) 452-1744; or check www.eriecountyhistory.org. The ***Erie Art Museum*** (411 State St.) has a small permanent collection and changing exhibits of fine art. Phone (814) 459-5477, or visit www.erieartmuseum.org.

To see contemporary American jewelry, studio pottery, carvings, and textiles, stop at the ***Glass Growers Gallery*** (10 E. Fifth St.; 814-453-3758; www.glassgrowersgallery.com). Upstairs are the creations of local and regional artists.

You've been through town, yet you haven't heard a word about the barges filled with lumber, coal, and hay. Where, oh where, is the ***Erie Canal***, you wonder. Answer: It's gone. It started on Elk Creek, a scant 20 miles down Route 5 from the city of Erie, and carried barges to the Hudson River, thus linking the Great Lakes and the Atlantic Ocean. The canal opened in 1844 and began to lose business to the railroads as early as the 1850s. When the aqueduct over Elk

That's Dinor to You

Don't ask me why diners in northwestern Pennsylvania are called "dinors." But they are, and one of the funkiest is the **Park Dinor** in Erie. *Diners of Pennsylvania,* the definitive study by Brian Butko and Kevin Patrick, calls it a classic—a tiny, trailer-shaped, 1948 Silk City model with room for 2 dozen diners (or dinors). Try the special Greek sauce, a spicy ground-meat gravy that tops everything from burgers to french fries. Located at 4019 Main St., outside the General Electric factory entrance; open Mon through Sat, 6 a.m. to 3 p.m.; call (814) 899-4390.

Creek collapsed in 1872, the canal closed. At least it survives in song. Beginning in 1918, commercial traffic began using the larger New York State Barge Canal.

Elk Creek flows through the town of Girard, which has a unique place in American history: Dan Rice lived there. Dan *who?* Dan Rice, the circus owner whose carnival spent summers in Girard. Dan Rice, whose flag-waving clown costume included a top hat and balloon pants. Dan Rice, whom Thomas Nast, an artist from *Harper's Weekly,* caricatured—and whose image became known as "Uncle Sam." *That* Dan Rice.

Wine Country

From Erie continue east on Route 5 to visit the local wine region, which stretches about 100 miles along the coast yet extends only 5 miles inland. Wine grapes flourish here because the lake creates a microclimate in which cold spring winds blow in from the lake, keeping the plants from budding too early and becoming vulnerable to frost. In the summer lake breezes cool the vineyards and keep the air circulating; in the fall the stored summer warmth from the lake delays frost. Because the lake once was much larger and has receded, the soils along the shore are especially fertile. Hence, fine wine. (Let's drink to that.)

In **North East** stop at the **Hornby School Museum** (10000 Colt Station Rd., Route 430), a restored one-room schoolhouse, built in the 1870s. With a reservation you can arrange to experience the kind of lessons that would have been part of a typical school day. The school is open Sun from June through Oct, 1 to 5 p.m. and by appointment. Call (814) 739-2720 for more information. It's free.

More fun than school, perhaps, **Lake Shore Railway Museum** (Wall and Robinson Streets) also has a lot to teach. Two children cried all the way there one morning because they hate museums, but at 5 p.m. attendants had to chase them out of the train cars to close up. The museum displays historical railroad items from the 19th and 20th centuries, ranging from dining car china to signaling devices. Outside the museum, which is in a station house by the tracks, you may tour a caboose and railroad cars on the siding—a Pullman sleeping car, diner, freight car, coach, and baggage car. The wooden caboose looks like one from the olden days, complete with a

trivia

So many fish are being fed at the Linesville Spillway, on Route 6 west of Meadville, that ducks can walk on the fishes' backs to compete for bread. It's part of the 17,088-acre Pymatuming Reservoir, the largest lake in Pennsylvania.

Petroglyphs on the Allegheny

For more than 300 years people have pondered the engraved graffiti on *Indian God Rock,* 9 miles south of Belmar along the Allegheny River. In 1889 a local newsman proposed that the strange runes were actually made by Norse explorers. More recent experts said that the animals, weapons, and other shapes were definitely made by Native Americans sometime before 1650. To protect the boulder from further vandalism—many 18th- and 19th-century visitors had added their names—the rock was placed on the National Register of Historic Places in 1984. There's a viewing platform near the 22-foot-high stone so you can look but not touch. If you're hiking or biking, take the Sandy Creek Trail.

stove and cooking area. In front of the station is a steamless locomotive, built in Erie in 1937. The schedule of the museum varies with the season and includes some special holiday events, so call (814) 725-1911, or visit www.lsrhs.railway .museum for specific details.

Mosey a half hour south of North East and you're in the land of biodiversity, home to French Creek and a national wildlife refuge. French Creek, named by George Washington for the former residents of this region between Meadville and Franklin, has recently been rediscovered as a stream of astounding diversity. The creek's glacial history and outstanding water quality make it a haven for all kinds of creatures, including peaceable humans.

French Creek and the Allegheny River used to flow north, as part of the St. Lawrence River system. However, the glaciers of the last ice age, which ended about 15,000 years ago, forced the creek to run south. As a result, 117-mile French Creek eventually began emptying into the Allegheny River. Today the creek retains species from the northern waterway as well as the Allegheny. It's home to 80 kinds of fish (an angler's dream), 2 dozen types of mussels, and a giant, very shy, rarely seen salamander—the hellbender, which some locals call a "mudpuppy." The hellbender can grow up to 29 inches long and live up to 29 years.

Canoeing is the perfect way to savor the beauty of the area, and there are plenty of launching spots. If you'd like to rent canoes or kayaks for day or overnight trips contact *Oars on the Allegheny* at 250 Elk St. in Franklin; (814) 388-9122, www.oarsontheallegheny.com.

As you drive toward the *Erie National Wildlife Refuge*—located in a marsh near Guys Mills, south of the lake—be on the lookout for bald eagles, which find good hunting in the wetlands. This federal site, one of two in the state, offers nearly 9,000 acres for hiking, hunting, fishing, and, of course, bird-watching. A new indoor bird observation area gives you binoculars, bird books, and even microphones to eavesdrop on 237 different species. Enter the refuge 10 miles east of Meadville on Highway 198. The visitor center is open weekdays from 8:30 a.m. to 4:30 p.m. Write to 11296 Wood Duck Ln., Guys Mills 16327; call (814) 789-3585; or visit http://erie.fws.gov.

Did you know that John Brown slept here? The abolitionist rabble-rouser lived in New Richmond, 13 miles north of Meadville, from 1826 to 1835, long before his Harpers Ferry raid. The farm was a "depot" on the Underground Railroad, helping some 2,500 slaves to freedom. You can't see the tannery where he worked, but you can visit the small *John Brown Farm Museum* near his home (if and only if you call ahead) Apr 15 to Oct 15 or in winter, and view interpretive displays at the tannery site. The site is located at the intersection of Routes 77 and 1033 at 17620 John Brown Rd. For information call (814) 967-2099.

Oil Country

Sharon is a very small town with some giant-sized attractions. In *Reyer's,* it has the world's largest shoe store; in *Daffin's Chocolate Kingdom,* the world's largest candy store; and in *Quaker Steak and Lube,* the self-proclaimed best hot wings in the USA.

Whether your teenager needs size 16 sneakers or your mom needs AAAAA width, Reyer's, with 150,000 pairs of shoes, can fit their feet. It's been in business for 120 years at 40 S. Water Ave. (800-245-1550). The store is open daily till 9 p.m. (abbreviated hours on Sun); shop online at www.reyers.com. Daffin's (496 E. State St.; 724-342-2892) boasts a chocolate menagerie that includes a 400-pound turtle and a 125-pound reindeer. It's open Mon through Sat from 9 a.m. to 9 p.m., Sun from 11 a.m. to 5 p.m.

Quaker Steak and Lube is, of course, a play on both the Quaker State and locally made Quaker State Motor Oil, and it carries the automotive theme to fantastic extremes, with real cars as overhead art. People come for the wings, but you can get all sorts of pub-style choices too. Insert your oil joke here. It's open from lunch to at least midnight 7 days a week at 101 Chestnut Ave.; call (724) 981-WING.

If you remember the Lettermen, you'll be pleased to know that the *Vocal Group Hall of Fame* is right here in the hometown of Tony Butala, one of their founding members. The small museum is housed at the Columbia Theater at 82 W. State St. Get details at (724) 983-2025, or visit www.vghf.org.

In the grand Richardson Romanesque style (seen also in downtown Pittsburgh) is the *Buhl Mansion Guesthouse and Spa* at 422 E. State St. Built in

BEST ANNUAL EVENTS IN NORTHWESTERN PENNSYLVANIA

MAY

Edinboro Art and Music Festival

Edinboro

www.edinboroartandmusic.com

Each May fans of traditional Appalachian finger-picking, stomping, and crafts flock to the Edinboro Art and Music Festival. The free 3-day event, held the third weekend of the month, happens all over town, with jam sessions, artisan exhibits, and everyone's-welcome workshops in the old-time arts of dulcimer, mandolin, and flat-foot dancing.

JULY

Presque Isle Bay Swim

(814) 838-5138

www.discoverpi.com

You don't have to paddle to Canada to enjoy Lake Erie. Just enter the annual Bay Swim, a one-mile race across Presque Isle each June. Get the details from the Presque Isle Partnership.

AUGUST

Dan Rice Days

Girard

(814) 774-3535

A stilt-walking Uncle Sam leads the parade at the annual Dan Rice Days in Girard. Held the first Saturday in August, the festival includes games, food, crafts, and such—and Uncle Sam, fashioned after local legend Dan Rice.

Celebrate Erie

Perry Square, Erie

(814) 870-1593

www.celebrateerie.com

Mid-August brings a three-day family-friendly street fair to the downtown's Perry Square that concludes with massive fireworks over the lake.

SEPTEMBER

Pennsylvania State Championship Fishing Tournament

Tidioute

(800) 624-7802

During the last full weekend of September in Tidioute (rhymes with "pretty suit"), you can participate in the Pennsylvania State Championship Fishing Tournament. Call the Warren County Tourism/Northern Alleghenies Vacation Region at (800) 624-7802 for rules and regulations.

Wine Festival

North East

(814) 725-4262

www.nechamber.org

If you've always wanted to do some grape-stomping, the town of North East will give you the chance each September at its Wine Festival. You can also sample wines by the glass and try a few champagnes—a local specialty.

OCTOBER

Eerie Horror Film Festival

Erie

(814) 873-2483

http://eeriehorrorfilmfestival.com

The Eerie Horror Film Festival is a scream. Literally. New sci-fi, suspense, and slasher flicks are shown annually at Erie's Halloween cinema celebration. Watch for your favorite stars at the accompanying Carnival of Carnage Expo.

1890 for a wealthy local couple, it's been restored to glory by owners Donna and Jim Winner (he invented the anti-theft device The Club®). Visit www.buhl mansion.com, or call (724) 346-3046.

Lake Erie's not the only swimming spot in northwestern Pennsylvania. Generations of families love **Conneaut Lake,** with its famous old hotel and amusement park. The amusement park has teetered on the edge of bankruptcy but still manages to reopen each season. The park's old-fashioned roller coasters, pony rides, and miniature golf course are classics, and admission to its beach is free. Plan a summer visit by calling (814) 382-5115, or visit www.conneautlake park.com. It's at 12382 Center St. in Conneaut Lake.

Let Meadville lure you off the interstate (off I-79, to be precise). Keep an eye out for a funky monument to the city as you enter along Route 6/322. That's where a bunch of **Allegheny College** students have created a 1,200-foot mural made entirely of recycled highway signs. "Read Between the Signs" is a light-hearted interpretation of local landmarks, including the Allegheny Mountains and French Creek. The state highway department provided the raw materials. The students figured out how to turn them into moving artwork—the mural even includes components powered by sunlight and wind.

Allegheny College, one of the oldest colleges west of the Alleghenies, has a good collection of Abraham Lincoln memorabilia in the Pelletier Library. Ida Tarbell, one of the college's first female students, majored in biology because she hoped to find God with what she could learn through a microscope. After graduating, she became one of the muckrakers famous at the turn of the 20th century: journalists who tried to expose the abuses of businesses and the corruption of politics. Tarbell wrote an extensive biography of the Lincolns and later donated the papers to her alma mater. The library also has many interesting papers, books, and artifacts related to Tarbell. Two college buildings, Bentley Hall and Ruter Hall, are listed on the National Register of Historic Places.

Meadville's downtown includes more than a dozen historic buildings that should interest those who care about old architecture. You can pick up a free self-guided tour to bygone Meadville at the **Market House** (910 Market St.). On the ground floor a farmers' market flourishes, as it has for more than a hundred years. You can eat at the lunch counter and shop for produce, flowers, baked goods, handicrafts, cheese, ceramics, and collectibles in the marketplace. Market House is open year-round (but not on Sun).

A handy 15-minute drive from Meadville's college population is **Sprague Farm and Brew Works** (22113 US Hwy. 6 & 19, Venango). This microbrewery offers a half-dozen varieties. They'll fill up your growler or give you a tour. Call (814) 398-2885 or visit www.sleepingchainsaw.com.

Approximately 30 miles east of Meadville, you can get a glimpse of the early influence of oil, before Texans thought of liquid gold. Start at Titusville with the **Drake Well Park and Museum** (814-827-2797; www.drakewell .org), site of the world's first successful oil well and an 1860s boomtown. The well is topped by a replica of the derrick. The museum details the early oil days and shows films about how the first well came to be drilled. (One vintage film stars Vincent Price. Now that's scary.) In the library are thousands of photographs and papers of Titusville native Ida Tarbell related to her famous exposé of the Standard Oil Company. Though the museum won't hold their interest, kids may enjoy dipping into "the pits." These are slight depressions in the ground, near the banks of Oil Creek, where Indians scooped oil off the surface of the water—tipping off white settlers to what lay 38 feet below. The oil still seeps to the surface in warm weather. The museum is open Tues through Sat from 9 a.m. to 5 p.m. and Sun noon to 5 p.m. every day, except November 1 to the end of April, when it opens only Wed through Fri from 9 to 5 p.m. Closed on major holidays. Summer admission is $6 per adult.

A short drive southeast on Route 27, then south on Route 227, brings you to Plumer. Go 1.5 miles farther south to the ghost town of Pithole which was an oil boomtown in the late 1860s and was abandoned when the oil business fell off. A visitor center contains a pictorial history and artifacts of the town. By far the most interesting activity is wandering the site where people and businesses used to thrive and where nothing remains but cellar holes, wells, and the depressions that used to be streets. Open June through Labor Day. Get details from Drake Well Museum at (814) 827-2797. Another way to see oil country and its history is to ride the **Oil Creek and Titusville Railroad,** sponsored by the Oil Creek Railway Historical Society. The 2-hour trip runs from Titusville to Rynd Farm, 4 miles north of Oil City, passing through the sites of several boomtowns and some lovely countryside in warm weather months. You can board a train at the Drake Well Museum, at the Perry Street Station in Titusville, or at Rynd Farm. The schedule of northbound and

Rolling Along the River

One not-to-be-missed country road is Route 62, which hugs the bank of the Allegheny River between Warren to the north and Tionesta and Franklin to the south. Those three towns, plus the vacation cabins scattered along the shoreline, are just about the only signs of human habitation you'll see as you drive through the forest, passing magnificent vistas as the river widens and contracts.

A River Lighthouse

Tionesta boasts a 2-acre island in the middle of the Allegheny River. The 50-foot-tall wooden octagon on the island is the privately owned *Sherman Family Memorial Lighthouse,* which is open for tours several times a year. While most lighthouses are antiques, this one's a baby—it was built in 2006.

southbound trains is complicated, may change without notice, and includes additional trains scheduled for special celebration weeks in the summer; moreover, you need advance tickets to guarantee a place on the train. If that doesn't deter you, call (814) 676-1733, or visit www.octrr.org. Tickets are $17 per adult.

If you'd like to make part of the same trip on bicycle, try the 10-mile paved trail along Oil Creek from Petroleum Center to Drake Well Park. The trail is open from 8 a.m. to dark. Whichever route you choose, you're still invited to spend the night on the tracks at *The Caboose Motel.* The 21 rooms—er, cars—have all the modern conveniences—heating, AC, phones, and TVs. Book reservations at (800) 827-0690 or get details at www.octrr.org/caboosemotel.htm.

Enjoy a more amusing kind of history at the *DeBence Antique Music World Museum* (1261 Liberty St.), not far away on Route 8, Franklin. The museum has more than a hundred antique music machines from the Gay Nineties and the Roaring Twenties. Hear the nickelodeons, band organs, orchestrions, and music boxes. The museum is open April 1 through October 31, Tues through Sat 11 a.m. to 4 p.m. and Sun 12:30 to 4 p.m.; November 1 through March 31, it's open by appointment only. Call (814) 432-8350, or visit www.debencemusicworld.com for details. Admission is $8 per adult. Sounds great!

The town of Franklin dates to 1753, when the French established Fort Machault here. Seven years later the British built Fort Venango. But, as with so much of this part of Pennsylvania, striking oil was what really gave life to the community. Take the time to check out the local history displays in the *Hoge-Osmer House* (corner of South Park and Elk Streets) and at the *Venango County Courthouse* (Twelfth and Liberty Streets). If you're on Twelfth Street on Wed or Sat, you can browse through the local farmers' market. Wander around town, or request a self-guided walking tour at the Franklin Area Chamber of Commerce (1259 Liberty St.). For further information phone (814) 432-5823, or go to www.franklinareachamber.org.

Allegheny National Forest

The 500,000-acre *Allegheny National Forest* is one of 15 national forests in the eastern United States and the only national forest in Pennsylvania. Hardwoods—black cherry, yellow poplar, white ash, red maple, and sugar maple—make up most of the timber. More than 65 million board feet of timber, especially black cherry, are harvested each year. The black cherry is used for fine furniture; much of the rest is used for pulpwood. *Hearts Content,* one comparatively small area of the forestland, has some of the oldest tracts of virgin beech and hemlock trees in the eastern United States.

You can access the forest from many points along Route 6 and Route 62 for some truly off-the-beaten-path travel. Just past East Hickory, at Endeavor, turn right on Route 666, heading into the forest.

From here, turn around and drive back about a quarter mile, where you see a dirt Forest Service road just before Mayburg. Turn left here, on Robbs Creek Road, also known as Forest Road 116. Drive on to Hearts Road (though the signs often disappear), and turn left again. In about 2 miles you'll come to *Hearts Content Recreation Area* in the Allegheny National Forest. From Hearts Content you can hike, camp, and picnic—you know, to your heart's content. Whatever you do, you must take the scenic walk marked by signs. It is short and easy, and it seems to invite meditation. Streams make light music. The old deciduous trees arch high above, letting through just enough blue sky and sunlight to nurture the carpet of ferns, which reach your knees. Pines and hemlocks, nature's original incense, perfume the air. The forest floor, softened with pine needles and leaves, absorbs enough sound to make the surroundings seem as quiet as a cathedral. A 6-year-old child walking through the area for the first time captured its mystery by asking, "Are we inside or outside?"

The *Hickory Creek Wilderness,* all 8,570 acres of it, is next to the campground. No motorized equipment is allowed. An 11-mile hiking loop takes you through rolling terrain. You will probably see deer, small wildlife, and all kinds of birds.

You can find a smaller—much smaller—peaceful, tranquil natural area in *Clear Creek State Park* by heading north from Sigel on Route 36, then north on Route 949. Call (814) 752-2368 to reach the park office. Scenically located in Jefferson County's Clear Creek Valley, the park encompasses 1,200 acres, with another 10,000 acres of natural resources in adjacent Kittanning State Forest. A highlight of the park is the outstanding self-guided Ox Shoe Trail, which depicts logging practices of earlier years. The area is noted for its abundant wildlife, its hunting and fishing, and the breathtaking beauty of its mountain laurel, which blooms from mid-June to early July, peaking in late June. See if you—or your kids—can identify some mountain laurel, the state flower. The plant grows from 3 to 6 feet high on rocky, wooded slopes. Look for petals that form a nearly perfect pink or white pentagon.

waterydepths

The icy fresh waters of the Great Lakes preserve a number of shipwrecks, from 19th-century schooners to steamers and scows. Professional divers Georgann and Mike Wachter have mapped the sites where a number of these historic vessels have been found. See the results at www.eriewrecks .com.

You're quite near **Cook Forest State Park,** which, in 1994, earned a *National Geographic* listing as one of the nation's top-50 state parks. One of the finest stands of virgin timber in the eastern part of the United States is located here, and the area has been designated a National Natural Landmark. The trees in this ancient forest are hundreds of years old, measuring up to 5 feet in diameter and towering nearly 200 feet. During a recent old-growth forest conference, three of the tallest trees in the East were identified here in Cook Forest. The old Cook sawmill, home to the Sawmill Center for the Arts, features summer theater, festivals, and craft markets and draws artisans to instruct classes in traditional arts and crafts. Much of the area exists almost as it was in the days of William Penn, when it was known as the Black Forest. Cecil B. DeMille used the park in his film *Unconquered,* starring Gary Cooper.

Silver Stallion Stables, just north of the Cooksburg Bridge, offers 1- and 2-hour trail jaunts daily in the summer for riders as young as 6 years old (summer forest temperatures hover from the mid-60s to mid-70s). No matter how dumb you might feel in the saddle, the stables' owners, Mark and Lori Mills, say, don't worry, the horses are smart. "We're particular to Appaloosa and paint, for their intelligence, their stamina, and their beauty," he notes. Riders with disabilities or other special needs are welcome. Check ride prices at Silver Stallion (814) 927-6636.

Cook Forest Scenic Rides and Dude Ranch, off Clarion-Miola Road, offers "dude packages" with lodging, meals, and rides. Prices start at $150 per person for 2 dudes. Call (814) 856-2081 for details.

In these parts you may hear a clarion call to slow down and smell the roses—or look at leaves. **Clarion,** calling itself the autumn-leaf capital of the known world, boasts the rugged beauty of untamed natural resources and the nostalgia of an old-fashioned Main Street. It is unmistakably off the beaten path. Stop in the Free Library, on Main Street next to the post office, in downtown Clarion to pick up a booklet outlining a historical and architectural tour of the town, noting 40 structures of interest. Enjoy the old-fashioned streetlights and nostalgic building facades as you stroll downtown. A parasol would be nice.

Places to Stay in Northwestern Pennsylvania

CAMBRIDGE SPRINGS
The Riverside Inn
1 Fountain Ave.
(800) 956-9490 or
(814) 398-4645
www.theriversideinn.com
This famous 19th-century inn on the banks of French Creek is open Apr through Dec.

CLARION
Clarion House Bed & Breakfast
77 S. Seventh Ave.
(814) 226-4996 or
(800) 416-3297
www.chouse.com
B&B adorned with woodwork from nearby Cook National Forest.

COOKSBURG
Gateway Lodge
Cook Forest, Box 125
Route 36
(814) 744-8017
www.gatewaylodge.com
Rough-hewn log inn with a welcoming stone hearth.

SHARON
Tara
2844 Lake Rd.
Clark
(724) 962-3535 or
(800) 782-2803
www.tara-inn.com
Dedicated to "the greatest movie of all time, *Gone With the Wind*," with rooms with names like "Rhett's Room" and "Belle's Boudoir." Tours by costumed guides, dining rooms, a spa, and a lake.

WATTSBURG
Timbermist
11050 Backus Rd.
(814) 739-9004 or
(888) 739-9004
www.timbermist.com
Fresh local eggs and ingredients are the breakfast stars at this Erie County B&B.

Places to Eat in Northwestern Pennsylvania

ERIE
Smuggler's Wharf
3 State St.
(814) 459-4273
www.smugglerswharfinc.com
Arrive at this casual Lake Erie eatery from land or sea.

SHARON
Quaker Steak & Lube
101 Chestnut St.
(724) 981-7221 or
(800) 468-9464
www.quakersteakandlube.com/sharon_pa
Located in a former gas station. Your dining companions are a 1936 Chevrolet on a grease rack and a Corvette suspended from the ceiling. Hot wings and cool cars.

NORTH CENTRAL PENNSYLVANIA →

Getting Your Kicks on Route 6

One of the best ways to see what Pennsylvanians call the "northern tier" is by jumping on *Route 6* and following it east through Warren, McKean, Potter, and Tioga Counties. This pleasant, flat two-laner stretches all the way to Pike County, home of the *Delaware Water Gap.* Running through the Brokenstraw Valley, with mountains on either side, the road is an easy (and in some cases, the only) way to get through this neck of the woods, connecting most of the county seats. It's also one of the state's designated bike routes.

With such dense forests, it's no surprise that fall is a popular time to visit the area. But the upper Allegheny River offers plenty of summer fun, too, and on a crystal-clear winter morning, the vistas from a snowmobile are glorious. And you're welcome anytime.

National Geographic called Route 6 "one of America's most scenic drives." (But don't neglect Route 59, which links the *Kinzua Bridge State Park* with Kinzua Dam and Allegheny Reservoir, offering scenic views at every turn.) Route 6 even has its own website to help you get your kicks: www.paroute6.com.

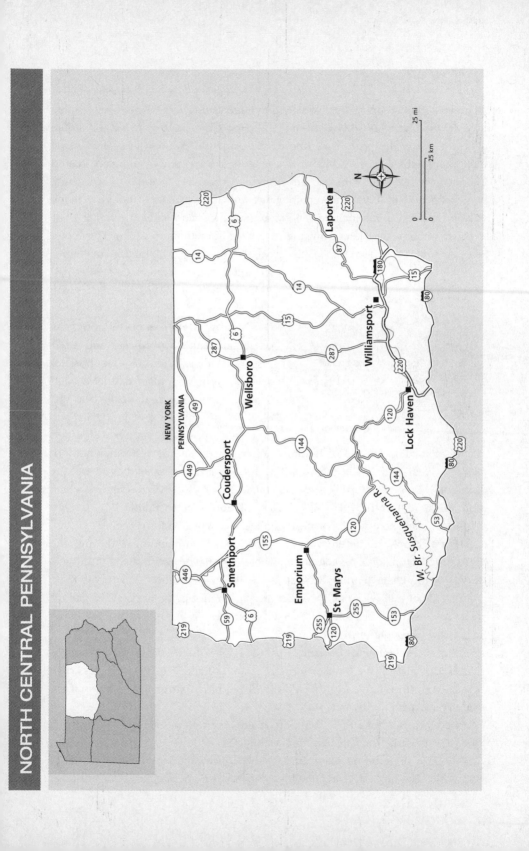

Wild Country

Start your wild-country trek with a fiery sightseeing experience—by visiting the **Zippo/Case Visitors Center** (1932 Zippo Dr.) in **Bradford,** off Route 219 just below the New York border. Zippo is the company that first made windproof lighters. (Legend has it that zippers had recently been invented, and the inventor liked the name, so he copied it.) Your visit includes the museum, which opened in 1994, the repair clinic, and the gift shop (though not the factory). Since Zippos include a lifetime guarantee, and since the repair shop receives about 400 lighters daily, there's always something to watch. The center is open Sun 11 a.m. to 4 p.m.; other days, 9 a.m. to 5 p.m. Look for streetlights shaped like giant lighters. Call (814) 368-1932 or (888) 442-1932, or flick www .zippo.com.

trivia

In Austin, just south of Route 6 on Route 872, a dam broke in 1911, leveling two towns and killing 89 people. The site is listed on the National Register of Historic Places.

Nearby **Glendorn** is the opposite of utilitarian. It's a plush inn and 4-star restaurant that's the grandest hostelry around, with room rates starting around $430 a night. For that price, you get elegance to the max. The Relais and Châteaux–approved property, nestled in the mountains outside of Bradford, offers skeet, tennis, and other outdoor activities year-round. Choose the Big House or the cabins; they're equally luxurious. Owner Holbrook Lawson is a member of the Dorn family, which built this retreat in the 1920s. It's at 1000 Glendorn Dr. in Bradford. Call (800) 843-8568, or reserve rooms or meals online at www.glendorn.com.

For a completely different dining experience, you might drive through the Bradford McDonald's on Main Street. There may have been billions of burgers served at the chain worldwide, but this is the only location that serves them with a side of real oil. Cline Oil #1 in the parking lot pumps dozens of gallons each day, just as it has since the 1870s. You'll see other private wells dotting front yards throughout the region.

Pop up to **Singer's Country Store** (814-368-6151) at the crossroads that is Custer City, just off the intersection of Routes 219 and 770 West. For less than a buck you can pluck a fresh pickle out of the briny barrel and chat about the countryside with the owner, Mary Dach.

Between Bradford and Smethport, make a vertigo-inducing stop at Kinzua Bridge State Park. The wooden railroad bridge built here in 1883—a trestle that stood higher than the Brooklyn Bridge—was once called the eighth wonder of the world. The view over a 2,000-foot gorge is still spectacular, but the bridge

AUTHOR'S TOP 10 FAVORITES IN NORTH CENTRAL PENNSYLVANIA

Cherry Springs State Park

Elk

elk burgers

Frenchville

Grand Canyon of Pennsylvania

Lookout Tower (which we climbed at Valley Forge)

Smethport

Wellsboro

Woolrich Company Store

Little League Baseball World Series

was felled by a tornado in 2003. Now a pedestrian walkway, similar to that on the rim of the Grand Canyon, includes a glassed-in floor that allows visitors to admire the view. The Kinzua Skywalk is free and open daily. Enter the park 4 miles from Route 6; it's 1721 Lindholm Dr., Mount Jewett.

Ride on to **Smethport,** a picture-perfect country town and county seat. Main Street boasts a solid core of restored Victorian homes and pleasant sidewalks for strolling. The McKean County Courthouse exudes stability, right down to the Civil War statue out front: He's a Bucktail, the local regiment of volunteers who formed the core of the Union Army's Forty-second Pennsylvania Regiment. The fact that every soldier decorated his cap with a deer's tail gives you a hint about the local wildlife.

Main Street is home to a mini-millionaires' row of superb mansions. It's also the address of the Smethport Diner, also known as the Route 6 Diner, and the Hub, a gas/convenience store named in honor of the Hubbers, the local high school nickname.

With over a century and a half of history, Smethport is home to the **McKean County Historical Museum** (814-887-5142) in the 1872 jail, open a few afternoons each week right behind the courthouse. Residents have also created the wonderfully named Planet Smethport website (www.smethporthistory .org). You can tour local landmarks by clicking up and down streets and learn (lots) about former residents. It's almost like peeking through their windows.

Head east on Route 6, through Coudersport. Across from Denton Hill State Park at Galeton, you reach the **Pennsylvania Lumber Museum,** an outdoor gallery that depicts the history and technology of Pennsylvania's prosperous lumbering activities. Two of the world's largest sawmills were located in Austin (24 miles southwest of the museum) and Galeton (11

What Can You See in the Dark?

Rural *Cherry Springs State Park,* off Route 44 south of Galeton, is one of the darkest spots in the country, making it a perfect spot for stargazing. It's Pennsylvania's first Dark Sky Park, and its hilltop Astronomy Field has a spectacular panoramic view of the nucleus of the Milky Way. Park at the nearby airport and walk to the field (if you've brought your own telescope or laptop, the field has power sources and concrete pads for setup). You can even rent one of four small (3- to 4-person) observatories for $10 per night. Public "star parties" are held several times a year, and there's entertainment at the family-friendly "Music and Stars" shows. A "clear sky clock" on the park's website, www.dcnr.state.pa.us/stateparks/parks/cherrysprings .aspx, forecasts the best times to visit. There's a modest entrance fee. Call (814) 435-5010.

miles southeast). The museum displays more than 3,000 artifacts related to the logging industry. Walk among the old buildings of the logging camp, the sawmill, and a logging pond, all surrounded by Appalachian Mountain wilderness. The visit re-creates the tough life of "wood hicks" in the days of lumbering. The men worked six days a week, from 5 a.m. to 9 p.m. (no, that's not a typo!), with time off for extended periods of downpour, though rarely for cold or snow. In about 1910 the workweek was reduced to six 10-hour days, and in 1920 to five eight-hour days. Lice and dirt were everywhere. Bathing facilities were nowhere.

Even though the workers' conditions weren't pristine, the forests and trees were, and the giant white pines were in great demand. Wood hicks felled the trees, tied them onto rafts, and floated them down the Susquehanna River and into the Chesapeake Bay, where they were exported to England to be made into ships. The Lumber Museum, administered by the Pennsylvania Historical and Museum Commission, is open 9 a.m. to 5 p.m. daily, Apr through Nov (except on fall holidays). Admission is $6 per adult. Phone (814) 435-2652; fax (814) 435-6361; write PO Box 239, 5660 Rte. 6, Galeton 16922; or visit www.lumbermuseum.org for more information.

sunrisetosunset

Every sunny day you can catch a perfect sunrise from Colton Point State Park. Enjoy the sunset from Leonard Harrison State Park. Both times, you luxuriate in a view of the Grand Canyon of Pennsylvania.

The most dramatic aspect of this section of the state is the mountainous and wooded *Pine Creek Gorge,* commonly known as the *Grand Canyon of Pennsylvania.* The gorge, comprising mostly state parks and wilderness, is 50 miles long and 1,000 feet deep, covering

300,000 acres of state forest. You can access the canyon by driving south on Route 660, midway between Galeton and Wellsboro.

Before the pharaohs built the pyramids, the headwaters of Pine Creek, near Ansonia, flowed to the northeast. Then came glaciers. As the glacial ice melted, it left a dam of gravel, sand, and clay, which blocked the creek's path. This natural dam forced Pine Creek to reverse direction and flow south. Thus formed the Grand Canyon, with land formations dating back more than 350 million years. In 1968 the National Park Service declared a 12-mile section a National Natural Landmark.

trivia

Guidebooks say the name Tioga comes from an old Indian word, but they disagree on what that word meant. Some say it meant "the meeting of two rivers," and others say it meant "gateway" or "place to enter." Either way, Tioga County is a hunter's paradise, serving as home to many species of white-tailed deer, bear, cottontail rabbits, wild turkey, ruffed grouse, and ducks.

At two state parks—**Leonard Harrison State Park** on the east rim of the canyon and **Colton Point State Park** on the west (570-724-3061 reaches both park offices)—you can stop at lookouts and pick up short hiking trails that don't require safari gear. Leonard Harrison State Park has a nature center (open spring through fall) and a relatively easy trail along the rim that gives you an orientation to the canyon. If you follow Turkey Path about a mile down to Pine Creek, you'll encounter more ambitious hikes that take in creeks and waterfalls. The area is noted for ferns, songbirds, and superb scenery in any season. In Colton Point State Park you can hike an easy mile-long loop through a hardwood forest rich in wildflowers and fragrant mountain laurel, the state flower.

One of the state's most spectacular rails-to-trails projects is the **Pine Creek Trail,** which runs 42 miles from Ansonia to Waterville. This level crushed-limestone path, closed to motor traffic, lets you explore by bike or by

The Tower That Traveled

The **Lookout Tower** in Leonard Harrison State Park affords views for 100 miles with the naked eye. The tower originally stood atop Mount Joy, in Valley Forge, where George Washington and his troops spent the winter of 1776 and 1777. Built in 1906, the tower was a birders' haven until 1988, when surrounding trees grew too tall for its use as an observation tower. At that time, it traveled 240 miles to its current home. Visit the tower daily, sunrise to sunset, weather permitting. Climb 125 steps to reach the top.

foot. If you're a hardbody, you might want to bike in with a tent and backpack and camp overnight at Harrison State Park; if not, there are 10 trailheads where you can exit the trail, and there are motels and inns at both ends where you can actually sleep in a bed. Hot water, too. For a map or information, contact the Tioga County Visitors Bureau at (888) 846-4228, www.visittiogapa.com; or the Lycoming County Visitors Bureau at (800) 358-9900, www.vacationpa.com.

Wellsboro, the Tioga County seat, is a beautiful little town, with old trees and gaslights lining the streets. In the public square, called the Green, a fountain splashes over a statue of Wynken, Blynken, and Nod in their wooden shoe.

lincolndoor house

So what if Abe Lincoln didn't sleep in Wellsboro? That's no reason not to claim his presence. Or presents. At 140 Main St. is the Lincoln Door House. Abraham Lincoln gave the door—now bright red—to Dr. and Mrs. J. H. Shearer when they bought the house in 1858. Mrs. Shearer and Mrs. Lincoln were friends in Springfield, Illinois.

When Wellsboro was incorporated in 1830, it had 250 residents. In the 1990 census, it had grown to 3,400, with another 5,000 within a 5-mile radius and 5,000 more within 10 miles.

Lots of cars in town sport bike racks, a clue to the popularity of the nearby trail, and Country Ski and Sports (81 Main St.; 570-724-3858) rents bikes right in town.

One person who fell in love with Wellsboro's slow pace is Nelle Rounsaville, who came here after 20 years as a flight attendant. "It's just a wonderful Victorian town," she says fondly. She started small, with a cozy Charles Street B&B on the town square that she dubbed *La Petite Auberge.* Then she bought the *Wellsboro Diner,* a classic 1939 eatery down the block. Then she bought the larger *La Belle Auberge* on Main Street. (Call Nelle at 570-724-3288.) Aside from being entirely made of porcelain, the Wellsboro Diner has another claim to fame: It was the subject of a "Zippy the Pinhead" cartoon by Bill Griffith. It serves breakfast all day, has daily specials, and is open daily until 8 p.m. at 19 Main St. Call (570) 724-3992, or check the menu online at www.wellsborodiner.com.

You can request an area map from the Wellsboro Chamber of Commerce, 114 Main St., Wellsboro 16901. Phone (570) 724-1926 or go to www.wellsboro pa.com.

The End of the World

Another near-wilderness park is *World's End State Park,* as remote as it sounds. To get there take Route 220 to Eagles Mere, which is about midpoint between Route 6 and I-80, then go west on Route 154. Part of the lure of World's End is its primitive quality and its ideal position for picnicking, fishing, swimming, and boating. The park phone number is (570) 924-3287.

trivia

Pennsylvania leads the nation in producing mushrooms and potato chips.

The town of **Eagles Mere** is the cosmopolitan village you turn to after exploring World's End. Eagles Mere, which used to call itself "the town that time forgot," is so earnest and simple that it might have inspired Norman Rockwell. In the 1800s wealthy folk from Philadelphia's Main Line visited the 2,100-foot-high mountain area, fell in love with the clean air and clear water, and set about causing development to happen. They built Victorian "cottages," similar to the gargantuan dwellings of the same name in Newport, Rhode Island. In 1892, with 90 rental cottages, the town had a summer population of 2,500. Since the roads were not paved, boardwalks covered the streets to protect the ladies' white dresses from dirt.

While the geology is a nature photographer's utopia, one human-made element also stands out. It's the **Slide,** a toboggan run built in 1904. When the first intrepid rider, sitting on a big iron shovel, tested the grooved, planed, wooden course, he whizzed so fast that he burned the seat off his pants. Today the slide is a 120-ton, 1,200-foot-long channel of ice, down which you can ride in relative safety at 45 miles per hour. An hour-long pass costs 15 or 20 bucks. Get the schedule from the Eagles Mere Slide Association at (570) 525-3244.

trivia

Bald eagles were once so rare that they were considered an endangered species. In 1980 Pennsylvania counted only three. Thanks to the national ban on DDT (in 1972) and the state Game Commission's introduction of eagles from Saskatchewan, Canada, by spring 1998 eagles were spotted in 27 nests. Eagle populations grow slowly, because pairs rear only one to three young each year, and it takes five years for the young to mature.

To relax after this thrilling plummet, treat yourself to dinner at the **Eagles Mere Inn,** the last remaining full-service inn from the 19th century. Its cozy guest rooms make you yearn for the days before cell phones. In the dining room, chef Toby Diltz's menu changes daily. If you prefer vegetarian or other special diets, call ahead to (570) 525-3273 or (800) 426-3273, or visit www.eaglesmereinn.com, and they'll try to honor your request. Find the inn at 1 Mary Ave., Eagles Mere.

Like hot dogs? Like peanuts and Cracker Jacks? Every August, **Williamsport** hosts the Little League World Series, attracting thousands of spectators and some of the best 12-year-old baseball players in the world. (Bonus: Tickets are free.) The thwack (or, perhaps, the ping) of the bat and the shouts of the kids remind you why the sport is the national pastime. The *Little League Museum* (570-326-3607; www.littleleague.org) honors Tom Selleck, Dan Quayle, George Will, Bill Bradley, Kareem Abdul-Jabbar, Nolan Ryan, and Mike Schmidt, to name a few. Admission costs $5 per adult. In June, the museum is open Mon, Thurs, Fri, and Sat from 10 a.m. to 5 p.m., and Sun from noon to 5 p.m. In July and Aug, it's open Mon through Sat 10 a.m. to 5 p.m. and Sun noon to 5 p.m. The rest of the year it's open Fri and Sat only from 10 a.m. to 5 p.m. It's located at 539 US Rte. 15, Williamsport.

trivia

In 1892 the first lighted nighttime football game was played at Mansfield University, Mansfield.

Little Lock Haven is home to a 5,000-student state university; a recently restored movie theater, the Roxy; and a new riverfront trail with pretty views of the Susquehanna. It's also home to the *Piper Aviation Museum* (1 Piper Way; 570-748-8283; www.pipermuseum.com), on the site where the famous Piper Cub airplane was manufactured until 1984.

Just north of Route 220, between Lock Haven and Williamsport, is the town of Woolrich. If the name sounds familiar, look inside the neckband of your hunting jacket. The company of *Woolrich,* in the town of Woolrich, makes sportswear and outerwear under both its own brand and that of other companies, including L. L. Bean and Lands' End. John Rich built his first woolen mill on Plum Run in 1830, and the rest, as they say, is red buffalo plaid. The actors in *The Horse Whisperer* wore Woolrich garb. Visit the original factory outlet store in Woolrich (570-769-7401 or 800-995-1299; www.woolrich.com), or at outlet malls in Grove City, Lancaster, and Reading. Visit the Woolrich Company Store from 9 a.m. to 6 p.m. Mon through Thurs, 9 a.m. to 7 p.m. Fri and Sat, and noon to 5 p.m. Sun.

In *Laporte,* the bustling little historical society can help you find local relatives. "Genealogy is very important in small towns," explains museum curator Melanie Norton. "Here we have 6,000 people, if everyone and their dog stays home. There are so many shared family names and so many shirt-tail relations." The museum can help you sift through 150 years of records on births, deaths, marriages, and other details. The complex includes the main brick structure, the Baldwin House (with authentic details like garden plants, outhouse, and playhouse intact), and two barns. The museum can also point you to Celestia, a mountaintop settlement 1.5 miles out of town. That's where a fervent 1850s Christian named Peter Armstrong and his followers planned a town, with a lot

Elk Lore

- May is the most popular month for elk to have babies.

- Female elk, or cows, usually hang out with the other ladies, disappearing for privacy a few days before childbirth. Mommy and baby remain solitary for about three weeks.

- In late summer the bull elk's antlers are usually white and ivory; they darken later as the animal rubs against shrubs and trees covered with juices and sap.

- Elk antlers, which can grow a half-inch a day, are among the fastest-growing animal tissues.

- Elk, like many humans, dislike thunderstorms.

- During the rutting season males mate with as many cows as possible, show off to shoo other males, and feed and rest very little. They may lose a hundred pounds in a month. That's serious rutting.

reserved for God himself. The museum shows his original street grid and offers a brochure for a self-guided tour. The *Sullivan County Historical Society Museum* is open mid-June through Labor Day, Thurs through Sat from 1 to 5 p.m. But whenever you see the "open" sign in the window on Meylert Street next to the county courthouse, says Melanie, just come on by. Admission is free. Call (570) 946-5020.

One treasure in this neck of the northern woods is the 23,000-acre *Bucktail State Park,* which extends southeast—and downstream—from Emporium to Lock Haven. Route 120, a good road between the mountains, essentially parallels the park, as does the Susquehanna River for half the distance. This pleasant, scenic drive takes you through state forests, parks, and wilderness areas. If you're in the mood for a more active experience, hike a trail or choose a private clearing for a view and a picnic. Almost always, you can count on being alone.

Incidentally, the park's name comes only indirectly from deer; the name actually commemorates Civil War volunteers, like the ones from Smethport.

A state-designated Scenic Byway also takes the Bucktail name. Take Route 120 from Ridgway to Lock Haven for views of hang gliders, elk, and more. This 100-mile stretch through the Sproul and Elk State Forests is another old Indian trail turned highway. Native Americans called it the Sinnemahoning Trail, and used it to travel between the west branch of the Susquehanna and the Allegheny River. Map it at www.visitpa.com/bucktail-trail.

West of Emporium is *St. Marys,* a town with a frothy claim to fame—*Straub Brewery* (303 Sorg St.). Straub's is one of the smallest independent breweries left in the United States. "Of course, that depends on how you define 'small,'" says owner Terry Straub. "A microbrewery makes fewer than 15,000 barrels per year and sells it only on the premises. We average over 36,000 barrels a year, and we distribute it in Pennsylvania and Ohio. So it's okay to call us 'one of the smallest.'" Bottoms up. Straub produces beer made of water, malt, grains, and hops; no sugar, syrup, or additives. The *Connoisseur's Guide to Beer* named Straub's one of the five best-tasting beers in the country. The company distributes only within a 150-mile radius, which means that to taste the beer, you must either visit the area or convince a friend to send you a six-pack. St. Marys is where Routes 255 and 120 intersect. Hours are Mon through Fri 9 a.m. to 4:30 p.m. (Sat until 1 p.m.) for free tours (for those 12 and over) and free tastings from Straub's "eternal tap." Be a good guest—wash out your own glass at the sink. To be sure you catch the brewery in operation, call (814) 834-2875 and hope to be placed on hold: The recording plays the sound of a tinkling brook, a subtle reminder of the all-fresh ingredients. Visit the website at www.straubbeer.com.

trivia

Pennsylvania has the nation's fourth-largest highway system—more than 44,000 miles of highways under state control. And the Keystone State has the eighth-highest count of highway miles—nearly 119,000 miles. Bottom line: Hit the road.

If you want to see some strikingly singular celebrities, head to Route 555, and keep your eyes peeled for elk. The 700-head herd of wild, free-roaming elk is one of the largest in the East. The St. Marys airport and the village of Benezette are prime viewing spots.

Elk are huge in Pennsylvania these days. Actually, they're always huge—bulls weigh nearly a ton, with antlers up to 5 feet long. But this state is big

Best Baked Goods?

If you live in Montgomery, Alabama; Madras, Oregon; or anywhere in between, Pennsylvania has an effect on your cookies. The packages of saltines, chocolate-chip cookies, and buttered biscuits that you buy near home may be marked REG. PENNA. DEPT. AGRICULTURE even if they were made in Madrid, Spain, or Minneapolis, Minnesota. Why? Because the Pennsylvania Department of Agriculture has the strictest standards in the country for packaged baked goods. The department inspects all Pennsylvania bakeries and requires copies of inspection reports for out-of-state and out-of-country bakeries that want to sell to Pennsylvanians. REG. PENNA. DEPT. AGRICULTURE indicates to oatmeal-cookie lovers everywhere that the package comes from a sanitary, safe facility.

on the prospect of big game, and the herd roaming Elk County provides a target of opportunity for both tourists who stay at a safe distance and hunters who dream of getting close enough for a shot. Elk don't outnumber people here—yet. But their population boom over the past 20 years has brought a steady increase in fall visitors. (In summer, elk, like humans, hang out in the shade.)

Above the tiny village of Benezette (population 237), the state-built viewing area at **Winslow Hill** overlooks meadows and magnificent hillsides. When fall colors explode through the Allegheny Mountains, the elk graze, gallop, and occasionally clash during the annual rut. The unearthly mating call of the bull elk is called a bugle. It sounds like a cross between a hyena's cry and a rusty hinge, and it is eerie and absolutely unmistakable. Making their most predictable appearances at dawn and dusk, the elk are the subject of a video at the Winslow Hill amphitheater that boasts of the state's success in reintroducing the animals.

Elk were hunted here until 1931, when they became protected by law. By the mid-1970s, their numbers had dwindled to only 38.

In the intervening years, north-central Pennsylvania dug deep into its hills for coal and lumber (HOUSE COAL: HARD OR SOFT signs still line the main road). But when those economic engines sputtered, a new one emerged. It turned out to be the elk. Coal strip mines, replanted with tasty grasses, provided a habitat that allowed elk to thrive. Ditto clearcut forest, streams, and farms, all of which dot the local hills. The state lent encouragement by sowing food plots and cleaning polluted streams. The resulting rebound gave Elk County its signature attraction.

trivia

Pennsylvania was the first state to issue "vanity," or personalized, license plates—in 1931.

It may seem a contradiction that the state now allows fall hunts to thin the herd, but hunters are thrilled at the prospect. (The viewing area around Winslow Hill is, of course, a no-hunting zone.) When the state announced its first lottery for 30 elk licenses in 2001, nearly 51,000 people leapt at the chance.

Frenchville used to be a place where you could go to *parler français,* but no longer. Mary Kay Royer, a seventh-generation Frenchviller, tells the story. Early in the 1800s a Philadelphia lawyer acquired a tract of land in upstate Pennsylvania. He advertised it in French newspapers at the bargain rate of 12 acres free with each 50 paid. And he found buyers. "You'll notice," says Royer, "that everyone came from within about 20 miles of one another,

BEST ANNUAL EVENTS IN NORTH CENTRAL PENNSYLVANIA

FEBRUARY

Ridgway Rendezvous
Ridgway
(814) 772-0400
www.chainsawrendezvous.org
Each February Ridgway hosts the Ridgway Rendezvous, where you can view chainsaw creations of ice and wood sculptures. Many of the results are auctioned off; all proceeds go to charity.

Winter JazzFest
Wellsboro
(570) 787-7800
www.endlessmountain.net
The final weekend of the month brings jazz artists to the Penns Wells Hotel for performances and open jam sessions.

MAY

Upper Pine Creek Trout Tournament
(570) 724-1926
www.wellsboropa.com
Everyone's welcome at this weekend fishing event, which offers cash prizes.

JUNE

Susquehannock Trail Pro
Wellsboro
(570) 724-1926
The first weekend in June, you can watch the Susquehannock Trail Pro auto racing rally in Wellsboro.

Pennsylvania State Laurel Festival
Wellsboro
(570) 724-1926
The third weekend in June, Wellsboro holds the Pennsylvania State Laurel Festival. The parade is on Saturday.

JULY

Endless Mountain Music Festival
(570) 787-7800
www.endlessmountain.net
This two week festival of classical and popular music takes places at open-air pavilions and theaters from Wellsboro to Elmira, New York.

AUGUST

Little League Baseball World Series
Williamsport
(570) 326-3607
www.roadtowilliamsport.com
Watch the Little League Baseball World Series in Williamsport during the last full week of August that does not include the Saturday before Labor Day. You'll see the eight top US teams (from the East, Central, West, and South regions) compete against the eight best international teams (from Canada, Latin America, the Far East, and Europe). Seats are free, and the only day you need a ticket is the Saturday of the championship, since the stadium holds only about 5,000 people. The stadium is

from Normandy and Picardy in France." Many were aristocrats fleeing the French Revolution: In the early 19th century, many settled in northern Pennsylvania and New York State. Men pioneered, she says, apparently walking overland from the ports of Baltimore and New York. When they signed their purchase agreements, they didn't understand that they were buying isolated land inaccessible by normal transport. Clearfield, which was just developing, was the closest town, and Bellefonte was next closest—yet neither of built into a hillside, so the other 30,000 or 40,000 spectators without tickets spend the day picnicking on the hill and watching from afar. For tickets write in January to the Little League Museum, PO Box 3485, Williamsport 17701 (No, you can't do it online, though the website answers some FAQs.) Mark the envelope "World Series Tickets."

SEPTEMBER

Wheel Around the Hub
Smethport
(814) 887-5815
http://smethportpa.org
Smethport's Wheel Around the Hub cycling race, held each September, features a 53-mile course through spectacular countryside, with prizes and a Family Fun Race.

1890s Weekend
Mansfield
(570) 662-3442
1890s Weekend is held the last weekend in September in Mansfield. The Victorian-themed event always includes a re-enactment of the world's first night football game, played by Mansfield University in Smythe Park on September 28, 1892. Call the Mansfield Chamber of Commerce at (570) 662-3442.

DECEMBER

Dickens of a Christmas
Wellsboro
(570) 724-1926
The first Saturday in December, catch costumed actors and carolers bringing "A Christmas Carol" to life. Main Street is lit by gaslight and lined with food and craft vendors.

those was (or is) a thriving metropolis. Eventually the men sent home for their families.

Even the inscriptions on tombstones are in French, though misspelled and grammatically incorrect. As new inventions came along—automobile, radio, television—the villagers incorporated English words into their speech. The few people in Frenchville who are still fluent in French speak a classically pure French, without an American accent and *sans* the slang of contemporary

French streets. But few French-speakers remain. Royer's father spoke French at home as a child but was prohibited from speaking it once he got to school, as were others of his generation. He's lost the French he once knew. Royer's parents grew up in Frenchville—"almost everybody is related somehow. And we don't get many newcomers. You can live here 10 years and still be the new person on the block."

The village of several hundred people hides in a pocket of hills and rugged woodlands in Clearfield County. The trip over pitted blacktop roads winds through the remains of played-out strip mines, some of them growing scraggly conifers planted as part of reclamation projects. The heart of the community, as always, is St. Mary's Church, a parish established in 1840. Its first home was a log cabin, where the cemetery now stands. The current building, of native hand-cut stone, was occupied in 1870, the year the town's picnic originated. It was a ceremony of thanks for the construction of the church, and it continues annually, during the third weekend in July, in recognition of that heritage. For more information about Frenchville, St. Mary's, or the Frenchville picnic, e-mail rectory@iqnetsys.net, or phone the rectory at (814) 263-4354.

Places to Stay in North Central Pennsylvania

COUDERSPORT

Millstream Inn
918 E. Second St.
(814) 274-9900
www.millstreaminn.com
There are 34 rooms, or choose one of the 6 suites for extra living and kitchen space.

RIDGWAY

Towers Victorian Inn
330 South St.
(814) 772-7657
www.towersinn.com
A 19th-century lumber baron's home.

ST. MARYS

Towne House Inn
138 Center St.
(814) 781-1556
A small-town gem on the National Historic Registry.

WELLSBORO

Coach Stop Inn
Route 6 West
(570) 724-5361 or
(800) 829-4130
www.thecoachstopinn.com
Near Pennsylvania's Grand Canyon in Tioga County.

Penn Wells Lodge and Hotel
62 Main St.
(570) 724-2111
www.pennwells.com
Modern facilities, or an old-fashioned country inn.

Places to Eat in North Central Pennsylvania

BRADFORD TOWNSHIP

Glendorn
1000 Glendorn Dr.
(814) 362-6511
www.glendorn.com
Gourmet dining at a 1,200-acre estate that welcomes overnight guests.

COUDERSPORT

Sweden Valley Inn
Route 6 at Route 44
(814) 274-7057
www.swedenvalleyinn.com
Country pub (hunters welcome) that goes upscale on the weekend dinner menu.

ST. MARYS

Station Inn
322 Depot St.
(814) 834-1010
The town gathering spot (closed Mon and Tues).

WELLSBORO

Antlers
Route 6 West
(814) 435-6300
www.antlersinnpa.com
Big-game mounts and a meat-lover's menu.

Steak House
27 Main St.
(570) 724-9092.
Dinner only, closed Sun. Burgers, pork, beef, lamb, and a full bar.

WILLIAMSPORT

Bullfrog Brewery
231 W. Fourth St.
(570) 326-4700
www.bullfrogbrewery.com
A dozen microbrews on tap. Try the Billtown Blonde.

NORTHEASTERN PENNSYLVANIA →

Promised Land State Park—the name suggests a Biblical desert, but it's actually a scenic wooded spot in Pike County, home of the Poconos. The good news is, it won't take 40 years to wind your way through this region of mountains and gorges, with heavenly panoramas, pre-Revolutionary history, and plenty of anthracite underfoot. The region's two major roads, I-80 and I-81, can get you from point to point fairly easily. When you reach water—the Susquehanna, Lehigh, or Delaware Rivers—stop and enjoy the view.

Hard-Coal Country

To understand northeastern Pennsylvania, you need to understand coal mining. Legend says that in 1791 in the quiet village of Summit Hill, in western Carbon County, Pennsylvania, a major discovery altered American history. While tracking game, a hardy backwoodsman named Philip Ginder accidentally kicked a piece of shiny black rock. He pocketed the stone and took it to Revolutionary War veteran Colonel Jacob Weiss, who took it to his colleagues in Philadelphia. Turns out,

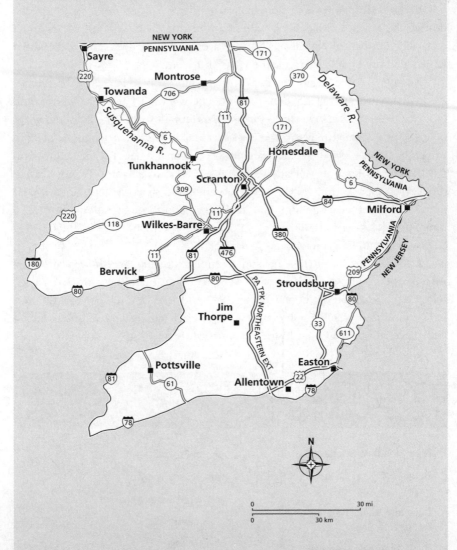

Ginder had discovered anthracite coal, often called "black diamonds" because of its value in the marketplace.

To recap your fourth-grade lesson, coal is a fuel substance composed of plants. You can inspect the raw material if you fail to rake leaves in your backyard for a few thousand years. The two primary types of coal are anthracite, or hard coal, and bituminous, or soft coal. Anthracite is more valuable because it has more carbon content and less moisture, thus it burns cleaner.

In the coal region some stretches of roadway through the hills are lovely, though the landscape has been marred by mining. The working mines aren't especially aesthetically pleasing, but the area is historically rich in details that let us see how people there used to live and work.

Nowhere is the legacy of coal mining more obvious than in Scranton. In downtown Scranton, on Cedar Avenue between Lackawanna Avenue and Moosic Street, the *Anthracite Heritage Museum* describes the lives and work of the ethnic communities in the region. Exhibits survey activities related to canals, railroads, silk mills, factories, and, of course, coal. The museum is on Bald Mountain Road in McDade Park. Take the North Scranton Expressway to the Keyser Avenue exit. Follow Keyser Avenue and signs to McDade Park. The museum is open year-round, 9 a.m. to 5 p.m. Mon through Sat and noon to 5 p.m. Sun; closed major holidays. Admission is $6 per adult. Call (570) 963-4804 or visit www.anthracitemuseum.org for details.

Also for viewing at the museum complex are the *Scranton Iron Furnaces,* open daily from 8 a.m. to dusk. These four huge blast-furnace stacks, built by the Scranton brothers between 1841 and 1857, are remnants of the iron industry around which Scranton grew, with coal mining and railroads falling into place as companion industries. Admission is free.

AUTHOR'S TOP 10 FAVORITES IN NORTHEASTERN PENNSYLVANIA

Blue Mountain Sports	Hotel Fauchère
Boulder Field at Hickory Run State Park	Inn at Jim Thorpe
Delaware Water Gap National Recreation Area	National Canal Museum
	Roebling Bridge
Hawk Mountain Sanctuary	Upper Mill
Historic Bethlehem walking tours	

McDade Park has picnic tables and barbecues, so you can grab a bite before going on to the **Lackawanna Coal Mine** tour, which begins next to the Heritage Museum. The tour takes you down into an abandoned slope mine to see what the miners did and what conditions were like. An electrical powered coal car lowers you from the loading platform to the mine interior. The big yellow car and hoist were designed especially for this purpose.

Inside the mine a retired miner or teacher takes you on a 600-foot tour along a wooden walkway, explaining the sights and answering questions. In the spacious underground area, mannequins in mining clothes and a life-size stuffed mule seem to say, "Hi." Although the mine isn't really dirty, it is underground, and coal can leave its marks, so consider blue jeans and walking shoes. The hour-long tours leave hourly Apr through Nov, more frequently during busy times. More exhibits and artifacts are housed aboveground in a building called Shifting Shanty. The box office opens at 10 a.m.; tours run from 11 a.m. to 3 p.m., but make sure you're there by 2:45 for the last tour of the day. Admission is $10 for adults. Call (570) 963-6463 or (800) 238-7245, or visit www .lackawannacounty.org/attractions_coal.asp.

Within walking distance of the mine is the **Steamtown National Historic Site,** the only place in the national park system that tells the story of steam railroading. The Steamtown Yard is open to the public. Visit the museum, which showcases coal-fired steam locomotives, restored cabooses, freight cars, and railroad coaches, offering a nostalgic journey to a period in American history when industry was on the move. The sights, sounds, smells, and even tastes of that era are brought to life in the presence of some of the most powerful machines ever built. It's located in the original Delaware, Lackawanna & Western Railroad Yard, which operated continuously from 1851 to 1963. The site boasts active locomotive and restoration shops, and a complex that includes a visitor center, history and technology museums, a 250-seat theater, and an operating roundhouse and turntable—the device that was invented to let trains turn around and start over again in the other direction. It's open daily except Thanksgiving, Christmas, and New Year's Day. All-day excursions to the **Delaware Water Gap,** East Stroudsburg, and other destinations are scheduled for select weekends. You can reserve ahead for those rides; short excursions within the Steamtown Yard are available without reservations beginning in late April. The park is open daily from 9 a.m. to 5 p.m. (9 a.m. to 4 p.m. Jan through mid-April). Adults pay $6 for the museum and additional fees for excursions. Although the entrance to the park is on Lackawanna Avenue, the mailing address is 150 S. Washington Ave., Scranton 18503. For more details visit www.nps.gov/stea/; call (570) 340-5200 or (888) 693-9391.

Magician Harry Houdini performed in Scranton, where the ***Houdini Museum*** (1433 N. Main) honors his memory. Ehrich (or Erik) Weiss (or Weisz)—who, abracadabra, became Harry Houdini—was born in 1874 in Budapest and moved to the United States when he was 4. He lived for years in Appleton, Wisconsin, of which he later said: "The greatest escape I ever made was when I left Appleton." In 1918, at the Hippodrome in New York City, Houdini first made an elephant disappear on stage. He performed underwater stunts, for which he practiced by holding his breath in the bathtub. In the museum you'll see Houdini's explanation of how he escaped from the incredible predicaments in which he put himself: "My brain is the key that sets me free." Since his parents spoke Yiddish, Hungarian, and German, his brain was probably also the key that taught him English.

The Houdini Museum also catalogs the history of Scranton and its coal and railroading industries. One exhibit, for instance, says that the Lackawanna Railroad created the image of Phoebe Snow, a delicate woman in a white dress, to foster the idea that riding coal-run trains was a clean event, hence the white dress. "Nothing could be further from the truth," it says. The old steam engines blew soot onto passengers riding the trains with open windows on warm days. Evening mystery events, too (reserve separately at 570-383-9297). Call (570) 342-5555, or go to www.houdini.org. Admission is $17.95 for adults and $14.95 for children.

Near Scranton is the ***Dorflinger-Suydam Wildlife Sanctuary,*** a 600-acre nature preserve and unique museum. The Dorflinger family manufactured glass until the 1920s, and eight US presidents owned some of it. Today the museum of cut glass is open May 1 through Oct 31, 10 a.m. to 4 p.m. Wed through Sat, and 1 to 4 p.m. Sun (weekends only in Nov); admission $3. On summer weekends the Wildflower Music Festival hosts open-air concerts. It's located on Route 6, midway between Hawley and Honesdale; the town is called White Mills, and the location is the intersection of Long Ridge Road and Elizabeth

Harry Houdini, Skeptic

Despite the annual Halloween séances in which people have tried to communicate with the ghost of Harry Houdini, the magician's spirit has been a no-show—perhaps not surprising for a man who delighted in exposing charlatans and fake mediums. After 10 years of trying, Houdini's wife, Bess, wasn't concerned. She wrote to friends that Houdini's permanent eternal silence "struck a mighty worldwide blow at superstition."

They Flip for Pizza

There are about 10,000 people in *Old Forge,* 5 miles south of Scranton, and they have one thing in common: They love pizza. In fact, they proudly dub the town the Pizza Capital of the World. There are at least a dozen pizza cafes on Main Street alone. Most of the pizza makers' ancestors hailed from the village of Felitto, near Naples, and most shops are still family businesses. While there are endless variations on ingredients, the rectangular pies served here, say the locals, are all "the best."

Street. Write to PO Box 356, White Mills 18473; call (570) 253-1185 or go to www.dorflinger.org for more information.

Ricketts Glen

Knowledgeable outdoorspeople consider *Ricketts Glen* the most spectacular of Pennsylvania's state parks. Its more than 13,000 acres of mountains, streams, waterfalls, and lakes spread through Sullivan, Columbia, and Luzerne Counties. The glen has 22 named waterfalls and a virgin hemlock forest with trees more than 500 years old. The only activity permitted in the natural area is walking. No picnics, campfires, camping, mountain biking, whining, or picking wild-flowers. Just hiking. You'll find bass, a swimming beach, and a summer-only concession stand on Lake Jean. The park has 23 miles of hiking trails, some strictly for the physically fit and some shorter loops that are less strenuous. The Falls Trail along the gorge gives you a view of all the falls in the glen and is breathtakingly close to the edge. It is possible to find deserted hiking trails almost any time and wander into the woods feeling that you're the only person in the forest primeval.

The hills are alive with the sound of RVs. You can rent cabins at Ricketts Glen (though not in the natural areas), and the park has good camping for

"Too Fast to Mow Grass"

That's the proud boast of the *Northeastern Pennsylvania Lawn Mower Racing Association,* whose souped-up racers cut a swath each summer at the Black Walnut American Legion on Route 6 in Tunkhannock. Tractor racing has quite a buzz all over the commonwealth, according to the Pennsylvania Lawn Mower Racing Association. Get the schedule at www.palmra.com.

recreational vehicles and tents. Reservations are recommended for overnight visits, especially on weekends during high season, which often lasts through October. Drive to Ricketts Glen via Route 487 or Route 118 north, depending on which side of the park you wish to enter. The grade is so steep that large vehicles should take Route 220, then turn north on Route 487 at Dushore. The park phone number is (570) 477-5675.

Working Valleys

From Scranton you can get to Hazleton quickly on I-81 or cross over to Route 11 and drive down along the Susquehanna River. From about Wilkes-Barre the drive becomes especially hilly in the narrow river valley. Almost any time you tire of it, you can pick up a short road back to the interstate to Hazleton, another formerly thriving coal burgh that was founded in 1837. Whether you follow the highway or your own way, you'll pass some little river towns—not the picturesque, renovated towns of shelter magazines, but real working towns inhabited by laboring folks. You may still see women wearing babushkas (head scarves), kids scuffing their shoes on the sidewalks, and town merchants sitting in front of their stores during idle moments.

Yuengling Brewery, in Pottsville, started brewing in 1829. During Prohibition the factory switched to nonalcoholic items—ice cream and dairy products. Four daughters in the fifth generation of Yuenglings (pronounced ying-LING) now run the firm.

The writer John O'Hara lived in a mansion once owned by the Yuenglings from 1916 to 1928. The National Historic Site is at 606 Mahatongo St. O'Hara set some of his major works in Pottsville. Thinly disguised as Gibbsville, the town is the backdrop for *Appointment in Samarra, Ten North Frederick, From the Terrace, Butterfield Eight,* and *The Big Laugh.*

Each fall 18,000 raptors get a bird's eye view of *Hawk Mountain Sanctuary,* just south of Pottsville. On routes that can begin at Hudson's Bay and end in Argentina, they soar down the Kittatinny Ridge, the southernmost ridge in the Appalachians, before cutting across Texas into Mexico, where they mass into millions. Hawk Mountain is one of the best places in the world for humans to catch the timeless spectacle. At this central Pennsylvania bird sanctuary, located off Route 61 near Pottsville, volunteers from all over the world annually track the flight paths of 16 species, from tiny kestrels to bald eagles, for the longest record of raptor population in the world.

Migration is hard work. Hawks, falcons, and eagles make it look easy, gliding at eye level past the sanctuary in numbers that can reach 1,000 per day in mid-autumn. It's easy to copy their laid-back style and sample their view by

River of Rocks

The white streak through the center of the valley below Hawk Mountain is the *River of Rocks,* boulder-sized leftovers from the glacier that pushed past this region 11,000 years ago. Visitors can hike a 4-mile circuit around the formation, circling down into the valley and back. Other hikers are just passing through: This is one of the most difficult stretches of the Appalachian Trail.

kicking back on a fall afternoon on the sunbaked boulders atop Blue Mountain. From the sanctuary's 1,300-foot summit, the views can extend some 70 miles. The Indian blanket of orange, yellow, and red foliage draping the ridge-and-valley landscape is *echt* ("pure") Pennsylvania.

Are you guaranteed to spot a golden or bald eagle? No. But here's a tip: Visit when the winds blow. "When there's a cold front over the Appalachians, we usually get northwest winds, and birds conserve energy by riding that deflected air current," says khaki-clad Jeremy Scheivert, an education specialist at the center. Trails are open dawn to dusk; adults pay $5 to enter, $7 on autumn weekends. From I-78, take the Hamburg exit (exit 30). Drive north on Route 61, then veer right to go north on Route 895. Turn right at Drehersville. You can write to the Hawk Mountain Sanctuary, 1700 Hawk Mountain Rd., Kempton 19529; call (610) 756-6961; or visit www.hawkmountain.org.

If you prefer valley views to mountain views, the old *Wanamaker, Kempton & Southern Railroad* still operates steam engines near Hawk Mountain. The 6-mile ride boards just past the intersection of Routes 143 and 737 on 737, just north of Kempton, on weekends from May through Oct. Tickets are $8 for adults and $4 for children ages 3 to 11. For a schedule call (610) 756-6469, or board www.kemptontrain.com.

Nine miles east of Hazleton, the *Eckley Miners' Village* gives you a chance to visit a spot that is part historic site and part living community. It is authentic, not because it has been re-created, but because it has never changed—the black silt heaps, open strip mines, and slag are ever present. Eckley was a company town from its settlement in 1854 until 1971 and is now administered by the Pennsylvania Historical and Museum Commission. Its population of retired miners, widows, and children has dwindled to about 15. The village, covering 100 acres, is off Route 940. Follow the signs to the site, which is open Mon through Sat 9 a.m. to 5 p.m., and noon to 5 p.m. Sun. It is closed holidays except Memorial Day, Independence Day, and Labor Day. Admission is $6 per adult. For more information write to the village at 2 Eckley Main St., Weatherly 18255; call (570) 636-2070; or go to www.eckleyminers.org.

Another coal locale is the ***Pioneer Tunnel Coal Mine*** in Ashland. The tunnel follows an anthracite vein that is nearly 200 feet thick in some places (huge by mining standards). You can take a half-hour tour ($9.50 per adult) in an open coal car pulled by a battery-powered mine motor. Another half-hour train tour ($7.50 per adult) goes around the outside of the mountain, not through tunnels. A steam locomotive, called a *lokie,* pulls the train past an open pit mine that was dug close to the surface with steam shovels and a "bootleg hole" where poachers dug out coal. To get to the Pioneer Mine, take Route 61 into Ashland, where it becomes Center Street. Turn left (south) on Twentieth Street and continue for 3 blocks. The mine is open from Memorial Day to Labor Day, 10 a.m. to 6 p.m. daily. Call (570) 875-3850, or go to www.pioneertunnel.com for hours in Apr, May, Sept, and Oct; closed the rest of the year.

Check out ***Nesquahoning,*** a mining town on Route 209, southeast of Hazleton. Nesquahoning is built on hills so steep that nothing seems level. Driving slowly, you can peek through a barbershop window to glimpse an elderly gentleman getting a haircut. In front of the homes, flowers spill from their beds over cement walls toward the sidewalk. In backyards women hang laundry to dry on clotheslines. Then you're through town, and signs usher you down the mountain into Jim Thorpe.

Little Switzerland

Until about 1950 ***Mauch Chunk*** was another Pennsylvania mining town whose economy fluctuated with the coal market, where miners lived in uncertainty and millionaires lived in mansions. Trying to survive, citizens of Mauch (rhymes with "hawk") Chunk and East Mauch Chunk donated a nickel a week to an economic development fund. In 1954 the towns merged and became ***Jim Thorpe.*** If you love small towns, you'll love Jim Thorpe.

Mauch Chunk's history is synonymous with coal mining and railway transport. Josiah White, a self-taught civil engineer and founder of the Lehigh Coal & Navigation Company, designed and invented a device to schlep his coal to his canal. He contrived the switchback railroad, which followed the Delaware Canal to Philadelphia and the Morris Canal to New York City, and which jokers refer to as the first roller coaster. The 9-mile Gravity Road was completed in 1827; 10 wagons, each carrying one and a half tons of coal, traveled down Summit Hill powered entirely by gravity. Mules pulled the empty cars up the

strangeas it **sounds**

Of the 26 millionaires living in the United States before World War II, 13 had homes in Mauch Chunk.

Northeastern Pennsylvania **133**

incline, then got a free ride down. After the demand for coal diminished, the train was used by tourists.

Driving down the highway into the heart of Jim Thorpe, you quickly realize why locals call their home Little Switzerland. Park in a public lot (or at a meter, where a quarter still buys an hour) to explore the narrow, winding streets on foot. This area at the foot of the hills is Hazard Square. It quickly becomes obvious how it got its name. Drive and walk defensively.

On the square, in the *Jim Thorpe Railroad Station,* you can buy tickets for rides on diesel-powered locomotive trains through the mountains to Old Penn Haven, round-trip, from Memorial Day through the weekend before Christ-

trivia

The town of Jim Thorpe has gone through several incarnations. At its founding it was known as Coalville. In 1815 it changed its name to Mauch Chunk, the local Native American term for Bear Mountain. Now it's named for one of the United States' greatest athletes.

mas. Tickets for a coach are $12 per adult; for the open air cars and caboose, tickets are $18 per adult. For complete schedules and rates, contact the *Lehigh Gorge Scenic Railway* at www.lgsry.com or (570) 325-8485.

Across the square from the station, you see the *Hooven Mercantile Company.* On the first floor, specialty shops laid out in emporium fashion, without partitions, feature coal jewelry, dolls, decorated eggs, and various other craft items and supplies. Upstairs is the *Old Mauch Chunk Scale Model Railroad*

"Thanks, King"

Controversy in the Olympics didn't start with murder in Munich or bribery in Salt Lake City. In 1912 in Stockholm, Sweden, Jim Thorpe, a Native American from Oklahoma, won gold medals in the pentathlon and decathlon. King Gustav V, presenting the medals to the 24-year-old, said, "You, sir, are the greatest athlete in the world," to which Thorpe replied, "Thanks, King." When the International Olympic Committee (IOC) learned that Thorpe had earlier played semipro baseball, earning $2 a game, it demanded that he return his trophies, which he did. He later played baseball for the New York Giants, Cincinnati Reds, and Boston Braves and football for the New York Giants and other teams. After retiring from professional sports, Thorpe played bit parts in several Hollywood movies. When he died of cancer, penniless, in 1953, Oklahoma refused to build him a monument, so his widow started looking for a place where her hero husband could be buried with honor. She found Mauch Chunk and East Mauch Chunk, which voted to consolidate their communities as Jim Thorpe Borough. In 1982 the IOC reinstated Thorpe's amateur status and gave his family replicas of his gold medals. Thorpe's grave is on Route 903.

trivia

In Mauch Chunk, now Jim Thorpe, miners in 1913 earned 23 cents an hour.

HO Display, a train-lover's exposition with 13 model trains that pull cars over more than 1,000 feet of track. Hours vary seasonally, so check ahead (570-325-4371; www.omctraindisplay.com). Admission is $4 per adult.

Drive up the hill on Route 209 to tour the **Asa Packer Mansion,** providing a dramatic contrast to the cabins of Eckley Miner's Village near Hazleton. Asa Packer worked his way from humble beginnings to become the founder and president of Lehigh Valley Railroad, founder of Lehigh University, and a philanthropist on a grand scale. In 1860 European craftsmen built the Victorian home, lavishly decorated and furnished in mid-19th-century opulence. It stands today as it did when the Packers celebrated their 50th wedding anniversary, preserved rather than restored. Among the outstanding pieces is the first-prize gas chandelier of the 1876 Centennial Exposition in Philadelphia, copied in the film *Gone With the Wind.* You'll find collections of carved walnut furniture, paintings, sculpture, crystal, and china. Hours are 11 a.m. to 4 p.m. daily, Memorial Day through Oct; weekends only in April, May, Nov, and through the first half of Dec. Admission is $8 for adults. Write to PO Box 108, Jim Thorpe 18229, call (570) 325-3229, or visit www.asa packermansion.com for more details.

Asa gave his son, Harry, the brick-and-stone Second Empire–style mansion next door as a wedding gift. This house is lavish, too, with hand-decorated ceilings and Victorian antiques, including some pieces that belonged to the Packer family. The **Harry Packer Mansion** (Packer Hill) operates as a bed-and-breakfast inn, with 13 rooms. The mansion has mystery weekends and sometimes turns over the entire establishment to special celebrations, so be sure to call ahead. Write to 19 Packer Ave., Jim Thorpe 18229, visit www.murder mansion.com, or call (570) 325-8566.

One block south of Broadway, Race Street winds along the path once taken by a millrace and passes old buildings, more specialty shops, and the stretch of stone facades called Stone Row, built by none other than Asa Packer in 1848. Today longtime residents and shopkeepers live side by side with newly arrived artists and writers.

Don't miss **St. Mark's and St. John Episcopal Church** at 21 Race St., considered one of the most notable late Gothic Revival churches in Pennsylvania. It was built in 1869 by Richard Upjohn, the architect who was responsible for the Third Trinity Church of New York City. St. Mark's is laid out in the form of a Latin cross, with an altar of white Italian marble, Minton tile floors, and two Tiffany windows. The reredos (which is the partition behind the altar), made of Caen stone, is a memorial to Asa Packer. Half-hour tours are held Tues through Sat, noon to 4 p.m. A $5 donation per adult is requested. Call (570) 325-2241, or visit www.stmarkandjohn.org for more information.

While Jim Thorpe is a historian's heaven, it's also a sportsperson's paradise. The 100-mile-long Lehigh River runs right past it. Hiking and biking trails attract athletes from hundreds of miles away. Of the several outfitters in Jim Thorpe, you can't do better than **Blue Mountain Sports** (34 Susquehanna St.). Owner Tom Marsden sells clothes and equipment and rents kayaks and mountain bikes, but his staff goes the extra mile: They know and love the area, and love to give advice about the best paths and routes. Visit their website at www.bike jimthorpe.com, or call (570) 325-4421 or (800) 599-4421. For more information about the town, call the tourist center toll-free at (888) JIM-THORPE (546-8467), or visit www.jimthorpe.com.

Just outside of Jim Thorpe, overlooking Route 209 at the base of Mount Pisgah, is a memorial plaque on a large rock where the village of Northern Liberties used to be. In 1861 virtually all the village males between the ages of 16 and 26 volunteered to serve the Union in the Civil War; their wholesale death effectively destroyed the village by killing off its reproductive population. All that remains is the plaque memorializing the soldiers.

Consider **Country Junction** a transition from the old world into the new. Country Junction may or may not be the world's largest general store, as it claims, but once you sing a few tunes with the life-size statues of the Blues Brothers and have a conversation with the parrot, you won't care. It's a hoot, this rural version of a shopping mall. Buy a wall plaque that says I FISH, THERE-FORE I LIE. Or you could shop alphabetically: Pick up potted plants, plaid pillows, or purple paint. Look at lawn ornaments, lumber, and lightbulbs. Country

Bitter Memories: The Molly Maguires

In the late 1870s a group of men were hanged in the Mauch Chunk Jail (now the **Old Jail Museum** in Jim Thorpe) for murdering two mine bosses. The men were members of a group called the Molly Maguires, Irish immigrants who fled the famine and found a dismal existence in the mines of northeastern Pennsylvania. Poor pay and rotten working conditions led to a strike, which led to management's hiring a spy, which led to long-term controversy. Before the trial, which the coal companies financed, all newspaper reports called the men killers. See Sean Connery and Richard Harris in the movie *The Molly Maguires,* and decide for yourself the guilt or innocence of the executed men.

Junction is open 7 days a week; Route 209 in Lehighton, 4 miles west of I-476. Call (610) 377-5050 or visit www.countryjunction.com.

Head down Route 209 to Route 33 for a respite from anthracite memories in two famous towns: Nazareth and Bethlehem. These namesakes of Biblical cities are blessed with charm.

In *Nazareth* a folk landmark strikes a chord: *The Martin Guitar Company.* Beck, Sting, and Johnny Cash are among the many famous musicians who insist on this brand, made locally since 1839. (Elvis Presley loved Martins, too.) The firm also used to manufacture banjos, ukuleles, and mandolins but now concentrates on its premier acoustic product. Stop in the little museum, or take a free 1-hour guided tour of the factory weekdays between 11 a.m. and 2:30 p.m. Yes, of course, they still sell guitars. The factory, museum, and store are located at 510 Sycamore St. (a great all-American name). Call (610) 759-2837, or visit www.martinguitar.com.

In *Bethlehem,* a thriving city of 72,000 that shares a metro area with Allentown, you'll find living history. Settled by Protestant Moravians on Christmas Eve, 1741, the city is still home to many members of that faith, which predated Anglicanism by a hundred years. Its famous multipointed star, called Moravian, is today a symbol of the town.

Bethlehem is home to several colleges. On the south bank of the Lehigh River rises the almost-vertical hillside campus of Lehigh University. Students and shoppers love Bethlehem's Main Street, a 19th-century gem with welcoming sidewalks, plenty of cafes, and Victorian storefronts. Its famous *Moravian Bookshop,* founded in 1745, claims to be the oldest bookstore in the world; some of its proceeds still go to support church charities. Over the years it has grown to encompass food items, a delicatessen, gifts (including Moravian stars of all sorts), and music. It's a friendly, very well-stocked place to browse. Open 7 days a week at 428 Main St. (610-866-5481), or shop online at www .moravianstar.com.

Engineering, a Team Sport

Lehigh University, founded by Asa Packer in 1865, prides itself on its excellent engineering department, so much so that its sports teams were nicknamed the Engineers. But in 1996, the school mascot became the Mountain Hawk. The school still uses the nicknames "Brown and White" and "Engineers" about teams of the past but uses the winged nickname in the present. Lehigh has the longest-running rivalry in college football with *Lafayette College,* in nearby Easton; the teams have clashed annually for 140 years.

Peeps!

Peeps, the fluffy, nutrient-free marshmallow candy chicks that nest in Easter baskets all over the country, are produced by the Rodda Candy Company in Bethlehem. The company makes 1.5 million of the little guys each year. Emory University researchers subjected Peeps to a number of experiments several years back, testing their resilience in ovens, vacuum chambers, liquid nitrogen, and more. They proved virtually indestructible.

In a huge 18th-century log home, the *Moravian Museum* (66 W. Church St.; 610-691-6055) offers 12 exhibit rooms. It's run by the Historic Bethlehem Partnership, which also operates five other period properties in town. In addition to workshops and the original living quarters of the first settlers, the sites include God's Acre, an egalitarian cemetery where Indians are interred alongside town leaders. Walking tours detail the industrious, God-fearing lives of those settlers, who were brutally attacked by local Indians in the 1750s. For details check www.historicbethlehem.org.

Shining just down the block, at 564 Main St., is the *Sun Inn,* which was the 18th century's place to see and be seen. It hosted Revolutionary War heroes in the 1770s; in 1792 51 chiefs and warriors of the Six Nations Confederation, including Red Jacket, Corn Planter, and Osiquette, lodged at the inn on their way to Philadelphia to meet President Washington.

How much is that doggie in the window? At *Pott's Doggie Shop* (known fondly as Pottsie's), 114 W. Fairview St. (610-865-6644), a great hot dog costs just over a buck. Get all-American takeout here.

As you might guess, Christmas celebrations are a big draw in this town—with stars everywhere, Christmas markets, arts events, and music by the city's famous Bach Choir. Get the full holiday lineup from the convention and visitor bureau at (800) 747-0561, or visit www.discoverlehighvalley.com.

The Poconos

The *Pocono Mountains,* northern foothills of the Appalachian Range, are a year-round playground for the Boston-to-Washington megalopolis. The highest Pocono—the impressively named Mount Ararat, in Preston, Wayne County—towers 2,654 feet above sea level. Well, maybe it doesn't tower—some jokingly call the Poconos "the Pinocchios." Nevertheless, they're huge with East Coasters. Best known for cheesy honeymoon hideaways, the Poconos also offer kitschy entertainment, including playing the slots at Mount Airy Casino and Mohegan Sun at Pocono Downs.

To see some of the more scenic and lesser-known parts of the Poconos, take Route 33 out of Nazareth and join Route 209 at Sciota. In its time Route 209 was a major highway, important enough for its construction to displace homes, cemeteries, and prize stands of sugar maples. This route has lost much tourist traffic to interstates; here and there you still see a failed group of tourist cabins predating today's motels or an abandoned gas station with weeds growing through the macadam. By today's standards 209 is narrow and slow due to the steep hills and curves, but the surface is in fairly good condition, trucks pull over to let traffic pass, and most of the countryside is lovely.

Continue north on Route 209, then turn right (south) on Old Route 115. Turn left on Lower Cherry Valley Road, and follow the signs into the *Cherry Valley Vineyards,* a friendly little winery run by the Sorrenti family. (From Route 33 take the Saylorsburg exit, then Old Route 115 south, and follow the signs.) For more information on visiting the Saylorsville vineyard, call (570) 992-2255 or visit www.cherryvalleyvineyards.com.

A quick jog back on Route 33 north takes you to Snydersville, which isn't much more than a gas station, a school bus stop, and antiques dealers in old homes. The names and proprietors may change, but this remains a good area for antiquing—the dealers are knowledgeable but not in the thick of the tourist stream.

At Snydersville pick up Business Route 209 (paralleling the 4-lane Route 209) going south. Turn right on Hickory Valley Road and follow the signs to *Quiet Valley Living Historical Farm.* (If you start in Stroudsburg, take Business Route 209 north, turn left on Hickory Valley Road, and follow the signs.) Alice and Wendell Wicks, with their daughter and son-in-law, Sue and Gary Oiler, saw the possibilities for this centuries-old Pennsylvania German farm. The Wicks and the Oilers have invested work, time, and money in researching, repairing, and collecting furnishings and farm equipment. In 1963 they opened Quiet Valley as a living museum, showing how the original Pennsylvania Dutch family lived on this virtually self-sufficient homestead from about 1770 to 1913. The families restored the existing buildings to full function and reconstructed

Appellation Lehigh Valley

With nearly a dozen vineyards sprouting between Jim Thorpe and Allentown, the area's terroir—the regional qualities imparted by soil and climate conditions—may one day be heralded for cabernets, chardonnays, and chambourcin, rather than coal. The vintners cooperate on special tastings and events year-round. Plan a day or weekend visiting the winemakers; go to www.lehighvalleywinetrail.com.

Pennhenge

While "new megalith" may seem like an oxymoron, the ones erected in the late 1970s at *Columcille* (2155 Fox Gap Rd., Bangor) are worth a look.

Trying to emulate the peaceful and mystical vibe of the Scottish isle of Iona, the pair of idealists who created this park named it for St. Columba (Colum Cille). The 6th-century founder of a monastic community, he protected the legacy of Celtic Christianity. The Pennsylvania park mimics its giant menhirs and stone circle and includes a meditation pond and an Infinity Gate. As Columcille's website (www.columcille.org) explains, it "suggests to all who enter that these are portals into a world of myth and mystery where the veil is thin between the worlds." All quarried locally, the stones are mind-bendingly old: 400 million years at their core.

Catch the ancient energy daily from dawn to dusk at *Columcille Megalith Park and Celtic Art Center.* It's located 3 miles from Quiet Valley Historical Farm. For more information call (610) 588-1174.

others that would have been there; for a while the Oilers lived in the top floor of the home. "We don't own it anymore," says Sue Oiler. "It's now a private, nonprofit organization. My home is in the middle of a nonprofit farm. In my head I know it's not really mine, but in my heart I care for it and love it as if it were."

After the tour, consider picnicking in the grove. Quiet Valley is open mid-June to Labor Day, 10 a.m. to 5 p.m. Tues through Sat, and noon to 5 p.m. Sun. The last tour begins at 3 p.m. Cost is $10 per adult. For more information write to Quiet Valley Living Historical Farm, 347 Quiet Valley Rd., Stroudsburg 18360; visit www.quietvalley.org, or call (570) 992-6161.

The Poconos offer options for every imaginable outdoor enthusiasm—as well as some unimaginable ones. For most of us, auto racing is a spectator sport, but the 2.5-mile race course *Pocono Raceway* is also home to the *Bertil Roos Racing School.* Go equipped with a driver's license, sneakers, gloves, and experience handling a standard shift. The raceway provides instruction, race cars, racetracks, colorful driving suits, and helmets. Your instructor will show you when to brake, when to accelerate, how to handle corners, and, presumably, how to pray for safety. Call Roos Mar through Oct at (800) 722-3669, or zoom to www.racenow.com. The office is on Route 115 in Blakeslee.

Consider popping into the *Pocono Cheesecake Factory* (Route 611, Swiftwater), where chefs prepare up to 100 cheesecakes daily. Watch through the giant window as almonds, raspberries, chocolate chips, and liqueurs blend into the dessert of your choice. As you choose between your wallet and your

From Tanneries to Tannersville

Whether or not you stop in *Tannersville,* you'll certainly drive through it. While you're waiting for the traffic light to change, a bit of deep background: Early on, the Lenni-Lenape Indians lived in this valley in the foothills of the Poconos. In about 1750 John Larned bought the land and built a log tavern and two gristmills. Twenty-nine years later General Sullivan and his army, en route to the Wyoming Valley, spent the night in tents next to the tavern. In 1834 Jacob Singmaster built a large tannery, which became the village's main industry and inspired the name change from Larneds to Tannersville. Fire destroyed several tanneries, but innumerable candle shops keep the heat on.

waistline, read the sign: LIFE IS UNCERTAIN. EAT DESSERT FIRST. Open daily 10 a.m. to 6 p.m. Call (570) 839-6844 or visit www.poconocheesecake.com for menus and calorie counts.

Heading north on Route 611, turn east in Mount Pocono on Route 940, then north on Route 191. Every roll of the tires takes you farther away from civilization. Stop in Cresco to visit the *Theo B. Price Lumber Company,* a singular hardware-and-quilts store with a distinctly down-home flavor. On the street level, with its uneven wood-plank flooring, amid the nails and feed, you can find solutions for problems you didn't know you had—until you see the solutions. Upstairs are hand-sewn and handcrafted goods for the home, the friends, and the soul. Shopkeeper Maryann Miller manages the emporium, started in 1908 by her grandfather Theo, who invented tools and devices for mines. His original cash register, capable of ringing sales as high as $20, sits in the back of the place. Hours are 8 a.m. to 5 p.m., except Sun. Call (570) 595-2501, or visit www.theobprice.com.

Eight miles up Route 191, in beautiful downtown LaAnna—wait, you missed downtown—you can visit *Holley Ross Pottery.* Daily from 9:30 a.m. to 5:30 p.m. (Sun from 1 to 5:30 p.m.), you can watch pottery being made and buy Fiestaware, gazing balls, and a variety of glass and ceramic items. The pottery showroom is closed mid-Dec through Apr, except by chance or appointment. Call (570) 676-3248, or go to www.holleyross.com for details.

Paintball is everywhere in the Poconos. If you like mayhem, paintball is for you. This competitive outdoor "sport" involves balls of water-soluble, biodegradable, nontoxic paint, which you shoot at your friends or enemies. (Yeah, it hurts for real when you get shot.) Ride a military troop transport to a mountaintop with a beautiful view—in order to inflict damage on your friends. Your $30-and-up all-day pass entitles you to 50 paintballs, all-you-can-use carbon dioxide as a propellant, and protective headgear and face mask. You can rent a camouflage suit, which might be a good idea since the games are called "attack and defend," "hostile takeover," and "total elimination." Call ahead to reserve a field at **Skirmish USA** (Route 903, Jim Thorpe; 800-754-7647; www .skirmish.com).

For the back-to-nature gang—and even for people who prefer their nature in *National Geographic* specials—**Hickory Run State Park,** especially the Boulder Field, is not to be believed and never to be forgotten. This area, now a National Natural Landmark (say that fast three times) has remained essentially unchanged for 20,000 years. Boulders up to 26 feet long cover an area 400 feet by 1,800 feet, and you're welcome to climb, scramble, or sit on them—if you can. Imagine a dish of 1-inch pebbles, and imagine an ant trying to navigate the terrain. The ground beneath the boulders is totally flat and free of vegetation. Staggering.

Of course, like any self-respecting state park, Hickory Run has trails, campgrounds, and picnic facilities. You may apply for hunting and fishing licenses and try your luck in the park's 15,500 acres. You can swim in summer and snowmobile, cross-country ski, and sled in winter. But what should lure you miles out of your way—and what will indubitably entice you back—is the **Boulder Field.** Hickory Run is immediately southeast of the intersection of I-476 and I-80, so it's hard to miss if you're in the area. You can write to the park office at State Route 534, White Haven 18661, call (570) 443-0400, or visit www.dcnr.state.pa.us/stateparks/findapark/hickoryrun/index.htm.

Perhaps you'd like to find the bluebird of happiness while you're in the Poconos? No problem. Take the 53-mile auto tour, with 12 stops and 6 suggested side trips, that follows John James Audubon's 1829 journey into the forests of the Lehigh River Valley. Audubon, who first settled in Pennsylvania at Mill Grove, near Valley Forge, is the famed 19th-century naturalist who observed, painted, and wrote about birds and other wildlife. He lived in Pennsylvania and traveled extensively throughout the state and the rest of the

Bike the Gorge

Want to enjoy world-class white water without getting wet? Bike the *Lehigh Valley Gorge Trail,* a 25-mile level path from Jim Thorpe to White Haven. This traffic-free rails-to-trails experience hugs the Lehigh River shoreline the whole way. Roaring rapids, breathtaking scenery. River outfitters at the trailheads in White Haven, Rockport, and Jim Thorpe can supply fat-tire bikes and shuttle services. Get the details at www .800poconos.com or (800) 762-6667.

country. The aim of Audubon's America Program is to help conserve, restore, enhance, interpret, and protect natural and cultural resources. From Hickory Run State Park, turn east on Route 534 to Albrightsville; south on Route 903 to Jim Thorpe; west on Route 209, then north on Route 93 to Hudsondale; north on Hudsondale Drive, through Rockport; then back to Hickory Run on Route 534. Download a map from www.audubonslehigh.org.

Delaware Water Gap

Here you are close to the *Delaware Water Gap National Recreation Area,* which runs along a 40-mile stretch of the Delaware River in New Jersey and Pennsylvania. Publicity calls it "the eighth wonder of the world." The town of Delaware Water Gap marks the southernmost point of the 70,000-acre recreation area, which became federal property in 1965. At the *Dingmans Falls Visitor Center* (off Route 209 north of Johnny Bee Road), you'll find park information and a bookstore. A full complement of programs includes a waterfall hike. For more information contact the Dingmans Falls office at (570) 828-2253. Since hours vary seasonally, you might want to visit www.nps.gov/dewa/planyourvisit/dingmans-falls.htm.

Even in the 19th century this gap attracted the well-to-do for resort holidays away from the heat. Horse-drawn carriages and rafts transported early visitors until about 1856, when the Delaware and Cobb's Gap Railroad Company opened a track to Scranton. Native Americans called the area Pohoqauline, Pahaqalong, or Pahaqualia, all of which mean "river passing between two mountains." Its beauty lies partly in the contrasting colors of layers of quartzite, red sandstone, and dark shale that have been revealed as the river carved its path over geologic eons.

With light hiking, you can appreciate the gap close up. Park in the Resort Point parking lot off Route 611, on the Pennsylvania side. Across the road stone steps take you to a trail paralleling a stream that goes up steeply for a short distance, then turns left onto a marked trail. The trail continues gently

Protecting Bog Turtles

The Water Gap Recreation Area adjoins Pennsylvania's newest national wildlife refuge. The *Cherry Valley National Wildlife Refuge* was created in 2008, protecting more than 20,000 acres in Monroe and Northampton Counties. Like all such federally mandated areas, it preserves the habitat of rare plants and animals, like the local bog turtle. But it also guards a scenic rural landscape of working farms.

Eagle Etiquette

"The eagles are getting so friendly," marvels Maria Vernon at the Delaware Water Gap Visitor Center. While they don't actually wave, the birds have gradually become less afraid of humans. But please, don't scare them. To view the dozen or so pairs of bald eagles along the upper Delaware shoreline, the Eagle Institute recommends using the observation blinds at viewing areas to remain hidden from view. Avoid loud noises, and use binoculars instead of moving close to the birds. And plan to do your bird-watching in midwinter—come spring, eagle parents don't want company while they're tending to their newborns (a sentiment most new mothers would share).

Maria recommends the Shohola Recreation Area, off Route 6, as a good viewing spot; Lackawaxen is good, too, she says. Basically, any spot with open, unfrozen water will afford an opportunity for viewing the raptors.

upward for about a mile; when you get to a waterfall, you can no longer hear the highway traffic. A little farther straight ahead, a large rock outcropping takes your breath away. It's picture-postcard pretty. In this area you can also drive into some well marked overlooks from which you have a spectacular view without hiking. At one such place a souped-up red Chevrolet once roared in; a couple of teenagers slurping diet colas looked out, said, "There isn't anything here," and roared away. Pushing these types of people over the edge is against park regulations. For complete information on the Delaware Water Gap National Recreation Area, write to Interpretation & Education, Delaware Water Gap NRA, Bushkill 18324; visit www.nps.gov/dewa or call (570) 426-2452.

One way to see some of this without driving is to ride the **Delaware Water Gap Trolley.** Guides discuss the history, points of interest, settlers and Indians, and the entire natural splendor of the gap. The trolley operates from late Mar through Nov; the depot is on Route 611 at the center of Delaware Water Gap. The cost for adults is $9.50. Call (570) 476-9766 or visit www.water gaptrolley.com.

The **Pocono Indian Museum** on Route 209 shows the history of the Delaware Indians in 6 rooms of collected artifacts. Some pottery is more than 1,000 years old, and weapons and tools have had only their handles reconstructed. The Delaware Indians wore simple deerskin garments, cut their hair short, and wore no feathers, except perhaps for ceremonies. Nor did they live in tepees. The museum and gift shop are usually open daily 10 a.m. to 6 p.m., but call first. Admission is $5 for adults. For more information visit www.poconoindian museum.com or call (570) 588-9338.

Even more glorious than the creations of any human hand, **Bushkill Falls,** called the Niagara of Pennsylvania, is easy to reach, 2 miles northwest of Route 209. Easy walking over rustic bridges and a nature trail of about 1.5 miles takes you through virgin forests and past a gorge with a view of 8 waterfalls, the largest of which is Bushkill, dropping 100 feet. Even with a simple camera it's possible to take spectacular pictures. You may picnic, boat, and fish in the park. Some food is available. The park is open daily 9 a.m. to dusk Apr through Nov. Admission is $11 for adults. The park's operating calendar varies depending on the season, so call (570) 588-6682, or go to www.visitbushkillfalls.com.

At Dingmans Ferry, farther north on Route 209 but still in the Delaware Water Gap National Recreation Area, **Dingmans Falls,** the highest waterfall in Pennsylvania, pours down over 100 feet of rock with awesome power. On the same easy trail, in woods of hemlock and ferns, Silver Thread Falls, not quite as high but equally beautiful, is another stop worth a few photographs. In the park's nature center, you can study an audiovisual program, pick up a map, and talk to a naturalist about the falls and good trails—including easy ones—to walk.

From Dingmans Ferry it's only about 10 miles to Milford, a good place to spend the night. As a kid I remember discovering the **Hotel Fauchère.** My grandfather loved taking us to the place, and I later found it has an interesting history, playing host to many New York celebrities in its heyday. One was D. W. Griffith, who filmed several early movies in the area. Now it's been transformed into a 4-star boutique hotel, so grandchildren aren't as welcome as upscale adults. But the food is still magnifique (401 Broad St.; 570-409-1212; www.hotelfauchere.com).

Can you picture one of Dingmans Ferry's most famous natives, Chief Thundercloud? If you've got an old nickel, it's easy. He's thought to be the model for the famous beaked profile on the obverse of the Indian-head coin (and for the last $5 gold piece minted in the United States). Though he was a Boy Scout in his youth, Thundercloud went on to quite a show-biz career, traveling with Buffalo Bill's Wild West show and P. T. Barnum. He also served as a model for sculptor Frederick Remington and artist John Singer. He's buried back in his hometown cemetery on Route 6/309 in Delaware Township.

The grandeur of **Grey Towers,** the Milford home of Gifford Pinchot, was the creation of 19th-century architect Richard Morris Hunt. Pinchot, a two-time governor of Pennsylvania, was a leading early conservationist and the first director of the US Forest Service. His wife Cornelia was a noted suffragette and gardener. Tour the National Historic Site, open 11 a.m. to 4 p.m. from Memorial Day to Oct 31, at 151 Grey Towers Dr.; adult admission $6. Call (570) 296-9630 or visit www.fs.fed.us/na/gt.

In Milford stop at the **Upper Mill,** a 19th-century mill where water rushing over a 3-story-high waterwheel used to power a grindstone. The mill building, on the National Register of Historic Places, is open year-round with an easy-to-follow self-guided tour, and the waterwheel operates from May to Thanksgiving. The only power generated in the mill these days is retail power, but that, fortunately, is thriving. From the cafe and bar, you can watch the waterwheel. While you're there you'll also want to visit the bakery, gift shop, bookstore, and dress boutique. The mill (570-296-5141) is on Sawkill Creek at Water and Mill Streets.

From Milford, driving west on I-84 for about half an hour brings you to the **Sterling Inn,** in South Sterling. It has 66 rooms, a third with fireplaces or Franklin stoves. The inn sits on more than 100 acres, with hiking and cross-country skiing trails, a tennis court, and a swimming and skating pond. Call the cuisine traditional American country gourmet, with vegetarian options. Saturday night entertainment is live jazz or contemporary music. For rates and reservations write Sterling Inn, 248 S. Sterling Rd., South Sterling 18460; call (570) 676-3311 or (570) 676-3320; or visit www.thesterlinginn.com.

trivia

Lake Wallenpaupack, an artificial lake north of Route 84, east of Route 191, covers old farmlands. Divers can still see stone walls, marking the perimeters of some farmers' pastures.

For a different kind of stay, go northwest from Milford on Route 6 to the **Settler's Inn,** a 20-room country lodge furnished in antiques and white wicker. The inn is run by Grant and Jeanne Genzlinger with help from family and friends. The menu, which features local produce and local trout and pheasant, changes every four months—"except for the smoked-trout appetizer, which we can't take off the menu," says Jeanne. The inn is near Lake Wallenpaupack, where you can go fishing and boating. For more information about Settler's Inn, write 4 Main Ave., Hawley 18428; call (800) 833-8527; or visit www.thesettlers inn.com.

Upper Delaware Wilds

The Lackawaxen area remains unspoiled. Although the land along the Delaware River and the Lackawaxen River is privately owned, the stretch of the Delaware from Port Jervis to Hancock (both towns in New York) is protected under the Wild and Scenic Rivers Act. You'll find most of the historic and natural attractions along or near Route 590. The village of **Lackawaxen** (an Indian word for "swift waters") is named for the river that flows into the Delaware. If

BEST ANNUAL EVENTS IN NORTHEASTERN PENNSYLVANIA

FEBRUARY

Kiwanis Winterfest
(570) 924-4224
www.sullivanpachamber.com
Mush! Each February the Kiwanis
Winterfest pits contestants in a Human
Sled Dog Race. The Presidents' Day
Weekend event also includes a Polar
Bear Plunge with prizes, ice carving, ice
fishing, and even a real sled dog race on
the frozen lake at Camp Brulé, off Route
154 north of Forksville. Bundle up.

APRIL

Endless Mountains Maple Festival
Alparon Park, Troy
(570) 673-8871
www.maplefestivalpa.com
The last weekend in April, the Endless
Mountains Maple Festival takes place in
Alparon Park, Route 14, Troy. Of course
it includes a pancake-eating contest.

MAY

Farm Animal Frolic
Quiet Valley Living Historical Farm
(570) 992-6161
www.quietvalley.org

In May (usually the last 2 weekends) is
the Farm Animal Frolic, a time for baby
people to touch baby animals. No tours,
just hens and chicks, sheep and lambs,
pigs and piglets—you get the picture.
Admission is charged (for humans).

Bach Festival
Bethlehem
(610) 886-4382
www.bach.org
Music from the maestro: Each May for
more than 90 years, Bethlehem's Bach
Festival has showcased its famous
all-volunteer choir, which has even
performed at the BBC Proms, the
annual London music festival.

JULY

Wildflower Music Festival
Dorflinger-Suydam Wildlife Sanctuary
(570) 253-1185
www.dorflinger.org
Strike up the band. The Dorflinger-
Suydam Wildlife Sanctuary holds its
Wildflower Music Festival, a series of
Saturday evening concerts, in July and
August. General admission is $22.

you're a fishing enthusiast, you'll like the Lackawaxen Fishing and Boat Access,
operated by the Pennsylvania Fish and Boat Commission, which provides good
fishing where the Delaware River runs deep and slow.

Across from the fishing access is the *Zane Grey Museum*, representing a classic American success story. Zane Grey was a dentist. He attended
the University of Pennsylvania, where he received his degree in 1896. "He
played on the Penn varsity baseball team and was quite well known," says Dot
Moon, curator at the museum. "Baseball was very different than it is today.
College baseball was a very big thing." After college Grey played baseball
for the Orange Athletic Club in the Eastern League, which was considered a

AUGUST

Blueberry Festival
Montrose
(570) 278-1881
Try the annual Blueberry Festival the first week in August in Montrose. Alongside blueberry dishes from buckle pie to ice cream, the ladies of the Crazy County Quilters raffle off exquisite homemade designs to benefit the town library.

Tomato Festival
Pittston
(570) 693-0704
www.pittstontomatofestival.com
Pittston holds a Tomato Festival each August. The highlight: the in-the-streets, in-your-face tomato fights on Saturday. The $5 tickets include protective glasses. Splat!

Riverfest
Towanda
(570) 265-2696
In late August Towanda concludes its weekend Riverfest with Fire Over the Susquehanna, a waterfront fireworks display. Babies can enter the Baby Crawl; adults can try the 5K Walk/Run.

OCTOBER

Shawnee Timber Festival
(570) 421-7231
www.shawneemt.com
With a backdrop of peak fall foliage, world-class lumberjacks pole climb, log roll, chop, saw, and chainsaw in exhibitions at the Shawnee Mountain ski resort.

DECEMBER

Christkindlmarkt
Bethlehem
(610) 332-1300
www.christmascity.org
A European-style Christkindlmarkt with daily outdoor music, food, trees, crafts, and St. Nick marks the holiday season in downtown Bethlehem.

"gentlemen's league." Moon says that means they played for money but did not play on Sunday as "professional" baseball players did. In the off-season Grey practiced dentistry.

Grey's first article, a fishing story, was published in 1902. He gave up baseball after the 1902 season at the urging of his future wife, who encouraged him to devote himself to writing. In 1903 he wrote his first novel, *Betty Zane*, the story of his great-great-aunt who helped save Fort Henry during the Revolutionary War. He moved to Lackawaxen in 1905 to devote himself to writing and later said the Lackawaxen area was where he first became familiar with "really wild country." Between 1902 and 1909 Grey wrote articles for popular magazines on fishing and adventure, and in 1908 he wrote about his adventures in the Grand Canyon. While he was on this trip, he began writing his first novel about the West, *Heritage of the Desert*.

After leaving Lackawaxen, Grey traveled extensively to exotic places, such as Tahiti and New Zealand, to research his books. They were so convincing that Hollywood took to them, and by 1918 he left for California to work with the people producing movies based on his books. His Lackawaxen home remains a museum containing mementos of his life. Grey and his wife are buried in the cemetery of St. Mark's Lutheran Church (built in 1848), along with an unknown soldier killed during the Battle of Minisink in 1779, during the Revolutionary War. The free museum is open in warm weather; for hours and details call the National Park Service at (570) 685-4871 or visit www.nps.gov/upde.

From the fishing access you can also see John Roebling's **Delaware Aqueduct,** the oldest suspension bridge in use today. Roebling (who designed the Brooklyn Bridge but died before it was built, and who also created the "Three Sisters" bridges in Pittsburgh) designed and built four aqueducts for the Delaware and Hudson (D&H) Canal; only this one remains. Completed in 1849, the aqueduct connected the canal between Lackawaxen, in Pennsylvania, and New York. The aqueduct fell into disrepair and was later restored by the National Park Service. Now it is sturdy enough to be used, a century and a half later, as an automobile thoroughfare. (Locals—and local signs—call it the **Roebling Bridge.**)

A nice place to stay, and where owner JoAnn Jahn is deeply engrossed in local history, is the **Roebling Inn** on the Delaware. It's on Scenic Drive off Route 590 in Lackawaxen. Jahn says the white clapboard inn with green shutters and roof was built around 1870 and was used as an office for the D&H Canal company. The 6 guest rooms, decorated with country antiques, are modified for contemporary tastes with private baths, televisions, and queen-size beds; some rooms have fireplaces. From the inn you can walk to canoeing, golf, horseback riding, a bait shop, a lunch restaurant, a general store, white-water rafting, tennis, river swimming, and a couple of great places for dinner. (Previous editions of this guide sent many visitors to the Roebling Inn because, says Jahn, "The title of the book says it all. We really are off the beaten path.") For full

trivia

A popular horse race that was 5 miles long used to take place between Camptown and Wyalusing. The race is believed to have inspired Stephen Foster, who was visiting his brother in Towanda, to write "Camptown Races." Doo-dah.

details and reservations, write 155 Scenic Dr., Lackawaxen 18435; call (570) 685-7900; or visit www.roeblinginn.com.

You can find considerably more rustic accommodations at the **Sylvania Tree Farm** on the Delaware River in Mast Hope. It's a tree farm—a naturalist's paradise—where you can stay in a modern cottage or pitch your tent at a campsite. Mast Hope is one of those you-can't-get-there-from-here places. From Milford take Route 6 about 14 miles, go north on Route 434 for 3 miles, take Route 590 west to Lackawaxen, then turn right toward Mast Hope. (Ask for a brochure with full directions when you make reservations.) The destination worth the trouble is 1,250 acres on the river with woods, fields, brooks, and

> ## trivia
>
> Joseph Smith, founder of the Latter Day Saints movement, lived in Susquehanna County in 1830 while translating the Golden Plates for the *Book of Mormon.* See the historical marker at the site on Route 11 between Great Bend and Hallstead.

seclusion. The property is in the Upper Delaware Wild and Scenic River corridor, administered by the National Park Service. Watchful visitors sight bald eagles and blue herons in the valley and white-tailed deer, black bears, beavers, and foxes in the woods and fields. The fly-fishing crowd loves the farm's private stream. You can cross-country ski in winter, hike other times, and take canoe and rafting trips with nearby outfitters. In addition, the National Park Service gives tours of the river valley and several historic sites. Write Sylvania Tree Farm, 112 Mast Hope Ave., Lackawaxen 18435, or call (570) 685-7001. Find out more at www.sylvaniatreefarm.com.

A Day Trip: Endless Mountains

Four adjoining counties—Bradford, Sullivan, Susquehanna, and Wyoming—form the **Endless Mountains Heritage Region.** More than 15,000 years ago, glaciers etched these stones, creating the North Branch of the Susquehanna River. Valleys that once held prehistoric agricultural settlements now hold modern farms—plus white clapboard churches, basket shops, and quaint bed-and-breakfasts.

Versailles, it turns out, is only a day trip from Scranton area. Early settlers thought the Susquehanna River vista looked like *la belle France.* So in 1793, those refugee royalists built an asylum for Marie Antoinette. Unfortunately, they waited in vain for the queen. Keep your head—and keep your eyes on the road—as you drive north on Route 6, above Wyalusing. The grounds are open May through Oct; hours vary. The $5 adult admission includes tours of the La

Porte house, a later structure. Call (570) 265-3376, or get the full history from www.frenchazilum.com.

For more information on the area, contact the **Endless Mountains Visitors Bureau,** 3367 Rte. 6 East, Tunkhannock 18657; (800) 769-8999 or (570) 836-5431. You can also visit www.endlessmountains.org.

Easton

My favorite Crayola color? Red violet. Nationally, folks vote for plain old true blue. Whatever your choice, take a tour of the **Crayola Factory,** which proves that crayon making hasn't changed much since it started here in 1885. The Crayola Factory is a happy place to visit, with craft stations, ball mazes, and clever depictions of the history of the company, now a subsidiary of Hallmark. The Crayola Store next door supplies a rainbow of chalk, glitter, clay, markers, and more. Both are at 30 Centre Sq. For more information call (610) 515-8000 or (800) CRAYOLA, or visit www.crayola.com.

The Crayola Factory shares Two Rivers Landing with the **National Canal Museum** (610-559-6613)—a natural for Pennsylvania, given the oceans of man-made waterways that crisscrossed the state in the 19th century. This is a well-designed little museum that illuminates the past with lots of hands-on displays, excellent short videos, and electronic timelines. One admission ticket ($9.75 for adults) admits you to the NCM and Crayola downstairs. Ten minutes out of town, at **Hugh Moore Park,** you can board the mule-drawn *Josiah White II* and float the 6 miles of the old Lehigh Canal that have been restored here. The

trivia

A plaque on the riverbank in Easton claims it's the site of America's first Christmas tree.

Josiah White II sails June through Sept; adult admission is $10.75. Get details from the museum at www.canals.org. For more information on Lackawanna County, call (800) 229-3526.

Places to Stay in Northeastern Pennsylvania

BETHLEHEM

Sayre Mansion
250 Wyandotte St.
(610) 882-2100
www.sayremansion.com
Mansion or carriage house accommodations on a downtown estate.

CLARKS SUMMIT

Nichols Village Hotel & Spa
1101 Northern Blvd.
(800) 642-2215
www.nicholsvillage.com
Renovated resort with indoor pool.

FRACKVILLE

Granny's Motel and Restaurant
115 W. Coal St.
(570) 874-0408
www.grannys-pa.com
Look for the 40-foot-high granny outside. Pet-friendly.

JIM THORPE

Hotel Switzerland
5 Hazard Sq.
(570) 325-4563
www.jimthorpedining.com
The town's oldest hotel, above the Molly Maguires Pub & Steakhouse.

Inn at Jim Thorpe
24 Broadway
(800) 329-2599
www.innjt.com
Relax on the cast-iron balconies in this renovated 19th-century landmark.

SCRANTON

Radisson Lackawanna Station Hotel
700 Lackawanna Ave.
(570) 342-8300
www.radisson.com
Grand neoclassical dowager near the Steamtown National Historic Site.

STROUDSBURG

Quality Inn
1220 W. Main St.
(570) 420-1000
Convenient to Camelback and Shawnee ski areas.

WILKES-BARRE

Woodlands Inn & Resort
1073 Rte. 315
(570) 824-9831
www.thewoodlandsresort.com
A full-service hotel with 2 restaurants, adjacent to Mohegan Sun Casino at Pocono Downs.

Places to Eat in Northeastern Pennsylvania

BETHLEHEM

Apollo Grill
85 W. Broad St.
(610) 865-9600
www.apollogrill.com
New American cuisine, serves lunch and dinner Tues through Sat.

EASTON

Pearly Baker's Ale House
11 Centre Sq.
(610) 253-9949
www.pearlybakers.net
Family-friendly pub in the heart of town.

HAZLETON

Library Restaurant
615 E. Broad St.
(570) 455-3920
Downtown near Hazelton General Hospital. Dinner only. Closed Sun and Mon.

JIM THORPE

Broadway Grille and Pub
Inn at Jim Thorpe
24 Broadway
(800) 329-2599
www.innjt.com
Hearty breakfasts, lunches, dinners, and plenty of specials.

Molly Maguires Pub & Steakhouse
Hotel Switzerland
5 Hazard Sq.
(570) 325-4563
www.jimthorpedining.com
Casual pub with a canopied deck.

MILFORD

Hotel Fauchère
401 Broad St.
(570) 409-1212
www.hotelfauchere.com
Elegant dining options in a hotel founded in 1852.

MOUNTAINHOME

Mountainhome Diner
Routes 191 and 390
(570) 595-2523
Comfort food destination near Buck Hill Falls.

SCRANTON

Cooper's Seafood House & Ship's Pub
701 N. Washington Ave.
(570) 346-6883
www.coopers-seafood.com
Look for the striped lighthouse and pirate ship. Really.

SHAWNEE-ON-DELAWARE

Saen
Shawnee Square
(570) 476-4911
Thai cuisine. Closed Mon.

SNYDERSVILLE

Snydersville Family Diner
Business Route 209
(570) 992-4003
A sure-fire bet for breakfast, served all day.

TANNERSVILLE

Smuggler's Cove
Route 611
(570) 629-2277
www.smugglerscove.net
Seafood and steaks for famished families, après-ski.

Appendix:
Uniquely Pennsylvania

A Selection of Pennsylvania's Covered Bridges

Adairs Covered Bridge Built 1864, rebuilt 1904. One of four covered bridges that span Sherman's Creek. Bridge is 150 feet long; Burr-truss construction. Route 274, east of Andersonburg, west of Loysville; southwest Madison Township, Perry County.

Aline Covered Bridge Built 1884, this bridge spans the North Branch of Mahantango Creek. Span is 67 feet long; Burr-truss construction. Route 104, north of Meiserville, Snyder County.

Bank's Covered Bridge Bridge is 121 feet long; heavily reinforced underdeck of Burr-truss system. Crosses Neshannock Creek. Halfway between Volant and New Wilmington, Lawrence County.

Bartram's Covered Bridge Built 1860 by Ferdinand Wood. Span is 60 feet long, 18 feet wide, 13 feet high; Burr-truss construction. Bartram family was instrumental in having bridge built. West of Newtown; Willistown and Newtown Townships, Bucks County.

Bells Mills Covered Bridge Built 1950. Bridge is 104 feet long; Burr-truss construction. Connects Sewickley and South Huntingdon Townships and connects Route 136 to I-70. Last remaining covered bridge in Westmoreland County. Near Wyano and Herminie.

Bistline Covered Bridge Built 1884. One of four covered bridges across Sherman's Creek. Also called Book's Covered Bridge. Span is 70 feet long; Burr-truss construction with multiple king posts. Route 274, southwest of Blain, northeast of New Germantown; Jackson Township, Perry County.

Blaney Mays Covered Bridge Built 1882, this bridge spans Middle Wheeling Creek. Queen-post-truss design, vertical plank siding, covered gable roof. Bridge is 31 feet long, 12 feet wide. J. Blaney once owned land near here. Southeast of West Alexander on Donegal Road, Claysville, Washington County.

Bogert Covered Bridge Built 1841, it's the oldest bridge in the country. Span is 145 feet long across Little Lehigh River. Fish Hatchery Road, south of Allentown in Little Lehigh Park, Lehigh County.

Bucher's Mill Covered Bridge Built 1892. Also called Cocalico Bridge, it crosses Cocalico Creek. Span is 64 feet long, 15 feet wide; Burr-truss construction. Cocalico Road, off Route 272, south of Denver; East Cocalico Township, Lancaster County.

Cerl Wright Covered Bridge Crosses north fork of Pigeon Creek. King-post-truss system. Has outlived records of its builder and date of construction. Great view from I-70. Sumney Road, northwest of Bentleyville overlooking eastbound I-70; Somerset Township, Washington County.

Crawford Covered Bridge Queen-post-truss construction. Bridge crosses Robinson Fork of Wheeling Creek, 6 miles west of Finley, then 0.7 mile north of town on Route 3037, Washington County.

Ebenezer Covered Bridge Spans south fork of Mingo Creek. Queen-truss construction. Mingo Creek County Park, Kammerer, Washington County.

Jack's Mountain Covered Bridge Built 1894. Crosses Tom's Creek. Bridge is 75 feet long, 14.5 feet wide; Burr-truss construction. State-owned; open to vehicles. Hamilton Township, southwest of Fairfield near Iron Springs, Adams County.

Jackson's Mill Bridge Built 1875. Span is 95 feet long, 14.5 feet wide; Burr-truss support. Drivable. Township Route 412, 3.5 miles south of Breezewood, Fulton County.

Kidd's Mill Covered Bridge Built 1868, restored 1990. Crosses the Shenango River. Span is 120 feet long; all-wooden-truss design patented by Robert Smith of Tippecanoe City, Ohio. Last historic covered bridge in Mercer County. Five miles south of Greenville on Route 18, then east.

Knapp's Covered Bridge Burr-arch timber bridge constructed about 1860 over Brown's Creek. Span is 88 feet, 10 inches long. Said to be the highest covered bridge in Pennsylvania, at 36 feet above the stream bed. Burlington Township, Bradford County.

Kramer Bridge C. W. Eves built the bridge in 1881 for $414.50. Named for Alexander Kramer, a local farmer, who also bid on its construction. Span is 50 feet long across Mud Run, a tributary of Green and Fishing Creeks, south of Rohrsburg on Rohrsburg Road, Columbia County.

PENNSYLVANIA'S CAVES

Crystal Cave
963 Crystal Cave Rd.
Kutztown
(610) 683-6765
www.crystalcavepa.com

Indian Caverns
5347 Indian Trail
Spruce Creek
(814) 632-7578
www.indiancaverns.com

Indian Echo Caverns
368 Middletown Rd.
PO Box 188
Hummelstown 17036
(717) 566-8131
www.indianechocaverns.com

Laurel Caverns
200 Caverns Park Rd.
Farmington
(724) 438-3003 or (800) 515-4150
www.laurelcaverns.com

Lincoln Caverns
Route 22, RR #1, Box 280
Huntingdon 16652
(814) 643-0268
www.lincolncaverns.com

Penn's Cave
222 Penn's Cave Rd.
Centre Hall
(814) 364-1664
www.pennscave.com

McConnell's Mills Covered Bridge Built 1874 over Slippery Rock Creek, just down-stream from McConnell's Mill. Span is 96 feet long; built with Howe-truss support system. McConnell's Mill State Park, Slippery Rock Township, Lawrence County.

Sachs Covered Bridge Built 1852 by David S. Stoner across Marsh Creek. Also called Sauck's Bridge. Red bridge is 100 feet long; lattice-truss design. Pedestrians only. Both Union and Confederate troops used the bridge in 1863. Waterworks Road between Cumberland and Freedom Townships; near Gettysburg, Adams County.

Thomas Mill Covered Bridge This rural bridge in the midst of the state's biggest metropolis is 97 feet long and 14 feet wide. Access it by foot, bicycle, or horse along Forbidden Drive (so named because cars were always forbidden) between Valley Green Inn and Bells Mill Road, or from Germantown Avenue down Thomas Mill Road. Chestnut Hill section of Philadelphia.

Wertz's Red Bridge Longest single-span covered bridge in Pennsylvania. Northwest of Reading on US Route 222; Bern/Spring Townships, Berks County.

Take a Hike

Appalachian National Scenic Trail Approach this 232-mile segment of the Appalachian Trail from Rouzerville, Franklin County. Its highest elevation is 2,000 feet. Along the beautiful route you'll find laurel and rhododendron blooming in late spring, historic sites, fall hawk migration, and fall foliage. For more information call (304) 535-6331, or visit www.appalachiantrail.org.

Black Forest Trail Start in Haneyville and hike a 9.8-mile loop trail that gains 1,220 feet in elevation. Allow about 6 hours, and you will be rewarded with a section of the Black Forest Trail along Pine Creek Gorge. Pass a waterfall and the historic remains of the Black Forest Railroad, built to log much of this area. For more information call Tiadaghton State Forest, (570) 327-3450.

Eddy Lick Run This trail is 7.3 miles long, and it takes more than 4 hours to hike. Starting at the trailhead at 2,292 feet, the loop gains another 950 feet in elevation. Walk past a logging railroad and traces of a splash dam, which permitted logging along streams that were too small to float logs, even in the spring flood. Most splash dams were made of logs and soil, so they were temporary, but this one was built largely of rock and is well preserved. For more information call Sproul State Forest, (570) 923-6011.

Maple Summit to Ohiopyle To walk this trail, the southernmost section—and one of the most scenic bits—of the Laurel Highlands Trail, start in Confluence. The 11.3-mile-long trail requires several steep climbs—all worth the effort—for a total elevation gain of 1,700 feet. Allow at least 6 hours. The trail is contained within State Game Lands, No. 111. For more information call (724) 455-3744.

Table Rock You can access this 4.2-mile easy trail near Dauphin and can cover it in a couple of hours. Allow time to take in the views from Table Rock. The wide swath cut for power lines allows for great vistas of the Susquehanna River.

For more trails—many more—visit www.trails.com. At last count it listed 265 Pennsylvania off-the-beaten hiking paths.

Final Resting Places of Prominent People

Adams, Earl John "Sparky" (1894–1989). Slick infielder for Cubs, Pirates, Cardinals, and Reds. Starting third baseman for Cardinals' "Gas House Gang" of early 1930s. Tremont Reformed Cemetery; Tremont, Schuylkill County.

Ashburn, Richie (1927–1997). Baseball Hall of Famer who was twice National League batting champ with the Philadelphia Phillies. Also an original New York Met and a Phillies broadcaster for more than 30 years. Gladwyne Methodist Church Cemetery, southeast corner, directly behind the church; 316 Righter's Mill Rd., Gladwyne, Montgomery County.

Bailey, Pearl (1918–1988). African-American vocalist and movie and stage actress. Began as dancer, won amateur contest in Philadelphia in 1933, sang with Big Bands. Starred in *Hello, Dolly!* Hosted a TV variety show. Autobiography: *The Raw Pearl*. Rolling Green Memorial Park; 1008 West Chester Pike, West Chester, Chester County.

Barry, Commodore John (1745–1803). Born in Ireland, Barry went to sea early and settled in Philadelphia by 1760. Commanded two ships. Became senior captain in US Navy. Called Father of the US Navy. Saint Mary's Catholic Church; 252 S. Fourth St., Philadelphia.

Barrymore, John (1882–1942). Stage and film actor, born in Philadelphia. Brother of Ethel and Lionel Barrymore, he debuted in 1903 and became a matinee idol. Triumphed as a stage Hamlet in 1922, then turned to films and radio. Married four times. Mount Vernon Cemetery; Ridge and Lehigh Avenues, Philadelphia.

Britt, Elton (1913–1972). "World's greatest yodeler" lies here—listen. Most famous song: "There's a Star-Spangled Banner Waving Somewhere." Independent Order of Odd Fellows Cemetery; Broadtop City, Huntingdon County.

Buchanan, President James (1791–1868). Fifteenth US president and the only one born in Pennsylvania. Woodward Hill Cemetery; Lancaster.

Calder, Alexander S. (1870–1945). Sculptor and painter, "Sandy" Calder was most famous for creating sculptures that move; artist Marcel Duchamp named them "mobiles." Artist Jean Arp named Calder's stationary sculptures "stabiles." West Laurel Hill Cemetery, Pencoyd Section, Lot 200; 215 Belmont Ave., Bala Cynwyd, Montgomery County.

Croce, Jim (1943–1973). Top-10 folk-rock singer and instrumentalist. "'Cause every time I tried to tell you, the words just came out wrong, so I'll have to say I love you in a song." Haym Solomon Cemetery, Section B/B; Frazer, Chester County.

Day, William Howard (1825–1900). Prominent abolitionist, minister of A.M.E. Zion Church, orator, editor, and educator. Born in New York City; traveled in United States, Canada, and Britain on behalf of antislavery and free blacks. Lived after 1870 in Harrisburg, where he edited the newspaper *Our National Progress*. First African American elected to the Harrisburg School Board; later served as its president. Lincoln Cemetery; Lincoln and Carlisle Streets, Steelton, Dauphin County.

Dorsey, Jimmy (1904–1957). One of the musical Dorsey Brothers, he was a saxophonist, playing with his trombonist-brother Tommy (1905–1956). Together they were key figures of the Big Band era. Began their musical careers in Shenandoah, Pennsylvania, performing together until 1935. Later they led separate orchestras for 18 years before

Pennsylvania Wineries

The website www.pennsylvaniawine.com offers a taste of wine-making activities throughout the state (though the most productive vineyards tend to be in the north-western counties, near Lake Erie, and the southeastern part of the state). Winemakers say that the climate and soil hereabouts is similar to the Bordeaux and Burgundy regions of France; ergo, it augurs well for wine-making. Since wine is a subject with as many opinions as there are tasters, you'll just have to find out for yourself.

Here are a few of the wineries that have been consistent award winners in national and international tastings the past few years:

Blue Mountain Vineyards
7627 Grape Vine Dr.
New Tripoli
(610) 298-3068
www.bluemountainwine.com

Chaddsford Winery
632 Baltimore Pike
Chadds Ford
(610) 388-6221
www.chaddsford.com

Clover Hill Vineyards
9850 Newtown Rd.
Breinigsville
(888) 256-8374
www.cloverhillwinery.com

Naylor Wine Cellars
4069 Vineyard Rd.
Stewartstown
(800) 292-3370
www.naylorwine.com

Nissley Vineyards
140 Vintage Dr.
Bainbridge
(717) 426-3514
www.nissleywine.com

Pinnacle Ridge Winery
407 Old Rte. 22
Kutztown
(610) 756-4481
www.pinridge.com

Presque Isle Wine Cellars
9440 W. Main Rd.
North East
(814) 725-1314
www.piwine.com

Winery at Wilcox
1867 Mefferts Run
Road Wilcox
(814) 929-5598
www.wineryatwilcox.net

reuniting. Annunciation Cemetery; Schuylkill Avenue, Shenandoah Heights, Schuylkill County.

Drexel, Saint Katharine (1858–1955). Raised with status and wealth, she devoted herself to serving Native and African Americans and established many missions. She was beatified in 1988, canonized in 2000. 1663 Bristol Pike, Bensalem, Bucks County.

Ennis, Del (1925–1996). Slugging outfielder for the Phillies in 1950s, three-time All-Star, and member of 1950 "Whiz Kids." Hillside Cemetery, Lawnview Section, Lot 102; 2556 Susquehanna Rd., Roslyn, Montgomery County.

Fine, Governor John S. (1893–1978). Governor of Pennsylvania from 1951 to 1955. Oak Lawn Cemetery; Wilkes-Barre, Luzerne County.

Forrest, Edwin (1806–1872). Actor born in Philadelphia; excelled in tragic roles. His rivalry with actor William Macready led to the 1849 Astor Place Riots in New York, where 30 people were killed during a fight. Episcopal Community Services; 225 S. Third St., Philadelphia.

Foster, Stephen C. (1826–1864). Popular 19th-century composer of folk songs and ballads. Penned "Oh! Susannah," "Camptown Races," and "Beautiful Dreamer." Lived in the Pittsburgh area most of his life. Allegheny Cemetery; 4734 Butler St., Pittsburgh.

Franklin, Benjamin (1706–1790). An American superstar, Franklin signed the Declaration of Independence; proved that lightning is an electrical phenomenon; wrote, printed, and published widely; and invented bifocals. Also known as diplomat, philanthropist, statesman, and scientist. The 18th century's most illustrious Pennsylvanian built a house in Franklin Court starting in 1763 and lived there the last five years of his life. Christ Church Burial Ground; southeast corner of Fifth and Arch Streets, Philadelphia.

Frick, Henry (1849–1919). A Pittsburgh industrialist and philanthropist, Frick was instrumental in the organization of the coke and steel industries. His controversial management style while chairman of Carnegie Steel led to the bloody Homestead Strike in 1892. Homewood Cemetery; 1599 S. Dallas Ave., Pittsburgh.

Furness, Frank (1839–1912). Influential Philadelphia architect. Designed Victorian buildings between 1870 and 1900. Laurel Hill Cemetery, Lot 94, Section S; 3822 Ridge Ave., Philadelphia.

Garroway, David (Dave) (1913–1982). Television host. Originally a disc jockey on Chicago radio, he appeared on NBC-TV. First host of *Today* show (1952–1961); hosted *Wide, Wide World* (1955–1958). West Laurel Hill Cemetery, Washington Section, Lot 49; 215 Belmont Ave., Bala Cynwyd, Montgomery County.

Gathers, Hank (1967–1990). Hank "The Bankman" Gathers was the last college basketball player to lead the NCAA in both scoring and rebounding. Mount Lawn Cemetery; Eighty-fourth Street and Hook Road, Sharon Hill, Delaware County.

Gridley, Captain Charles Vernon (1844–1898). Commander of Dewey's flagship USS *Olympia* in the Battle of Manila Bay, 1898. Dewey's order, "You may fire when you are ready, Gridley," opened the battle in the Spanish-American War. Lakeside Cemetery; East Lake Road, Erie.

Hopper, Hedda (1890–1966). Gossip columnist, born Elda Furry in Hollidaysburg, Pennsylvania, one of nine children. Worked in theater, became a fashion commentator on a Hollywood radio station. Eventually her column appeared in 85 metropolitan papers, 3,000 small-town dailies, and 2,000 weeklies. Rose Hill Cemetery; Altoona, Blair County.

Jarvis, Anna (1864–1948). Her mother had hoped "sometime, somewhere, someone will found a Mother's Day." When her mother died, Jarvis, living in Philadelphia, did it. The first Mother's Day was May 12, 1907. President Woodrow Wilson made it official in every state, and the day is celebrated now in more than 40 countries. West Laurel Hill Cemetery, River Section, Lot 499; 215 Belmont Ave., Bala Cynwyd, Montgomery County.

Kahn, Louis I. (1901–1974). This 20th-century architect designed the Salk Institute for Biological Studies in La Jolla, California, and the Yale Center for British Art and Studies in New Haven, Connecticut. He taught at Yale and Penn. Montefiore Cemetery; 600 Church Rd., Jenkintown, Montgomery County.

Mansfield, Jayne (1933–1967). Actress born Vera Jayne Palmer in Bryn Mawr, Pennsylvania. Known for sultry movie and stage roles, including *Too Hot to Handle* and *Will Success Spoil Rock Hunter?* Fairview Cemetery; Plainfield near Pen Argyl, York County.

McKean, Thomas (1734–1817). Signed the Declaration of Independence. Laurel Hill Cemetery, Section G, Lot 210; 3822 Ridge Ave., Philadelphia.

Mead, Margaret (1901–1978). Anthropologist who redefined and expanded the field of anthropology, the science of human culture. Born in Philadelphia, she was ambitious and always controversial. Did field work in Polynesia, Melanesia, and Nebraska, among other sites. President Jimmy Carter awarded her the Presidential Medal of Freedom. Buckingham Friends Cemetery; Lahaska, Bucks County.

Moore, Marianne (1887–1972). Modernist poet. Studied at Bryn Mawr College and Carlisle Commercial College; worked at US Indian School. Famous for her eccentricity, devotion to baseball, and keenly intelligent poetry. Evergreen Cemetery, Lot 91, Area G, Grave 5; 799 Baltimore St., Gettysburg, Adams County.

Peale, Charles Willson (1741–1827). Portrait painter who was a Democratic member of the Pennsylvania Assembly. He established the Portrait Gallery of the Heroes of the Revolution (1782) and founded the Peale Museum of natural history and technology (1786). His most famous painting is *The Staircase Group* (1795), portraying his sons, Raphaelle and Titian. Married three times, he had 17 children, many of whom were

PENNSYLVANIA WEB ADDRESSES

www.1fghp.com/pa.html
fishing guide

www.pennsylvaniawine.com
wineries

www.fallinpa.com
a virtual tree of autumn leaves

www.paroute6.com
virtual drive across the northern tier

www.visitphilly.com
tourism in Philadelphia

www.visitpa.com/shopping
from one-of-a-kind to outlet malls

http://golfinpa.com
link to the links

www.trails.com
off-the-beaten-highway paths

www.groundhog.org
eternal replays of February 2

www.visitpa.com
tourism in Pennsylvania (official state site)

www.pahuntandfish.com
visit 17 million acres of forest

www.visitpittsburgh.com
tourism in Pittsburgh

artists. St. Peter's Churchyard; occupies a city block bounded by Third, Pine, Fourth, and Lombard Streets, Philadelphia.

Pitcher, Molly (1754–1832). Mary Ludwig Hays McCauley was dubbed Molly Pitcher while carrying pitchers of water to her husband and other thirsty soldiers during battle; heroine at Battle of Monmouth. Old Graveyard; South Hanover Street between Walnut and South Streets, Carlisle, Cumberland County.

Rizzo, Frank (1920–1991). Commissioner of police department of Philadelphia, where he lived all his life. Called himself "toughest cop in America." Twice elected mayor of Philadelphia (1972 and 1975). Holy Sepulchre Cemetery, Section S, Range 1, Lot 136; Cheltenham Avenue and Easton Road, Cheltenham Township, Montgomery County.

Rush, Benjamin (1742–1813). Signed the Declaration of Independence. Christ Church Burial Ground; Fifth and Arch Streets, Philadelphia. Other signers buried at Christ Church Burial Ground include Jacob Broom (1752–1810), Pierce Butler (1744–1822), Joseph Hewes (1730–1779), Francis Hopkinson (1737–1791), Robert Morris (1734–1806), and George Ross (1730–1779).

Russell, Lillian (1861–1922). Actress and singer born in Clinton, Iowa. This popular, flamboyant blonde beauty was known for her unreliability. Starred in 24 musicals between 1881 and 1899. Allegheny Cemetery; 4734 Butler St., Pittsburgh.

Sully, Thomas (1783–1872). Learned art from relatives, began painting portraits in 1801. Studied with Gilbert Stuart and Benjamin West. Returned to Philadelphia; painted technically polished and elegant portraits. Laurel Hill Cemetery, Section A, Lot 41; 3822 Ridge Ave., Philadelphia.

Index

Already "Been There, Done That"?
Then Get Off the Beaten Path!

OFF THE BEATEN PATH®
A GUIDE TO UNIQUE PLACES →

"For the traveler who enjoys the special, the unusual, and the unexpected."—*The Traveler* newsletter

Alabama	Kansas	Nevada	Quebec
Alaska	Kentucky	New Hampshire	Rhode Island
Arizona	Louisiana	New Jersey	South Carolina
Arkansas	Maine	New Mexico	Southern California
British Columbia	Maritime Provinces	Metro New York	Tennessee
Colorado	Maryland & Delaware	Upstate New York	Texas
Connecticut	Massachusetts	North Carolina	Utah
Dakotas	Michigan	Northern California	Vermont
Florida	Minnesota	Ohio	Virginia
Georgia	Mississippi	Oklahoma	Washington, D.C.
Hawaii	Missouri	Oregon	West Virginia
Idaho	Montana	Pennsylvania	Wisconsin
Indiana	Nebraska	Philadelphia	Wyoming
Iowa		Puerto Rico	